The Saigon Zoo

Vietnam's Other War:
Sex, Drugs, Rock 'n' Roll

A very different
Vietnam memoir

Pete Whalon

INFINITY
PUBLISHING.COM

Copyright © 2009 by Pete Whalon

Cover-Picture Photographer: Bill "Ozzie" Oswald
Cover Photo: Members of the Fab 50 form a "chain gang" in the "prison yard" next to Warehouse 32 (The Saigon Zoo), July 1969
Interior Photographs: Bill "Saigon Bill" Harper,
Bill "Ozzie" Oswald, Pete Whalon, and Dave Schrunk
Book editor: Paul Wilder, USN
Cover Concept & Cover Copy: Robin Quinn

ISBN 978-0-7414-2045-9

Published by:

PUBLISHING.COM

Info@buybooksontheweb.com
www.buybooksontheweb.com
Toll-free (877) BUY BOOK
Local Phone (610) 941-9999
Fax (610) 941-9959

Printed in the United States of America
Revised Edition Published November 2012

This book is dedicated to Gene Bellotti, Mark Goodman, Dave Schrunk, Bill Harper, Jerry Judge, Lee Mills, Bill Oswald, and Larry Pratt:

*Proud members of **The Saigon Zoo**,*

AND

*To **Paul Wilder**, the smartest man I have ever known. His command and precise knowledge of the English language is truly a marvel. With his continued encouragement and unrelenting insistence on perfection, The Saigon Zoo is now a product of superb editing.*

Though the text of this book has undergone painstaking proofing, any errors and inaccuracies that may remain are the sole responsibility of the author.

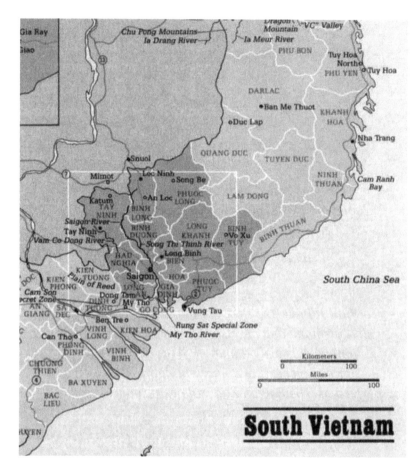

South Vietnam

Notice how close together and how far south both Saigon and Long Binh are? The boys further north, fighting Charlie in the bush, had a name for guys like me—REMFs—Rear Echelon Motherfu**ers! Now, was that nice?

Acknowledgments

I would like to thank the special friends who, through their encouragement early in the writing process, gave me the inspiration to continue. These people include Beverly DiSarno, my earliest and most dedicated fan; Dave Siemienski, a true friend who provided me with honest, well-thought-out criticism and encouragement that helped keep me on track; and Chris Devilbiss, who believed every word I wrote deserved a Pulitzer. And to Nancy Ferris—an elegant woman and modern-day sage.

Also, special thanks to my old Army buddies I have located over the past two years: Dave Schrunk, Larry Pratt, Gene "Buzz" Bellotti, Bill "Ozzie" Oswald, Bill "Saigon Bill" Harper, Lee Mills, and Jerry "The Judge" Judge. Their memories and encouragement truly inspired me. And thanks to Karen Goodman, wife of my good friend from those days, Mark Goodman, who passed away in 2001. Through her words, I realized how much Mark would have loved being involved in this project.

Thanks to my cover-copy editor, Robin Quinn.

And last, to my loving parents, Philip and Irene, who will be reading my book from their place in Heaven. I hope you enjoy the book and it makes you smile. Thanks for my sense of humor and the ability to avoid taking myself too seriously. I'll see you down the road.

Private Whalon on roof of the Hung Dao Hotel
in downtown Saigon, Vietnam in 1969

Introduction

When I returned to the U.S. in March 1971, after twenty-two months in Vietnam, most people were understandably curious about my experience and wanted to know just how horrific it had been in the jungles over there. I always replied with the same canned answer: "It wasn't too bad at the swimming pool where I was a lifeguard." I loved seeing the confused looks on their faces. Most people had watched the horrors of war on the nightly TV news; they expected to hear harrowing tales of life in the "bush" of Vietnam, and about the battles with the Vietcong that I'd been involved in. They wanted a little "blood-and-guts" talk.

As those close to me soon learned, I had no such "war stories" related to Vietnam. Mine were outrageous accounts of bizarre characters, drug addicts, overzealous lifers and a tight-knit group of misfits in constant search of their next cheap thrill. My friends at home never tired of my wild tales, and they badgered me constantly for more tantalizing Vietnam stories. Often my buddies would request an anecdote they had heard many times before. "Pete, tell these guys about the pool party you threw with over eight hundred drunken GIs." Or, "Whalon, what was it like being on that street in Saigon with all the bars and hookers?" Often my pals would want to impress a chick they were with. "Hey Pete, tell Sally about all the junkies in Nam and all the different drugs you could get there." Many of my accounts of Vietnam took on a life of their own.

Occasionally, upon hearing the stories, a friend or acquaintance would tell me that I had enough great material for a different type of Vietnam book. They believed that my experiences were so contrary to perceptions of Vietnam, and so remarkable, that it would show another side of the war.

At age forty-five, twenty-three years after my discharge from the Army, I began writing *The Saigon Zoo.* I worked on the book sporadically for the next eight years. However, I never took the project too seriously until after retiring in January 2002. At that time, I decided that I would finish the book whether it ever got published or not. I also took on a related project. I began searching for old Army buddies who had served with me during those raucous, out-of-control days of 1969 and 1970. With the use of the Internet, I became proficient in tracking down these old friends I had not seen in over thirty years. By the time I had written this Introduction, I'd located eight old friends and, unfortunately, also discovered that two others had passed away. The more buddies I found, the more inspired I became to complete this humorous account of my undistinguished military service. Our little group of over-the-hill vets still stays in contact with each other and we are in the process of scheduling a reunion.

This book begins in June 1968 on the devastating day that I visited the Army recruiter's office with my best friend John. It ends on the glorious day when the Army discharged me in March 1971.

In 1968, the fear of being drafted was on the mind of every eighteen-year-old male in the country. Everybody had a friend or knew of a friend of a friend who had been wounded or killed in Vietnam. It appeared that the war would last for years and many more innocent young men would lose their lives.

Still, the war seemed so distant to my friends and me. We lived a dreamlike existence, only blocks from one of the finest beaches in Southern California. For a teenager in the USA, there was no better place to live in the late '60s. Southern California had it all: suntanned chicks roaming the beaches on hot summer days, endless parties, movie stars, the Los Angeles Dodgers, and a permissive lifestyle perfect for an eighteen-year-old male and his friends! "Make love, not war!" was the Southern California creed. The only downside was the looming fear of being drafted and sent to Vietnam.

I remember the day someone told me that a friend of mine from church had gotten his parents' permission to join the Marines at the age of seventeen. Nine months later, I learned "friendly fire" had taken his life somewhere in Vietnam. This strange time in our history would have dramatic effects on the youth of the day for years to come, and still affects thousands of middle-aged men today.

This is not a war book, but rather an account of my Vietnam experience. At the time, the events seemed normal to me. However, today those memories have taken on a surreal quality. From my assignment to a Saigon warehouse working with a motley gang of malcontents, to conning my way into a position as head lifeguard at an Army swimming pool in Long Binh, my time spent in Nam was an extraordinary journey. Maybe after reading this book, you'll understand why it was also one of the most memorable, rewarding and enjoyable periods of my life.

I have changed many of the names in this book, but the events are true. These are the old friends whose real names I have used in the book, with their permission: Bill Harper, Dave Schrunk, Gene Bellotti, Jerry Judge, Bill Oswald, Lee Mills, and Larry Pratt. Mark Goodman was another good friend; he passed away in 2001. I have contacted Mark's wife, Karen, and she has given me permission to use his name.

One final note. I have conspicuously omitted the "F" word from this book, for two reasons. First, my mother, God rest her soul, would haunt me for the remainder of my days on Earth if I included it. Second, it would make this read entirely too lengthy.

I hope you enjoy reading *The Saigon Zoo* half as much as I enjoyed writing it!

Main Characters
Everyday People
(Sly and the Family Stone, 1968)

The GIs

Gene "Buzz" Bellotti: Gene was Mr. Cool with a constant buzz on. From San Francisco, he epitomized the 1960s hippie culture.

Mark Goodman: A lifer's worst nightmare. Mark's verbal confrontations with those in charge were highly anticipated events.

Charlie Hardy: A tougher-than-nails guy from Philly. Hardy and Willie Stuart were the only two blacks in our tight-knit group.

Bill "Saigon Bill" Harper: My sharp-tongued, pool-hustling buddy from North Carolina.

Jerry "The Judge" Judge: Jerry's acerbic wit and rapid-fire retorts were a thing of beauty.

Lee Mills: One of Florida's finest, known for his laid-back style.

Bill "Oz" Oswald: Wild Bill from New York was always in search of the next party.

Larry Pratt: Larry was as honest as a saint, as friendly as a puppy, and as naive as an Amish toddler.

Paul Price: Paul's NYC style and accent made him unique.

Dave Schrunk: My informal guardian and roommate.

John Soranno: My best friend from Redondo Beach, California; he later joined me in Vietnam.

Willie Stuart: Always funny and always loaded.

Lifers Assigned to Warehouse 32

Sergeant "Papa Bear" Foster: NCOIC (noncommissioned officer in charge) of Warehouse 32.

Sergeant "Uncle Remus" Aaron: The guys at the warehouse regarded this sergeant as their favorite.

Sergeant "Popeye" Chester: Operations sergeant at the warehouse.

Sergeant "Barney Fife" Macking: The lowest ranking of the six warehouse sergeants.

Sergeant "Crabs" Otto: Meanest warehouse sergeant.

Sergeant "Bulldog" Netton: The toughest sergeant, Bulldog loved busting the GIs at the warehouse.

Warrant Officer "Mr. Peepers" Edwards: The officer responsible for all warehouse personnel and operations.

Lifeguards at the Long Binh Pool

Frank "Monte" Montecalvo: The lifeguard who hoped to play for the Green Bay Packers after leaving the Army.

Wade "Sleepy" Fossett: The lifeguard who never met a drug he didn't like.

Buddy Beard: The lifeguard who just wanted to be "cool" someday.

Contents

PART III—Doin' Hard Time at the Long Binh "Bayou"

Cronauer: *Speaking of things controversial, is it true there's a marijuana problem here in Vietnam?*

Funny voice: *No, it's not a problem; everyone HAS it.*

From *Good Morning, Vietnam,*
starring Robin Williams
as Nam disc jockey Adrian Cronauer

Part I

Road to Nam

August 1968 - May 1969

Chapter I

It's All Over Now

(Rolling Stones, 1964)

June 9, 1968, the day I reluctantly joined the United States Army, remains as vivid in my mind's eye today as this morning's sunrise. I awoke that morning with the intention of going to the beach to begin working on my summer tan. Unfortunately, it was a typical June day in Redondo Beach, California—cloudy and overcast. Undaunted, I showered and put on my new Hawaiian Hang-10 trunks. Before heading outdoors, I grabbed my Bob Dylan beach towel, Styrofoam cooler, and transistor radio.

The phone rang just as I closed the door behind me. I momentarily debated whether or not to answer it. The fear of missing a better offer than a cloudy day at the beach sent me running for the phone. That decision would turn out to be the first of numerous small mistakes I would make in the course of that fateful day. The call came from John Soranno, my best friend who lived up the street.

"Hey Peety boy, I gotta go somewhere important— wanna go with me, dude?"

"Where?" I asked.

"I can't tell you—it's a surprise. But you'll be glad you came, I swear to God." With that, John let loose his all-too-familiar cackle—one I had heard too many times before. It signaled a clear warning. John, who loved practical jokes, had something up his sleeve.

"If you don't tell me, I ain't going! No way, man."

"It involves chicks and a party tonight with a keg."

I gave in, unwilling to take the chance of passing up two of my favorite things in life.

3

"Are you driving?" I asked.

"Yeah, I'll pick you up in ten minutes. Be outside." John hung up.

I quickly changed and went out on my front lawn to wait for John. I knew he was lying but decided I had nothing to lose by tagging along. John and I had been best friends for eight years and we did everything together. I soon heard the familiar roar of John's '55 metallic-blue Chevy coming from just up the street. Seconds later, the car screeched to a stop in front of my house. John was laughing as I got in and closed the door.

"Okay, funny boy, where we goin', and don't BS me," I demanded.

"Guess," John said cackling.

"Lenny's work?"

"No."

"Danny's sister's house?"

"No."

After six or seven incorrect guesses, I gave up. By now, we were a few miles from home, cruising down Hawthorne Boulevard toward the city of Inglewood.

"John!" I screamed, "tell me what's up or I swear to God, I'll jump out at the next stoplight! I swear to God, man!" I hoped the two "God" references would convince him to let me in on his little secret.

"Okay, okay, don't have a cow, dude. It's groovy, it's cool." Funny boy started laughing again. "I'm joinin' the Army, man. Gonna be a medic—can you believe that shit? I leave for Fort Ord next week to start basic training and then I go to Fort Hood, Texas—does that blow your mind? Kinky

4

(John's nickname) is gonna be a soldier boy." John began shaking his head up and down at the prospect.

"Okay Kinky, real funny, you're a real Red Skelton. Now where are we really going? Your lazy ass wouldn't last three days in the Army—make that three hours, Kinky."

John pulled the car to the curb and stopped laughing for the first time since he had picked me up. He pointed out my window. I turned and read the sign hanging over the red-brick building. An icy chill rushed through my body. The sign read, "United States Army Recruiting Office—Inglewood." Just under the sign hung a large tacky red, white and blue painting of Uncle Sam. He was pointing at me, staring in my eyes and declaring, "I want you!" My mind raced as I tried to make sense out of this surreal situation. This couldn't be happening! There had to be a logical, rational explanation.

"John," I said slowly, "first of all, you are shittin' me, right? This is one of your tasteless, idiotic jokes, right?"

I waited for him to confess and point out the car window at Allen Funt and his *Candid Camera* crew emerging from behind the building. Instead, between his aggravating laughs, John laid out the unbelievable details.

"Pete, I'm dead serious, man. I brought you with me so we could enlist together and go in on this cool deal the Army calls the 'buddy plan.' It'll be cool dude, together in Texas, training to be medics. How cool would that be? It's only three years. Whatdaya say, Pete? Are you my buddy? Have you got the balls to join with me?" More grating laughter came from this complete stranger behind the wheel of John's car.

It was now clear to me: I wasn't on *Candid Camera.* Instead, I had entered *The Twilight Zone.* Surely, Rod Serling would appear any moment, cigarette in hand, to clear up this nightmare. The situation called for logic and clear, rational thinking—something I was well-known for.

"You are crazy, man—out of your empty skull, you idiot!" I was yelling and pointing at this person who had kidnapped me. "It's 1968, ass-wipe—ever hear of Vietnam, ass-face? Yeah, that's right, there is a war there, asshole—people are getting blown away daily, ass-licker—you are an idiot, ass…" I paused. I had completely run out of derogatory ass references. "You're a moron—what in the world is wrong with you? Really man, I mean it. What the hell is wrong with your rotting brain? This makes no sense, John—none! I thought this was gonna be our best summer ever, John. Ever! The beach, chicks, beer and parties. Remember those things? Don't go in there. Let's go home now. Please, man! Have you signed the papers yet? When did you decide to do this, and why didn't you tell me? You're a real dumbshit, I mean a real dumbshit! Let's go home now—I don't feel good; my stomach hurts." I was completely drained.

"Funny stuff Pete, really funny," John remarked. "Now let's go inside, I'm late."

"What? I'm not going in there with you. You are C-R-A-Z-Y. Don't do this, John; you'll regret it. It will ruin everything—please."

John just laughed, saluted me with the wrong hand, tossed me the keys so I could listen to the radio, and then strolled toward the recruiter's office. Just before going inside, he glanced over his shoulder to see if I'd follow, but I held my ground.

My head began spinning in all directions. How could anyone—especially my best friend—want to join the Army now? It was bad enough sweating out the draft every day, never knowing if the mailman would deliver my notice. The daily mail delivery had become a stressful event in my life since the day I turned eighteen and had to register for the military draft. One thing I never considered was joining the military. If I had to go in one day, I'd do so only kicking and screaming. Human nature got the best of me and, I thought, better John than me.

I settled down a bit, turned on the car radio, and tuned into my favorite station, KRLA. I closed my eyes as I sang along with the lyrics to Barry McGuire's classic song, "Eve of Destruction."

Suddenly, a rapid knocking on the passenger-side window jolted me from my musical reverie. I looked up and saw one of the Army recruiters smiling down at me. I instinctively locked the car door, but said nothing.

"Pete, how's it going today?"

How did he know my name? John! I made my first vow of the day: in the near future, I'd inflict severe pain on the body of John Soranno.

"Pete, come in and have some coffee or a cold drink with us. John will be a while. Come on, it's cooler inside." The sergeant widened his phony smile and beckoned me from the Chevy.

I froze in place and stared straight ahead. Nothing could extract me from the car. He went for the door. Nice try, soldier boy, but it's locked! The door opened. I suddenly remembered that all of John's door locks didn't work. As I stood on my buckling legs and submissively followed the man inside, I mentally decided on the tools I would use for John's torture.

How had this happened? An hour before, I was relaxing safely in my room, listening to "Light My Fire," "Ruby Tuesday," "The Letter," "Judy in Disguise," and other timeless songs on my Pioneer 8-track tape player. Now I was shuffling through a door held open by a massive Army sergeant whose occupation required him to trick young, naive, unsuspecting males (like me) into enlisting in the United States Army. I hastily devised a plan to sit still and say nothing. Don't ask questions and do not, under any circumstances, answer questions. Simple, yes, but foolproof.

"Pete, this is Sergeant Johnson and I'm Sergeant Wilkins." I nodded slightly. "Would you like some coffee or a

7

Pepsi?" Sergeant Wilkins politely asked. I shook my head from side to side. "John is going to be about half an hour. Would you like to look at some opportunities the Army has to offer young men like yourself?" Here comes the bullshit, I thought. Once again, side to side. I was doing well. "How old are you, Pete?" Wilkins casually asked.

"He turned nineteen in March—March 6." John smiled as he cheerfully answered for me.

"Is that correct, Pete?" Wilkins asked. "Nineteen years old and you haven't gotten your draft notice yet? I'm surprised. It could be coming any day now."

Why is Sergeant Wilkins torturing me like this? Why couldn't he just leave me alone? Why had I come with John today? What is that large, wet, sticky ball in my throat? In my desperate search for clarity and inner peace, I hadn't noticed Sergeant Johnson making a phone call. When I heard him mention my name, I focused on the conversation.

"Yes, Pete Whalon, that's correct. He's nineteen years old, born on March 6, 1949," Johnson said to the person he was talking to on the phone. "Can you tell me when his draft notice is scheduled to be sent? Sure, I can hold."

My good buddy, Benedict Soranno, had kindly supplied the sergeant with my last name. Sergeant Johnson smiled and gave me a wink. I hastily made the decision that if some day I ended up in Vietnam and had enough fortune to meet up with my old friend John, I would empty an entire magazine from my M16 into his body.

I had not uttered a single syllable since I entered the recruiting office. I held true to my plan but things were unraveling quickly. With every ounce of strength remaining in my body, I asked with a cracking voice, "What are you doing?"

"I'm just checking to see if you've been assigned a draft date yet, Pete. Thought you might like to know if and when you will be drafted. Hold on, Pete." Johnson began talking on the phone again. "Repeat that please. Thank you very much." With a concerned look, the sergeant began writing on his notepad as soon as he hung up the phone.

"Interesting," Johnson muttered as he joined Sergeant Wilkins toward the back of the room. I strained to hear but they were intentionally speaking softly. I glared at John. He smiled back, giving me another left-handed salute. Was he saluting me with his left hand on purpose, I wondered, or was he just a dumbshit? I decided that he was a dumbshit—the thought made me feel better momentarily.

Smiling, the two sergeants approached me.

Why was everyone in such a good mood? In contrast, I had cold sweats and a roaring stomach, my head ached, and I couldn't feel my legs.

Johnson spoke first. "I'm going to give it to you straight, Pete." The sergeant placed his hand on my right shoulder. "You're not being drafted in July..." The words echoed in my head—"not being drafted." Thank you God and all the saints! My prayers had been answered. I now knew how a death-row inmate felt when a governor granted him a last-minute stay of execution, thus sparing his life. It felt great to be alive.

Sergeant Johnson continued. "But you will be receiving your draft notice sometime in August, Pete."

"What?" I gagged.

"Pete, don't worry," Wilkins said, chiming in. "The Army has many options for you to consider. There are ways you can avoid the draft by joining instead. If you join for three years, you are guaranteed the school of your choice." Wilkins continued to jabber; however, I didn't listen.

My arms had gone numb. John was laughing, pointing at me, calling me Private Whalon, and repeatedly saluting me with his left hand. The two sergeants took turns talking, trying to get me to look at their list of Army Occupational

Specialties. Wilkins smiled down at me like a vulture watching a severely wounded wildebeest take his final gasps for air. My body felt as though it was getting smaller, as though I was shrinking.

Maybe I misunderstood what he said, I thought.

Mustering up every ounce of strength in my decomposing body, I meekly whispered, "What?"

Johnson, instinctively sensing that they had broken my spirit, returned to his desk to complete the process of committing John to three years of military service.

"Well Pete," Wilkins persevered, "I think we can help you choose the right school for your training."

"Come on, Pete, go for it. Sign up and be a man," John contributed.

"Shut the hell up, asshole!" I screamed at my former best friend. John laughed heartily, deriving great pleasure from my mental breakdown.

"Yes sir, Private Whalon," John responded.

The two sergeants now laughed along with this person who had once cared about my welfare. My spirit was crushed. I was physically and mentally exhausted and it was only 11:15 in the morning.

"Anyway," Sergeant Wilkins began again, "you're going to get your draft notice in late August, which means you will have two years of military service to fulfill. You will be sent to basic training at Fort Ord for eight weeks and then, most likely, sent to infantry training for another eight weeks. Pete, I have to be honest with you. Upon completing infantry training, most privates are sent to Vietnam."

There it was—that dreaded seven-letter word, "VIETNAM"! An intrusive word, it was capable of provoking bizarre behavior from otherwise rational young men. It had sent some men sneaking off to Canada, and caused otherwise honest men to fake physical injuries. The word had motivated thousands of college students to study harder and get better grades. I despised the sound of that word; it scared the hell out of me. I wanted no part of Vietnam. I listened more intently.

"Now Pete, it's not as bad as it appears," Wilkins said in a comforting voice. "We can avoid the draft by enlisting for three years."

What did he mean, "we"? Did he intend to go with me to basic training?

"That way," he continued, "you get to pick the training you want from our MOS list, which offers over one hundred and sixty-five specialties. The Army has many exciting opportunities for young men." I'd soon learn that the U.S. Army had an acronym for everything.

"Okay Pete, I'm sure you have some questions for me. Go ahead."

Yeah, Sarge, I do, I thought. Can I borrow your gun? Out loud I replied, "Are you sure I'm getting drafted in August?" It was the only question that seemed relevant at that moment.

"Absolutely, Pete!" the sergeant said, raising his right hand as if he was taking an oath.

"If I get drafted, are you sure I'll be sent to infantry training?"

"Yes, you will be a grunt and you will go to Nam," Sergeant Wilkins assured me.

"Hey Pete, go medic baby and ship out with me next week—buddy plan, dude!" John started up again.

Yeah, John, that's a great idea, I thought. They don't need medical personnel in Vietnam, you brain-dead circus clown! But instead, I said, "No thanks, John. I'd like to live through this experience if possible." I had lost track of my vows for revenge at this point.

I turned to Sergeant Wilkins. "Sergeant, I planned to take a few trips this summer with some of my friends. If I join, what is the latest date I could go in? Can I put this thing off for a year?" I asked optimistically.

After a short courtesy laugh, he answered, "Not that long, Pete. But we could have you start in late August."

I gave it one more half-hearted try. "How 'bout late September?" I had always been a poor salesman.

Like a pit bull on a kitten, the sergeant went for the kill. "Okay Pete, it's time to get serious here." The smile vanished and his voice was somber. "If you're going to do this, we need to get it done today! I'll give you some time, but I'm busy, son, so make a decision soon."

After this declaration, Sergeant Wilkins returned to his desk. John was busy with Sergeant Johnson, signing papers and asking questions.

Occasionally John would turn around and give me a wink or wiggle his tongue at me like a fool. I didn't care anymore about John's attempts to aggravate me. Decision time had arrived and the options equally nauseated me. I had two mind-numbing choices: I could say, "No thanks," shake everybody's hand, and walk out the door with the knowledge that I would be drafted in August—or I could join the Army, pick a training program I thought would keep me out of Vietnam, and spend most of the summer a free man.

I sat there sweating with my legs stuck to the cheap plastic chair, deep in thought for about fifteen minutes, though it seemed more like an hour. Neither sergeant spoke to me. They knew what I would do. These two hucksters had gone through this drill hundreds of times before. They had the best possible sales tool at their disposal—fear of death! It is what ultimately drove me toward enlistment. I was a thoroughly beaten man-child, ready to make the biggest decision of my young life. I would join the United States Army in 1968, at the height of the Vietnam War.

This was, by far, the absolute worst day of my short existence on the planet. I was sickened and depressed at the same time. Hard as I tried, I could find no solace in thoughts of family, friends, or visions of better days. I could muster no inner strength of character that day. I would reluctantly opt for the safe (or so I believed) route and join the United States Army for three years.

I stood, creating a disgusting sound as I separated my sweaty legs from the moist chair. Like a wounded lamb, I walked over to Sergeant Wilkins's desk.

"Okay," I sighed, "let me see the choices I have for the different schools."

John clapped noisily and whistled. Sergeant Wilkins smiled and shook my wet, limp hand. Sergeant Johnson looked up, nodded his head, and proudly proclaimed, "Pete, you made the correct decision. Welcome to the United States Army!" With that, he gave me my first and proper right-handed salute. I struggled to keep down my breakfast of French toast and Bosco.

The morning passed as a blur in my mind as we drove home. Although I thrilled John by joining the Army, he knew he pissed me off. John had pressed hard for me to join on the "buddy plan," but I needed more than a week to prepare myself mentally for this ordeal. The hardest part of the day would be returning home to inform my parents and friends of my new occupation. In seventy-eight days, I would enter a world I knew nothing about. From that day forward, life as I knew it would cease to exist.

Chapter II
Ticket to Ride
(Beatles, 1965)

"Give 'em hell, Private Whalon," my good friend Larry howled as he pulled away from the curb. I said a short, silent prayer wishing Larry would return home to find his draft notice waiting for him in the mailbox. Misery loves company! August 28, 1968—my personal D-Day—had arrived. Larry had just abandoned me in front of the induction center on Broadway Street in downtown Los Angeles. It was my first day as a United States Army recruit and I was scared shitless.

My best buddy, John Soranno, had called me two days earlier from his advanced training company in Texas to relate horror stories about the induction process and basic training in general. It gave me little consolation knowing that many of the tales John told me were pure bullshit. When John casually informed me that three or four guys actually die during every basic-training cycle, I decided to end our conversation. We promised to keep in touch with each other throughout our Army tours.

I had arrived ten minutes early for my 8:00 a.m. appointment. Not wanting to grant the Army one second more of my life than the three years it had tricked me into giving up, I decided to wait outside across the street until 7:59 a.m. I'd never felt more alone.

I passed the time observing the arrival of other freaked-out young men. In front of the induction center, the procession of cars grew longer, each waiting its turn to abandon the next lost soul. Every face veiled a restrained fear and hopelessness. When I stood to make my way across the street, a classic Bob Dylan song came to mind: "The Times They Are a-Changin'."

The verbal assault began the instant I opened the oversized wooden door. "What are you lookin' at, fairy?!" the first corporal I encountered screamed in my face. "Follow the yellow line on the floor, shit-bird! I'll put my boot so far up your ass it'll come out your ear—move it, punk! Are you smilin' at me, little girl? Follow the yellow line to Station 1, asshole!"

I merged with the endless line of would-be soldiers. At Station 1, a sadistic corporal with short cropped hair and front teeth like Bugs Bunny greeted us. The corporal checked off our names from a list he held, handed us a folder crammed with papers, and directed us to Station 2. I continued to follow the yellow line.

When I reached Station 2, a pissed-off sergeant waited. "Did your fat-assed mother have any kids that lived, punk?" Bits of saliva flew out of his mouth and onto my face. "Open your files ladies, we ain't got all day!" The sergeant quickly grabbed the top paper from each file, then began screaming again. "Your bus will be leavin' for Fort Ord at three today, and you will be on it, dead or alive! Convicts, fairies, and crybabies follow the blue line; all you other Girl Scouts follow the yellow line to Station 3!" The sergeant pointed in all directions at once as he barked his orders.

Assuming I was in the "Girl Scout" category, I continued following the yellow line. As I would learn throughout the process, the yellow line was the normal route to each individual station. If you were singled out at a station for any reason, you would then be instructed to follow the blue line. I had no clue where the blue line went and I didn't want to find out.

When I reached Station 3, I saw a plump long-haired kid doubled over, heaving his guts out while two sergeants hollered obscenities at him. The two sergeants, who resembled bulldogs from the same litter, appeared to be having a good time at Chubbie's expense.

At Station 3, a corporal divided us into groups of twenty-five. Things slowed down at this point, and the insults became more personal. I was number 23 in my section. Most of the guys in our cluster had shoulder-length hair or longer. Our clothing varied greatly. I wore a pair of Jack Purcell sneakers, Hang-10 shorts and a "Go Army" T-shirt I had received as a gag gift at my going-away party. I had intentionally picked that particular T-shirt to wear, thinking it a good idea to disguise myself as a person about to become a proud member of the United States Army. A majority of the other guys in my bunch wore torn, faded Levi's jeans with T-shirts that sported a variety of slogans and advertisements.

Toward the front of the line, I caught sight of a long-legged guy with a bulbous nose and grimy hair. He had made the idiotic mistake of wearing a T-shirt that read "Make Love, Not War!" on the front, and featured a picture of Jim Morrison (lead singer for The Doors) on the back. This was equivalent to throwing raw meat to a pack of wolves. At every station, the sergeants assaulted and brutally degraded him for his wardrobe choice. A dark, sadistic part of me took pleasure in the young fool's suffering.

Soon we headed toward Station 4. Once in earshot, I listened closely to the two sergeants at the front of our line. One by one they verbally mugged the victims preceding me. By the time I reached the front, I had learned to stare straight ahead and, more importantly, not to talk, smile, sneeze, cough, blink, twitch, or breathe. The burly sergeant with matching sweat rings under both armpits grabbed the pile of papers out of my hand, glanced at the first sheet, and started laughing in my face. He quickly thumbed through my papers, making a check mark with his pencil on each one.

When the sergeant handed the papers back, he barked at me like a seal: "Joined, huh Whalon? What a dumbshit! Bet your recruiter said you were gonna be drafted—for your information, Whalon, a recruiter can't get draft info. It's classified information, dimwit! That's the oldest trick in their book, retard. Don't feel bad, Whalon—there's a shitload of dumb-asses like you passing through here every day. You're just another dumbshit screwed by his recruiter so the man could meet his quota for the month. You *are* a dumbshit, right Whalon?" The sergeant stood inches from my sweating face.

I stood silent, not quite sure if he really wanted a reply.

"Answer me or I'll kick your skinny ass right here in front of all these other fairies—answer me!"

I realized that no matter what I did, it would be the wrong move. Answer him or remain silent, I was doomed.

"Answer shit-bird, NOW!" he roared.

My mouth felt as dry as desert sand. I replied, my voice barely above a whisper: "Yes, sir."

His face instantly became beet red. "Did you call me 'sir,' shit-bird? I'm a sergeant, not a fairy officer." For a moment, I thought the sergeant would head-butt me. "You had better get your vacant head screwed on straight Whalon, or you ain't gonna make it outta here alive today. I will cut off your tiny balls and stuff them down your throat if you ever call me 'sir' again. Move your syphilitic ass outta here now!"

As I quickly moved forward and around the corner toward Station 5, I took my first full breath in three minutes.

Our demoralized herd moved quickly through Stations 5 and 6. As we waited for our arrival at Station 7, we espied a corporal with canary-yellow teeth and bad breath. The corporal's responsibilities included recording our height and weight. Corporal Canary Teeth had a different insult for every person in line, making this process much longer than necessary. Finally, I stepped on the scale, wondering what would happen if I hocked a big ole mucus-filled loogey in Tweety's face. Would I be drummed out of the Army on the spot or ushered into a small room where two or three sergeants would kick the livin' shit out of me? I knew the answer.

After the weigh-in at Station 7, the corporal handed each of us a medical questionnaire attached to a clipboard. He instructed us to fill out the form and return it to him when we finished.

After all twenty-five zombies had handed in their forms, we were herded into a miniature, dingy, musty-smelling room with three vending machines, eleven chairs, and a severely coffee-stained wooden table with the phrase "Welcome to Hell!" etched in it. Someone instructed us to take a ten-minute break. I decided to use the time to silently retrace my life.

Six minutes into our break, a corporal burst into the room and screamed at us to get off our "dead asses." He told us to follow the yellow line to Station 8, which he announced would be the medical exam. Now I had my chance to end this nightmare—Whalon's Last Stand!

I had carefully prepared for this moment. A few of my civilian friends and I had been working on a "Nose Plan" for two months. It was simple but foolproof—or so we had convinced ourselves while we chugged Colt 45 Malt Liquor and devised it. Since the age of nine, I had broken my nose five times while playing various sports. I had what was medically termed a "deviated septum," and could barely breathe through my nose. It was obvious to anyone looking at me that my nose had been broken. My mother had taken me to a specialist years before. He had advised us to wait, and to fix the nose after I reached adulthood and had finished playing sports.

My buddies and I decided to use this defect to my advantage. With my most pitiful look (one I had practiced before the mirror many times), and using the pathetic voice I had so skillfully honed, I'd relate to the doctor the extreme

18

difficulty I experienced when physically exerting myself. I'd inform him of the problems I endured with hyperventilation during periods of stress and mild exercise. I had done my homework and felt totally prepared to relate the Nose Plan in detail to my medical examiner. After hearing the facts, the Army doctor would, of course, sympathize with my plight and classify me 4-F—physically unfit for military service!

After Station 4, I had cleverly worked my way to the front of our pathetic bunch of recruits. I was now the first person in line. I had calculated that it would be better to see the doctor first, before he had tired of looking at the medical questionnaires of the twenty-two boys ahead of me.

"Whalon, get your flat ass in here!" a voice from the office boomed.

Before entering, I turned to the motley crew lined up behind me and confidently gave them a wink and flashed the peace sign, secure in the knowledge that the doctor would soon declare me unfit for military service and send me home where I belonged.

After taking a deep breath through my mouth, I hurried inside the room. Without looking up, the Army doctor gruffly ordered me to sit. He carefully studied my medical papers. When he put my file down, he leaned back in his chair, looked me in the eyes, and smiled wryly.

"I see you broke your wrist when you were twelve years old—any problems with it since then?" he inquired.

"No sir, it is fine now," I answered respectfully.

"Now, what about that broken nose of yours? Any problems there?"

This was too easy. My months of rehearsal were about to pay off—good-bye Army, hello Redondo Beach.

"Yes sir, I have extreme difficulty breathing when I exercise and in stressful situations…"

"Stop it, Whalon!" he barked, cutting me off abruptly. "You're going to make me cry like a baby."

Gazing at me with a smirk, he said, "Look at the bright side, boy—when you go to Nam, you won't be able to smell all that shit you'll be shoveling on latrine detail." He laughed loudly at his own joke; I didn't! "Now get your whining, pansy ass outta my office and follow the yellow line to Station 9." As I stood to exit his office, the doctor began laughing even louder.

So that was it. The Nose Plan had taken a nosedive. I knew, as I entered the hallway, that the entire group in line had heard every word. I made a quick left toward Station 9 but couldn't resist looking back, over my shoulder, at the guys waiting. They were all laughing, winking, and flashing me the peace sign. I gave a double middle-finger salute and disappeared around the corner.

At Station 9, they began combining groups. A section of about forty survivors waited silently in front of a large metal door, cleverly marked "ST. 9." Soon the door flew open, revealing the most enormous, towering hunk of flesh I had ever seen in my life.

Borrowing a phrase from the renowned wrestler, Freddie Blassie, the giant bellowed at the silent flock, "All you pencil-necked geeks get your asses in here and press 'em against the wall! Move it you sissified, long-haired fairies— get against the wall and keep your filthy traps shut!"

While the sergeant barked out his instructions, the disoriented herd charged inside and scrambled for a position along the wall. The massive room grew deathly silent when the behemoth slammed the door and stepped to the center. The temperature in the room must have hovered over 90 degrees— however, I had a chill.

"Ya look like a bunch of pansies and fairies. Well, bad news: two of you lucky fairies are gonna be Marines—jarheads." The sergeant began laughing.

The door swung open and two more Goliaths, bigger than our giant, entered the chamber.

"This is Sergeant Olsen and Sergeant Fann of the United States Marine Corps." With that, the Army sergeant then exited the room, slamming the door behind him.

It had somehow gotten even quieter.

"You look and smell like a boatload of rotten mackerel!" Fann boomed.

As Fann did his best to degrade and humiliate his terrified quarry, Sergeant Olsen strolled around the Circle of Fear. Abruptly, Olsen stopped, pivoted, and then maneuvered his body in front of the shortest quivering puppy in the room. Olsen came nose-to-nose with his puffy-faced prey.

"You're a gross, obese, greasy-faced, lard-assed pumpkin. I wouldn't let you kiss a Marine's ass, Fatty Arbuckle." Olsen turned and began circling again.

Howling like a jackal, Fann reported, "We're gonna grab two of you fairies to be in the Marine Corps. Anybody thinkin' he's got big enough balls to fill a Marine's jock, step forward."

No one in the room moved a muscle. Olsen began slowly approaching my position on the wall. I prayed to God and the Virgin Mary above: please, please, please don't let this vicious, menacing thug stop in front of me. God let me down that day.

"You scrawny, bony, long-haired fairy—what are you lookin' at, Tinkerbell?" Olsen's hot breath increased the amount of sweat pouring from my head. "You wanna be a Marine; is that it, punk?"

21

For some unexplainable reason (that I am still unaware of to this day), I smiled at the fire-breathing sergeant.

"I'll knock out your buck teeth and shove 'em up your bony ass if you don't wipe that smirk off your face!" Olsen roared.

He grabbed me by the neck with his left hand, squeezed my testicles with his right hand, and pressed his forehead hard against mine. He then began growling like a rabid dog. It took every ounce of the bodily self-control I had to keep from pissing through my boxer shorts and on his right hand. I knew that would be my death warrant. When he finally let go, the psycho Marine screamed in my face, showering me with saliva and small chunks of an unknown vegetable.

"You couldn't fill a Marine's jock with those tiny marbles—fairy!" Already heard that line asshole, I thought to myself.

Olsen returned to the center of the room near Fann and then whispered a comment into the sergeant's ear. Fann nodded his approval and walked up to the largest casualty in the room.

"You lose, queer bait!"

Sergeant Fann grabbed the trembling kid by the hair and dragged him outside. Olsen smiled as he circled the remaining carcasses like a vulture. I was still coughing and gasping for air from the chokehold when the sergeant stopped in front of the second-largest recruit in the room.

"Another loser—get your fat ass outside. You're in the Corps now, crybaby!"

He grabbed Loser Number Two by the scruff of the neck and ushered him towards the exit.

Before slamming the door, the brutal Sergeant Olsen fired a parting shot at the survivors. "Army fairies!" he screamed.

At this point, I was exhausted, confused, and severely depressed. Somehow, something had transported me to another world where the inhabitants spoke a strange, harsh language and wore peculiar outfits. I seriously wondered how I could possibly survive three years of this living hell. I wanted to cry, but knew it would be a fatal mistake in this bizarre world where the rulers devoured their young.

After the "Marine Lottery," we ate lunch in the main dining room, which actually looked more like a deserted airplane hangar. I had no appetite, so I grabbed a carton of milk from the counter and sat at a table in the back of the room. It amazed me to see how little the inductees conversed among themselves. The fear of doing something wrong had kept everyone silent during our processing. Now everybody was still petrified of talking to anyone for fear of drawing attention his way. Although hundreds of nervous inductees filled the building, the place was as quiet as a Sunday church service. When the sergeants weren't screaming at us, the place reminded me of a convention for severely depressed mutes.

The processing at the final two stations consisted mostly of signing papers and filling out forms. At 2:30 p.m., we returned to the dining area. Soon after all the inductees had gathered in the room, a sergeant marched into the area, stood on a wobbly table up front, and addressed the assembly.

"Okay ladies, listen up. Everybody with a last name beginning with a letter A through M proceed through those doors." The sergeant pointed to five open doorways located toward the rear of the room.

About three minutes later, the sergeant made a similar announcement for the remaining recruits, whom I dutifully followed into a gymnasium-like room outfitted with slow-moving overhead fans. On one wall hung a faded portrait of George Washington and a striking photograph of Mount

Rushmore. In the front of the room stood a podium with a microphone; an American flag hung from a pole. Within minutes, two sergeants and a major entered the room. The major smartly marched to the podium.

"Stand up, men," the major ordered.

We all stood.

"Raise your right hand and repeat after me—I do solemnly swear…"

Everyone obediently repeated his words. When we had completed the oath, a twisted smile appeared on the major's face.

"Congratulations men, you are now proud members of the United States Army."

He flashed a stiff arm salute, snapped it back to his side, and exited the room. The two sergeants followed.

Nobody cheered.

Chapter III

Only the Lonely

(Roy Orbison, 1960)

We spent our first three days at Fort Ord at the reception center, completing the necessary processing. Fort Ord was located in Northern California, two hours south of San Francisco. It encompassed the basic training site for new recruits from the Western states. The main job for the sergeants assigned to the reception center was a simple one— get the "new meat" prepared for their short truck ride to the "Hill," the place where we'd train. Getting "prepared" meant having our heads shaved (an extremely traumatic experience for us longhairs, who believed our extended locks contained the secret for picking up on chicks), being issued our stylish, olive-drab (OD) Army fatigues, filling out dozens of forms, and signing official Army documents which I really didn't understand. We also learned the proper way to salute officers, received numerous, painful shots designed to protect us from diseases common to our new occupation, and discovered an even deeper meaning of the phrase "verbal abuse." The highlight of my three days at the Reception Center was the popular physical exam, complete with the "turn-your-head-and-cough" maneuver.

At 8:00 a.m. on August 31, as we stood at attention for morning formation, the sergeant in charge commanded us to orderly board the trucks parked behind the barracks. The 160 head-shaven recruits piled onto the three colossal trucks waiting to transport us to "Hell on Earth"—at least that's what the sergeants had been calling the Hill for the last three days. I jumped onto the second truck and took a seat toward the back.

I had learned one valuable lesson during my first few days as an Army recruit: blend in. You didn't want to be noticed or singled out for anything—your weight, height, voice, accent, habits, birthplace, race, religion, or physical abnormalities. Be average. Recognition is bad, anonymity is good, I had come to believe. Hearing your name screamed out was very bad, but hearing someone else's name screamed out was very good. During the next eight weeks of training, I'd learn numerous, useful rules that would serve absolutely no purpose outside of the Army structure.

Within seconds of our trucks coming to a stop in front of the barracks, a swarm of drill instructors (DIs) began circling, screaming obscenities and barking orders to the herd of terrified sheep. Recruits scrambled from the trucks, jumping out the back and off the sides of the vehicles. More rabid DIs stood on the cement slab in front of the building, growling and pointing at the disoriented group. It was chaos personified. After the DIs had corralled all 160 of us, they stood us at attention in semi-straight rows of ten. Then the company commander appeared and addressed the soldiers.

"My name is Captain Wilder. I am the company commander of C-2-1. Company C—2nd Battalion—1st Brigade. We are Charlie Company, mighty, mighty Charlie," he informed us in a singsong voice with obvious pride.

"You will spend the next eight weeks being trained in the Army way of doing things. Forget what you learned back on the block (an often-used Army reference to your hometown). It has no significance here. In many aspects of your training, you will see..." He babbled on for fifteen minutes, spouting the Army party line.

It was all bullshit as far as I was concerned—the continual screaming, the personal insults, the orders, the intimidation, and the obsessive need to instill fear at every turn. Of course, I had decided this wasn't a good time to share my theory with the DIs. It became crystal clear to me, as the captain rambled on, that the army had locked me in for a long, bumpy ride. This daily nightmare would continue for three years. For the next thousand-plus days, I'd wake up as a member of the United States Army, would eat Army chow, wear Army uniforms, sleep in Army bunks, and listen to Army propaganda. The reality of the situation deeply depressed me.

As Captain Wilder had explained, the general purpose of basic training was to teach us the Army way of thinking and behaving. More specifically, the Army wanted to transform each of us from the piece of human garbage he was upon arrival, and into a proud soldier who would take orders and obey commands, without question, from all superiors. The army had no interest in our petty concerns or grievances. In basic training, the weak were scorned and ridiculed. If you had a fragile recruit in your platoon, the DIs would punish us with PT (Physical Training). The DIs insulted and taunted everyone daily, but no one dared respond. If you displayed a physical or mental weakness, the DIs would seize the opportunity, never letting you forget your defect. It was truly another world, with a rigid system that had proven successful for almost 200 years.

After Captain Wilder's speech, the DIs divided us into four equal platoons of forty soldiers each. A platoon consisted of four squads, ten recruits in each. I was in the 4th Platoon, 4th Squad. The 3rd and 4th Platoons were housed on the second floor of the barracks.

The 4th Platoon DIs, Sergeant Lugar and Sergeant Vogel, quickly began insulting our parents, wives, girlfriends, and pets as we stood at attention in front of the barracks. Just to our right, the men of the 3rd Platoon had their asses reamed by the head DI, Sergeant Hopper. He ordered them to "haul your sagging asses into the barracks and upstairs and put your bunks and footlockers in Army shape or I will climb down your throat and eat your liver!"

A few minutes after the 3rd Platoon had disappeared through the doors, Sergeant Lugar gave us a similar order. "You douche bags had better be ready for inspection in ten minutes," Lugar screamed, "or your asses are mine—did you hear me, MINE!! Move it, move it—all I wanna see is assholes and elbows!"

The other thirty-nine 4th Platoon recruits and I charged through the barrack doors and up the stairway. Unfortunately, Sergeant Hopper, the DI of 3rd Platoon, had just ordered his men back outside for some PT, because some homesick, baby-faced recruit had broken down and started crying. Our platoon had climbed halfway up the stairs when the third Platoon came charging down. The confused members of both platoons slowed down and started peacefully filing past each other.

When Sergeant Lugar (easily the most sadistic drill instructor assigned to Company C) saw this, he let out a blood-curdling scream. "Get up those stairs, 4th Platoon. You better not let those dingleberries from 3rd come down here! Kick their asses! Kick their tutti-frutti asses! Run 'em over—don't you let one of them perverts down the stairs or I will PT your asses all night!"

When Sergeant Hopper heard the challenge from Sergeant Lugar, he issued one of his own. "Third Platoon, kick those sleazebags out the damn door! Run their asses over—don't you let those peckerwoods up here! If one of those maggots makes it up the stairs, you all die tonight! Forget 'bout goin' to Nam—you die *tonight*!"

In an instant, "Stair Wars" began. 3rd Platoon started violently pushing down, trying to get past us, and we began the difficult journey to the top of the stairs. It got ugly fast. No one knew who belonged to what platoon. Recruits shoved each other onto the stairs and the platoons trampled each other. Everybody screamed and swore. Punches flew, bodies were kicked, but nobody backed off. The fear of what the DIs would do far outweighed the potential for a black eye or busted lip. I ducked my head and pushed forward. I was three steps from the top when a nasty looking guy standing at the peak of the stairwell dove into the crowd, sending a group of us crashing to the ground.

As I struggled to my feet, I heard a familiar voice screaming instructions. "Knock it off—knock it off now or you'll be repeating basic training! Sergeant Lugar, Sergeant Hopper, get your asses over here!" yelled a visibly unhappy Captain Wilder.

"You DIs had better get your men squared away now." The captain's voice echoed through the stairwell. "Clear this stairway! You have one minute to clear this stairway!"

Slowly we moved past each other, 4th going up and 3rd coming down. Wilder ordered the two DIs outside as the confused members of the 4th Platoon entered the bay where our cold, steel-framed bunks awaited us.

One of the guys in our platoon spoke up. "I'm Simon Gentry—I'm a reserve and have some experience with this kind of stuff. We should all find a bunk and stand at attention in front of it. Sergeant Lugar will be in soon and he is gonna be pissed off!"

Nobody questioned Gentry. We were all thrilled to have someone else make a decision for us. I found an upper bunk in the middle of the bay and set my duffel bag on top.

Seconds later, the door burst open. Sergeant Lugar, followed by Sergeant Vogel, stomped to the middle of the room, stopped, and proclaimed, "YOUR ASSES ARE MINE, MAGGOTS! Every minute of every day, your sagging asses are mine! You swingin' dicks just caused me an ass chewin' from the CC (company commander) and that ain't the way I planned on startin' my day!"

Lugar began picking up empty footlockers and throwing them across the room, pushing over sets of bunk beds, and ripping mattresses to the floor. His crimson face radiated heat, and froth shot out from the corners of his mouth. Sergeant Vogel silently stood in the center of the bay, scowling at the terrified members of the platoon.

"Drop and give me fifty, and I mean fifty!" screamed Lugar. The group immediately began counting out push-ups.

"Any of you buttercups who can't do fifty push-ups will be runnin' all night tonight!" The enraged DI stopped yelling and began circling, staring at our pitiful attempt to complete the command. For another five minutes, Sergeant Lugar ranted about how he would work us to death, how we wouldn't last two weeks in his platoon, and how we resembled pieces of dingo shit that should be flushed down the shitter.

When he completed his tirade, the ruby-faced sergeant heaved one last footlocker, walked to the double doors at the head of the room, turned, and gave us a final order: "You have ten minutes to get this slum in shape!" he bellowed. "Get your footlockers together—when I come back, there will be an inspection!"

I had arrived on the Hill only an hour earlier and depression now crushed me more than ever.

Surprisingly, the days of basic training took on a routine. The training exercises varied slightly but the schedule was predictable. Lights went on at 5:00 a.m. every day. We dressed quickly, made our beds, straightened our footlockers, *dand* raced outside for the dreaded morning run. The DIs always waited in the same spot for us when we arrived, and they always gave the same command: "Drop your jackets and flat hats—left face—forward march—double-time march."

In the early morning we ran six laps around a half-mile track. At the end of the three miles, the DI du jour would always inquire, "Who wants more?" The first few days of basic, some gung-ho wiseass would scream, "I do, Drill Sergeant!" and we would run another mile. It didn't take long for word to spread throughout the four platoons—anybody opening his big mouth after the run would get his ass kicked while he slept! After one week, the gung-ho loudmouths fell silent.

After the run, we lined up for breakfast in front of the mess hall. It didn't matter where you stood in line; you had fifteen minutes to eat from the time the first recruit grabbed a tray.

We filled our days with traditional forms of training: drill and ceremonies, marching, rifle range, bayonet, hand-grenade toss, the despised obstacle course, and the never-ending PT.

Once a week, the DIs treated us to archaic Army training films that covered a wide range of subjects the Army believed would keep us from trouble in the future. My personal favorites included the one on venereal disease, circa 1948, and the classic on the evils of smoking marijuana, released in 1955. I loved film day. If someone could keep his head from bobbing forward, he could catch a few surreptitious z's. Of course, anyone caught dozing ended up in front of the group, standing at attention and sucking his thumb, while singing "Mary Had a Little Lamb" or "Pop Goes the Weasel."

For the entire eight weeks of basic training, our movements were restricted to the barracks and the company area, unless accompanied by a DI for a specific reason. Although Fort Ord was larger than most small cities, our world included only the places necessary for training. When we had rifle practice or obstacle-course training, we would march to a location, perform the activity, and run back to our barracks. After dinner, we usually cleaned our rifles, scrubbed the bay and bathrooms, and shined our boots. If we hustled, we could complete all our responsibilities by 8:00 p.m., giving us one hour before lights out. If exhaustion hadn't felled us by then, most guys usually wrote letters or broke off into small groups and talked about home. The days grew long and physically demanding. If someone in the platoon didn't screw up during the week, the DIs gave us Sundays off. For a group of us, that meant poker day. Our little group of gamblers would play cards from early morning until just before lights out.

As the days turned into weeks, the routine became more bearable. I made many friends during this period of rigorous training. I had also come to grips with the fact that I was stuck in the Army for three years and, like it or not, should try to enjoy myself whenever possible. As our graduation day grew closer, the insults and verbal barrage lessened and, surprisingly, the DIs began acting like civilized human beings.

The day before our graduation, I was assigned KP (kitchen police) duty in the mess hall. While working in the dining room alone, cleaning the tables after lunch, I heard truck engines in the company area next to ours. I walked to the back of our dining area and looked out the last window. I viewed three trucks pull up, with bodies flying everywhere. New recruits for D Company had arrived for their first day of basic training. I watched in amusement as the DIs assaulted the confused, frightened young men scrambling to line up in straight rows.

A strange, satisfying feeling swept over me as I watched the mad scramble. Had it been only eight weeks since I had gone through this ordeal? I watched and laughed out loud at this comical, entertaining sight. The last row of terrified recruits, lined up on the pavement, stood only about twenty feet from my perch.

I couldn't resist the temptation. "Hey, asshole—asshole. Over here."

A skinny, ashen-faced guy at the end of the line glanced around to see where the voice was coming from.

"Get out now—go AWOL (absent without leave) tonight," I said in a voice just loud enough for him to hear. "They'll kill you here—it's Hell, living Hell!"

He turned away, and then turned back.

"Have fun for eight weeks, shit-bird," I said as I began laughing at the twisted look on his face. "I'm gettin' out tomorrow and you got eight weeks of torture to look forward to!" Like a grade-schooler, I stuck out my tongue and waved to him.

His expression never changed. In a sick and twisted way, the confusion and fear on his shrunken face elated me. He was just beginning his introduction to this brutal military transition period and I was almost finished. Better him than me, I selfishly thought, as I watched the all-too-familiar routine. A chill swept through my body as I imagined having to repeat this ordeal, but it passed quickly. The longer I watched the new recruits, the more satisfied I became. The perverse pleasure I derived from their suffering didn't faze me in the least. I had survived my basic training and was stronger for it—physically and mentally! Graduation would follow the next day. Soon afterwards, the Army would ship me to my next duty station for more training. For whatever bizarre reason, the few minutes I enjoyed spying on the terrified amateurs from D Company gave me complete peace of mind for the first time in eight weeks.

Graduation morning brought with it a bag of mixed emotions for many of the 160 newly minted Army privates. Although most were thrilled that they had completed basic, many of them would go on to infantry training—11 Bravo (11B). The common belief at the time was that 11B provided a sure ticket to the jungles of Vietnam. Because I had joined for three years, I had been guaranteed the school of my choice. I'd travel to Fort Gordon, Georgia to become a Teletype Operator (72B).

After graduation, I had two hours to say my good-byes to the many close friends made during the past eight weeks. To my surprise, it proved to be an extremely emotional experience. For the first time, I realized how strong a bond I had developed with this random group of strangers. I fought hard to hold back the tears as I shook hands for the last time with my platoon mates. Chances were that I'd never see them again. There was also the strong possibility that some of these guys wouldn't return from the battlefields of Vietnam.

I waved to a small group of my new Army friends and then ran over to the waiting taxi that would take me to the Oakland Airport.

"Oakland Airport, please," I informed the driver after hopping inside.

I could no longer hold in my overwhelming emotions. For the second time in two months, I was leaving my friends behind, traveling to another unknown place. I slumped in the seat and pulled my cap down to cover my watery eyes.

The concerned driver turned and asked if I was okay.

"No, but just drive to the airport," I replied quietly.

Chapter IV

Georgia on My Mind

(Ray Charles, 1960)

On November 2, 1968, the military shuttle bus I rode in drove cautiously through the iron gates of Fort Gordon, Georgia—my new temporary home. Fort Gordon served as the Army training site for the Military Police and the Signal Corps. This was the place where I'd receive my advanced training to become a teletype operator for the United States Army. This period was also the genesis of my thirty-one month odyssey in the Army—an unforgettable journey filled with extraordinary characters, bizarre events, and exhilarating adventures. I had no idea at the time, but many of us who became friends at Fort Gordon would spend our entire military careers together. We formed a human concoction of misfits, malcontents, and apathetic Army privates; this coterie would wreak havoc on lifers and test Army limits whenever and wherever possible.

Like a paper clip to a magnet, our passionate desire to roam freely again in the streets of Hometown, USA drew us together. We didn't consciously develop into a gang of rabble-rousers, attempting to disrupt the Army way; however, we did draw strength from each other's actions and over time developed into a contentious band of agitators looking for our next cheap thrill at the Army's expense. Though we lacked the sophistication and experience necessary for our many schemes, we nonetheless came armed with enough street smarts to spread our developing cancer: a dreadfully poor attitude toward military service. Whether or not it was our youth, resentment of authority, desire to outdo each other, loathing of military structure, fear of death, or a combination of all of these factors, collectively we dispised Army life and sought our retribution on any lifer who got in our way. At our core, we were a collection of spoiled youth, awkwardly making the

35

transition to manhood without the benefit of critical thinking, respect for authority, or an appreciation for the role we had to play in the preservation of freedom and the American Dream. These factors combined to create a collective human albatross that would hang around the neck of the United States Army for the next three years.

I spent my first weekend at Fort Gordon exploring my surroundings, meeting some of the guys I would train with, and playing poker. Card games such as poker, hearts, and spades would develop into my favorite pastime. It provided an excellent way to kill time and an even better way to pick up a little extra cash. A gambler at heart, I always prepared myself to offer or take a bet on anything—sports, politics, dice, cards, or whether it would rain that day. I loved the action and the thrill of putting my hard-earned money on the line.

No one would consider many of the young men in the military in 1968 among the sharpest tools in the shed. Simply put, an abundant supply of plain old dumb-shit guys protected our country during this turbulent time in our history. It was a reality of the military draft system—dumb, poor guys in; smart, rich guys out. Fortunately for a few other players and me, many of these "educationally challenged" young men loved playing cards and actually had the delusion that they excelled at it.

In the Army, it didn't take long for many of the guys to pick up reputations based on arbitrary factors, such as physical characteristics, accents, hygiene, stereotypes, rumors, the state they hailed from, etc.

Fortune smiled in this regard, simply due to where I had grown up. As a Californian in 1968, I enjoyed instant cult status in the Army. My being from Redondo Beach, a city mentioned in the 1963 Beach Boys' classic song, "Surfin' U.S.A.," also served me very well. Southern California was the "in place" to live in the late '60s and early '70s. California had the beach, the music, the hippies, the drugs, the movie stars and, most of all, a never-ending supply of blonde beach chicks. That was the prevailing wisdom anyway.

For my entire three years in the Army, my coming from California created amazing opportunities and kept me away from numerous bullshit assignments. Without hesitation, I used this status to my advantage whenever possible. Many evenings, with ten or twelve wide-eyed guys huddled around my bunk—including New Yorkers, Texans, college grads, high school dropouts, city slickers, and country rednecks—I would spin wild tales of my life in Redondo Beach. I entertained the gathering with anecdotes of drunken parties, where the suntanned chicks outnumbered the guys two to one, or of my exploits surfing fifteen footers at Huntington Pier, Malibu, and Hermosa Beach. I embellished these yarns with a combination of partial truths and outright lies, but my audience didn't care; neither did I. Soon I became known as Cal, the guy from Redondo, or just Whalon. I also earned status as the preeminent poker player in the company—a well-deserved reputation, I might add.

Calling my teletype training boring would be the understatement of the millennium. For five days a week, nine hours a day, we talked about typing, practiced typing, and took typing tests. Sometimes boredom so overwhelmed me that I actually regretted not going to infantry training. An all-male class did nothing to make the days pass more quickly. At least in high school when I got bored in class, I could play grab-ass with some cute chick. Goldfish had more personality and charisma than the typing instructors at Fort Gordon. I knew our sergeant tutors had earned their certificates from the "How-To-Be-Extremely-Monotonous Academy," and proudly displayed them on the walls at home. After seven tedious weeks of training, I completed my final typing test by successfully passing the thirty-five-word-per-minute minimum standard.

The following Monday a sizeable group of teletype school graduates gathered in the huge hall at the training facility for a brief graduation ceremony. After a few mind-numbing speeches from some of the pedantic instructors, a major addressed the gathering. He informed us that the graduates in the top five percent of the class would go on to some type of advanced training. The remainder of the grads would take assignments at new duty stations by the end of the week. In a striking example of my previous declaration relating to the intelligence of many draftees, I somehow finished in the top five percent, despite my less-than-illustrious previous academic performance. I had worked hard to maintain a "C" average in high school (the lowest qualifier to keep the parents off my back). I had also attended a partial semester at a community college and, before dropping out, had maintained a solid 1.5 GPA. Needless to say, most of the smart guys back home had figured out how to beat the system by staying in college and getting good grades. They were now safe and sound, sleeping in their own beds at night and eating their moms' home cooking.

The names of the lucky top-fivers were posted on the company bulletin board on Friday. We would attend a mandatory meeting Saturday morning to hear the details of the advanced training to come.

"Good morning men!" the much-too-jovial major bellowed across the room. "You should be proud of yourselves. You are the best and the brightest the Signal Corps has to offer." Oh shit, I thought. The Army is in serious trouble now. "You men have been chosen as the first trainees for the Army's new computer system, known as DSTE" (Digital Subscriber Terminal Equipment.)

The major beamed proudly as he continued. "You fifty men are the top of your class—the cream. Your contribution to the Army will go down in history—mark my words."

For the next forty-five minutes, between hollow platitudes, the major explained in excruciating detail exactly what we would carry out: the Army's "Master Plan" for its new computer system. Also during his speech, he dubbed our group the Fab 50 (a rip-off of the Fab Four, the Beatles). This name would stick with us throughout our military service.

The Army would install its first computer systems in five sites throughout the world. The fifty men selected for training would be divided into five groups of ten, with one group training at each site. The plan called for us to operate the system and, more importantly, to train other Army personnel to operate the equipment. I took this as fantastic news, since none of the five sites was located in Vietnam. The following Monday, we would transfer to the newer barracks on the north side of Fort Gordon to begin another training phase.

The "new" section of Fort Gordon, where we went for our advanced training, was a vast improvement compared to the old buildings. The private toilet stalls—a luxury!—contrasted strongly with the open, group "shitters," where two rows of twelve toilets faced each other, like two football teams squaring off for scrimmage. (I had often walked nearly a mile to the base PX, just to use its private restroom and avoid taking a crap in a small, poorly ventilated room with ten or twelve other guys squatted around me producing noises and smells that could make a grown man whimper.) The two-story red-brick buildings housed large, eight-man rooms (only seven guys lived in our room) and newer bunks. Even the doors locked! I compared it to moving from skid row to an upper-class gated community. Being one of the "smart" guys had its privileges.

We moved into our new living quarters two days before Christmas. Our training would begin in the new year on January 6. We had two weeks off for the Christmas holiday. During that period, I met most of the other members of the Fab 50.

The day after Christmas, I rounded up a few of the guys and we began a poker game. It turned into an on-again, off-again match lasting ten days. Although we limited the game to seven players at a time, at some point during the ten-day span, twenty-six different members of the Fab 50 played in it. During this marathon session I met and became acquainted with the guys who would become my best friends over the next couple of years.

A poker game is the perfect setting in which to learn what makes a person tick. The financial ups and downs of a game tend to bring out the true personalities and emotions of the players. During the game, I closely studied those twenty-six players and how they related to others. By the time our DSTE training began, the nucleus for a small band of nonconformist dissidents had been formed. Although we had many things in common, one powerful sentiment coursed through our veins—we hated being trapped in the Army. By the time the last hand folded, I had met six guys I really liked and wanted to make my friends. Four of the six played in the game, while the other two dropped in occasionally to observe and shoot the shit with the players.

Bill Harper, from Rocky Mount, North Carolina, was the only poker player who possessed the skills to play at my level. I would later learn that Bill was an accomplished hustler at 9-ball (a pool game). Harper intentionally used his Southern drawl to make people underestimate him. After an hour of playing poker with Bill Harper, I knew he was a sharp card player and a master at reading people. Bill possessed an abundance of street smarts and a marvelous sense of humor.

By the end of our first hour playing together, I knew Bill Harper was my kind of guy.

Jerry Judge, from Boston, Massachusetts, was a sharp-tongued dart thrower. Jerry loved instigating little feuds between two card players, and then adding fuel to the fire. I rated him the third-best card player in the pack of gamblers, although he falsely considered himself the best. Jerry Judge, much like me, loved getting in the last word of any conversation.

Hailing from the Bronx, Bill Oswald was a party guy. Like a mosquito in the tropics, Oswald hovered anywhere he'd find action. He squeezed every drop out of life and always stayed until the end of any gathering. Our combative arguments on the virtues of California versus New York became legendary during our military service.

San Franciscan Gene Bellotti epitomized the hippie culture of the late '60s. Bellotti, the "coolest" member of the Fab 50, related astonishing stories of growing up in the city of "Peace and Love." Gene displayed a terrific sense of humor and loved to laugh.

Mark Goodman and Dave Schrunk didn't care for playing poker, but they enjoyed passing the time observing the game.

I took an instant dislike to Mark Goodman of Wilmington, Delaware. He began his sarcastic comments the minute he first walked into the poker room. Any time someone made a bad move at cards or mispronounced a word, Mark would unleash a mocking string of comments aimed at the offender. Goodman, one of the older college guys, wanted everyone to know of his superior intelligence. His swift wit, searing retorts, and love of debating proved deadly for many who came his way. After a few days of sitting through Mark's acerbic attacks, I began to sense the depth of his comic genius. I often fired back at him; he enjoyed the challenge. By week's end, Mark and I started hanging out together and teamed up against defenseless young men not as skilled in such verbal assaults.

Dave Schrunk, from Dubuque, Iowa, often joined us in the poker room but never played. Dave, another older college guy, was more of a fatherly figure. He would always look for the logic in a situation and calculate his move accordingly. Dave became known for offering sound advice to us youngsters. However, instead of seriously listening to his counsel, we would often take the opportunity to make fun of his opinions and ruthlessly rip his ass. Our attempts to ridicule his ideas seldom discouraged Schrunk, and he never got mad at us. Deep down, I knew Dave was usually correct, and I made a point of having him as my roommate at each new duty station. I understood well that I needed an informal guardian during my Army stint—someone to protect me against myself. Dave Schrunk was the perfect man for the job.

This unique group of American youth possessed some common traits that drew me toward them. In varying degrees, all of them revealed a razor-sharp sense of humor, quick wit, and a love of adventure. They also sought to test Army limits and travel with the lead pack. They were rebels with an edge; that's exactly what I needed to help pass the time.

On January 6, the Fab 50 began the five-week training course for the Army's DSTE computer system. The entire system consisted of seven separate machines, lined up next to each other in a large, temperature-controlled room. The equipment measured over twelve feet long, and formed the military's first computer system. These machines, when perfected, would drastically improve the communication ability of the Army, or so thought the Department of Defense. I had no clue what a "computer" was or what it did. Harper, Bellotti, and I often joked about the system. We couldn't see the future value of a machine that sent messages from one place to the other. We believed these so-called computers would go down in history as another Army boondoggle. Obviously, Bill Gates didn't hold membership in the Fab 50.

The concept of the system was rather simple. The seven DSTE machines stood together in a row. The teletype operator would type a message on the standard teletype machine (not part of the DSTE system), producing a long, thin perforated tape. This tape, containing the message to be sent, the operator fed into the first DSTE machine. This tape produced a number of perforated cards that shot out into the tray of the second machine. The operator would then stack the cards in the card hopper of the third machine. The cards would automatically weave their way through the next three units and end up in the hopper of the sixth machine. The message had traveled instantly to its destination. The seventh unit was the receiving machine. Perforated, secure cards were spit out at the receiving end. A technician could then feed the cards into a card reader, which produced a typed message. The system, much faster than the old, cumbersome teletype machines, resembled e-mail, though it lacked the latter's blazing speed.

During the final week of classes, the Fab 50 received the greatest news we would ever hear during our three-year stint in the Army. It occurred at our daily morning muster. A young sergeant delivered the surprising news bulletin.

"Men, your training here is almost complete," he began. "You will be shipped to your new duty station at the end of next week. Once there, you will be assigned general duties until your Top Secret Clearance background checks are completed. This process usually takes about six or seven weeks."

I had mentally prepared for the worst locations: Kansas, Texas, North Carolina, or Alabama. You know, some shit-hole Army base in the middle of a cow pasture, where I could do nothing except watch prairie dogs pick ticks off their asses. Someone informed us early in our training that the

Army would station us at a base somewhere in the United States. There we would stay until the five sites had the DSTE system installed.

"You unbelievably lucky ladies," he continued with obvious envy, "are being sent to Hawaii for the next phase of your processing. You shit-birds have hit the Army jackpot!"

Had I heard him correctly? I glanced at Dave Schrunk to confirm the remarkable statement the sergeant had just revealed to us. Schrunk was smiling along with everybody else in the formation.

"Anybody here want to stay in Georgia with me?" the sergeant sniped sarcastically.

"No thanks, sergeant!" Mark Goodman loudly replied.

As the sergeant droned on, I closed my eyes and mentally conjured up a glorious image of myself, lying on the beach in Honolulu, Hawaii. In my fantasy, three gorgeous, suntanned Hawaiian hula girls fanned my bronze body as I sipped on a mai tai. Of course, a fitting Doors' tune, "Light My Fire," played in the background.

Chapter V

Blue Hawaii

(Billy Vaughn and His Orchestra, 1959)

"Pete, check it out man—does y'all beach in Redondo look like this one?" Harper, seated next to me on the flight to the island of Oahu, Hawaii, was being a wiseass. He often intentionally exaggerated his Southern drawl for effect. After gazing out the window and pointing, Harper turned my way and broke out in laughter.

"No, Billy Boy," I countered, mimicking his drawl, "ours has more sand, more surfers and lots more chicks lying half-naked on the beach."

Our plane made its final approach to the Honolulu Airport, banking left over Waikiki Beach. Our military flight held more than two hundred energized GIs, all headed for their new duty stations in beautiful Hawaii. As the plane touched down, every enthusiastic GI cheered and screamed.

Upon exiting the plane, I noticed something intriguing at the bottom of the stairs: two stunning Hawaiian women placing colorful flower leis on the necks of the disembarking GIs. Never one to pass up a corny line, Dave Schrunk remarked how great it was to get laid on his first day in Hawaii.

After we retrieved our duffel bags from baggage claim, a corporal instructed us to board the two OD-green Army buses waiting outside the terminal.

Fifteen minutes later, we pulled up in front of our living quarters, Fort Shafter. Our new home stood just five minutes from the crystal-clear waters of Waikiki Beach! A corporal advised my band of fifty DSTE operators to go inside to the second floor, pick bunks, put our gear in lockers, and then meet in the mess hall in an hour for orientation.

When we had gathered in the mess hall, a captain marched to the podium resting on the right side of the small stage and addressed our group. "Men, I am Captain Sewell, the man responsible for your actions at Fort Shafter. Welcome to Hawaii. I've been informed that you men will be stationed here awaiting Top Secret clearance approval from headquarters. We're happy to have you here, but be advised that you must comply with all orders and directions from your superiors, or you will be in a world of hurt—I shit you not! At this point in time, I am not sure just what duties you'll be performing yet. At Monday morning formation, we'll have our shit together and you'll get an assignment at that time. Since it is Friday, you may take the weekend to familiarize yourself with Shafter and the surrounding area. You may obtain a weekend pass from the company clerk, Corporal Rikker, tomorrow morning at 0800, but be advised—watch the sunburn if you visit the beach. Some of you swinging dicks are whiter than rice." The captain giggled at his rice line. "Also, stay outta the queer bars or you will end up in the brig—I shit you not! If you have any questions, the company clerk will be glad to assist you. And don't go to town and get drunk and end up in jail or your asses are mine."

The captain turned and smartly left the room.

A potbellied lieutenant with a paper-thin moustache and a shaved head took over. For the next thirty minutes, he bored our group with details on what we could and, more importantly, could not do while at Fort Shafter. As had become my custom, I didn't listen to a word he said. I spent the time fantasizing about the chicks I would meet on the beach that weekend, and wondering if they sold Colt 45 Malt Liquor on the island. When the lieutenant finished, he dismissed us, then ordered us to the barracks and "get our shit together." In the Army, lifers overused the popular phrase "get your shit together" as often as store clerks today spout the hackneyed phrase, "Have a nice day."

Our first weekend in Hawaii was magnificent! We invaded the beach like a swarm of locusts. To prepare properly for action that Friday night, I made a trip to the base PX and armed myself with all the necessities: a transistor radio, a pair of gaudy, fluorescent sunglasses, a bottle of Coppertone suntan lotion, a tourist guide to the islands, a pair of orange-and-yellow Hang-10 swimming trunks, and a bottle of expensive Hawaiian coconut oil that promised to make my bronze skin glisten in the noonday sun. I also purchased a large cooler to house the numerous cans of beer we would consume over the weekend. And to Jerry Judge's and my delight, the first liquor store we visited had a large supply of cold Colt 45 Malt Liquor.

As the resident expert on "beach protocol," I felt obligated to pass on my vast knowledge and experience to the beginners in our gang. I spent that first day on the beach giving bodysurfing lessons to the "Easterners," sharing my most successful pickup lines, explaining what to do when caught in a riptide, and pointing out the various chicks on the beach who didn't belong in bikinis. We concluded our first day on the beach with a raucous debate on the controversial subject of blondes vs. brunettes. By the time we settled the issue, it was too late to catch the last military transport back to the barracks. Since we didn't have to return to Shafter until Sunday night, we decided to stay at a Motel 6 near the beach. At 7:00 p.m., twenty-one drunken or semi-drunken Army privates staggered across the busy street by the ocean, stopped traffic, and booked four rooms for the night.

Although it had been one of the greatest days of our lives, we did suffer a few casualties from the long, sizzling day at the beach. About half of the group returned severely sunburned and in agonizing pain. One of the guys, whom we had badgered into drinking Colt 45 instead of Pepsi, vomited in the lobby of the motel and had to take a taxi back to the barracks. We decided that the best medicine for those "wounded in action" was the consumption of large quantities of Colt 45.

That night in our rooms, we drank, laughed, sang, told derogatory stories about the guys back at Shafter, and dropped water balloons from our balconies on anyone who looked as if he wouldn't retaliate. Later that night, we ventured out to some local clubs for an evening of dancing, obnoxious behavior, and trying to score on some local chicks.

When Sunday morning rolled around, we got up, showered, used any means necessary to relieve our well-deserved hangovers, and then headed for the beach to begin the grueling process all over again. That raucous weekend in Hawaii turned out to be one of the most enjoyable of my undistinguished military career.

The lifers at Shafter found it challenging to keep our pack of indolent privates busy. There were simply not enough "shit details" at the fort to keep fifty guys busy all day. After two weeks of listening to our snide comments and inane questions, they gave up! After their surrender, they required us to be present only for roll call at the 0800 morning formation. By 0830, the Fab 50 was dismissed until 0800 the next day. The superb life we enjoyed had just gotten better!

I had come to believe that our group's negative attitude toward the military and its horde of lifers was a development of several factors. Like me, most of the Fab 50 had joined the Army to avoid the draft and a tour of duty in Vietnam. The majority of the fifty did not respond well to authority; they also enjoyed the daily challenge of verbally mixing it up with the lifers. The guys in my circle of friends had quick wit and rebellious natures. Much like a street gang, we fed off each other and competed to outdo the last defiant act. We thoroughly enjoyed showing off for our peers by displaying the prowess for delivering stinging remarks to inferior lifers.

We derived benefit from two distinct advantages over our military leaders—youth and an extreme sense of invincibility.

We descended on the beach daily, like a herd of cattle released each morning to graze freely on the open range. For the most part, we were an overbearing, obnoxious gang of young, cocky, beer-swilling, foul-mouthed Army immigrants in search of our next cheap thrill. One day during our first month on the island, someone came up with the brilliant idea of chipping in and renting an apartment across from the beach. One week later, we had the keys to our own small one-bedroom apartment, only one block from Waikiki. It would serve as a crash pad, beer hall, place to shower, and general hangout; in other words, a military commune for the Fab 50.

We tastelessly furnished our pad with beach chairs, a nineteen-inch black-and-white television, a record player, and two refrigerators to house our brew. We voted Colt 45 Malt Liquor as the official beer and called our new place the "Black Hole." We made two mandatory rules—first, replace within twenty-four hours all beer you drink and, second, flush the toilet after every use. Later, we added an amendment to the second rule: if at all possible, after eating Mexican food, take your "dumps" at the filling station on the corner. Nobody followed these regulations very closely.

One morning, Willie Stuart, one of the two blacks in our group, charged into the barracks. He rushed up to Harper, Judge, Oswald, and me as we sat on my bunk playing poker. He was overly excited, incoherently babbling a mile a minute. Although it took some effort to slow Willie down and extract the relevant details, we eventually pieced together what he had seen and heard.

Stuart had gone to the company commander's office to get a weekend pass. Then he overheard Corporal Rikker talking to the CC, Major Winder. Our spy was sitting in a

49

chair, out of their view, waiting for the corporal to come out of the office. Soon, the two men started discussing the fate of "the computer guys from Georgia." Apparently, the Army had experienced mechanical problems with the DSTE equipment. As a result, Army brass decided to delay the system's projected operational date for at least one year. Stuart heard the major tell Rikker that he had no need for the DSTE operators; therefore, he would assign our group to Hawaii permanently. Stuart quietly left the office and rushed back to give us the incredible news.

Stuart started laughing after delivering his big scoop. The rest of us began cheering and shaking hands. I celebrated with everyone else, but felt a gnawing ache in the pit of my stomach. I had always believed in the old adage, "If it seems too good to be true, it probably is."

Mario, one of the college guys and a clear-headed, rational thinker, wanted to be sure that Stuart didn't have his information screwed up. He asked deliberately, "Are you sure, Willie—really sure? Don't screw with us. If you're not sure, tell us. This is no time to jump to conclusions. You're sure you heard him say our group would stay in Hawaii?" Mario stared into Stuart's eyes looking for telltale signs of doubt.

Willie was adamant. "I'm sure, Mario—I'm positive I heard what I heard. They didn't see me sitting 'round the corner by the water cooler. I heard every word. We're stayin' in Hawaii, we're stayin' at the beach. I ain't shittin' nobody. I shit you not!"

That was it!—a firm confirmation. Most of the Fab 50 had gathered around Willie by this point. The barracks erupted again. We howled, danced, hugged, backslapped each other, shook hands all around, and giggled loudly. My nagging feeling went away. We'd live in Hawaii for the next two-plus years. Unbelievable! Utterly unbelievable! With the war raging in Vietnam, we would serve our country as we kicked back at the beach in Hawaii.

After settling down, we all agreed it was best not to mention the news until the CC officially notified us. We geared up for a wild, wild weekend on Waikiki Beach. Lock up the women and children and remove Granny's hearing aid! It's party time for the Fab 50!

Ten days had passed since Willie Stuart dropped his bombshell and still we hadn't received official word on our status. I grew slightly concerned, but wrote it off to Army incompetence, governmental red tape, and a jealous reluctance to give us the good news.

In Hawaii by this time, more acquaintances from our training in Georgia had become my good friends. Paul Price from New York, Lee Mills from Florida, Charles Hardy from Philadelphia, Willie Stuart from South Carolina, and Larry Pratt from Maine all became part of my inner circle of close buddies. Army life could not have been any better had I planned it myself. But then came "Black Friday."

As the Fab 50 stood outside in front of the barracks for morning formation that day, we heard the news. On that cool, dreary Friday in late May 1969, a military "hammer" dropped on our collective heads. Sergeant Trundle began slowly, clearly savoring the moment. "Ladies (he always called us ladies, as if we hadn't heard it a hundred times before), I deliver great news to you today."

Here it comes, I thought—the announcement we had waited for! I smiled and winked at Harper standing next to me. He smiled and winked back. My euphoria was short-lived, however.

"It's days like this that make me proud to be in the United States Army." Trundle was much too happy, I thought. "You men are being given the opportunity to serve your country at a time when it needs you most. You men are being sent to The Republic of Vietnam—you will now be given the chance to fight for the preservation of our freedom!" He continued, but I had gone suddenly deaf.

My heart skipped a beat, my legs felt like boiled spaghetti, and my eyes began watering as my throat closed. I gasped for precious oxygen. This must be some sort of cruel, vicious Army prank, designed to make us tougher, I thought in disbelief. On my right, Paul Price collapsed to his knees, while others joined me in choking and gasping for air. To me, it was no different from having a doctor tell me I had terminal cancer. To a bystander, it must have looked as if a horde of invisible aliens had descended on our formation and begun beating the shit out of us.

The stunned assembly of suntanned soldiers glanced around for reassurance that this was just a sick, twisted mistake. The more distress we exhibited, the wider the shit-eating grin on Trundle's face became. He truly enjoyed the group's pain. What happened to Stuart's discovery about our orders to remain in Hawaii? I looked ahead two rows at Stuart, but he just stared at the ground. It wasn't Willie Stuart's fault, but I blamed him anyway.

How could this happen to me? I wasn't even remotely prepared for Vietnam—only for partying at the beach. Nine months ago, I was home playing grab-ass with my friends; today a pock-faced, malicious sergeant told me to prepare to fight in a war I didn't understand. I didn't know whether to cry or charge Trundle and choke the life out of him. I stood silently staring at the blue sky overhead, trying to conjure up visions of better days.

Through a friend in the CC's office, I would learn the next day that Major Winder *did* know that Willie Stuart sat around the corner, and he had made up the story of our getting orders to remain in Hawaii. Apparently, the major just wanted to screw with our heads and get a little payback for our blatant disregard of the Army and its leaders. Everyone around Shafter knew the lifers despised our rebellious group. They thought of us as hippies, and one thing old-school lifers despised was hippies. Apparently, it rather pissed them off that we could drink beer, and soak up rays at the beach every day, while they had to stay confined on the base to work.

Sergeant Trundle wasn't through messing with us that day. He gleefully continued: "With your help, the war in Vietnam will be won in the next two years! We are on the brink of a historic event..." Mississippi native Farrell Farmington, a skinny, pimple-faced kid with an anemic look and bad teeth, interrupted Trundle's "victory" speech by heaving his guts all over the pavement.

Trundle displayed his compassion. "Hey Barney (an often-used derogatory Army reference to Barney Fife of *Mayberry* fame), whattaya gonna do when Charlie (nickname for Vietcong soldiers) starts firing his AK-47 at your skinny ass—puke on him?" The cheerful sergeant tittered like a co-ed.

Farmington had started a mini chain reaction. Two more distinguished members of the Fab 50 deposited their breakfast of chipped beef and biscuits on the pavement. The smile quickly vanished from Trundle's face. The sergeant was losing control of the formation and he knew it.

Our gathering of spoiled soldiers was ill-prepared for the bitter news we had just received. The fear of Vietnam in most of us was as real as the war itself. A couple of nut-jobs in our group, inflicted with John Wayne Syndrome, relished the idea of fighting in the infested jungles of Vietnam. However, they were the exceptions.

After Trundle finished his obscenity-laced tirade (filled with classic Army clichés about shaping up and facing our duties like men), he regained control of the shell-shocked gathering. As he rambled on about malaria, vaccinations, Purple Hearts, jungle rot, mosquitoes, and a host of other nauseating Vietnam-related possibilities, my mind wandered. Orders to serve in Vietnam had remained my biggest fear since the day I had registered for the draft. As a result, I—like my brethren—had grabbed onto the belief that we'd be staying in Hawaii, far from the conflict in Southeast Asia. That dream, however, had been violently crushed!

The formation now fell deadly silent, resigned to the reality of our situation. We were going to Nam!

We spent the remainder of Black Friday getting vaccinations, watching a rerun of my favorite film on venereal diseases, and packing our few belongings for the trip. As an added bonus, a crazy-eyed, one-legged Vietnam vet from Hawaii treated us to a lecture. Captain Sewell introduced him as Curly (though his bald pate shone brighter than Mr. Clean's) Lamar, a "badass" dude who had served two tours in Nam and knew more about the bush than most gooks living there. In his Edward G. Robinson-like voice, Curly proceeded to scare the living shit out of us with graphically violent stories of body parts flying here, heads exploding there, while the VC soldiers burned babies in huts as they simultaneously executed the babies' parents in the street. He was one freaky-looking dude the Vietnam War had completely destroyed.

Shortly afterwards, as I carefully prepared my treasured record albums for the journey home, one of the sergeants walked past. He noticed one of my albums and just couldn't keep his big mouth shut. "That's right, Whalon. Send that Bob Dylan Communist-shit album home to mama. That Dylan fairy ain't gonna do you no good when you're face down in a rice paddy, eatin' water buffalo shit and pickin' bullets from a Cong sapper outta your ass!" He laughed like a donkey.

I had absolutely no clue what he was babbling about, but it sent a bitter chill down my spine. I don't think anyone slept well that night.

The next morning at 0600, an irritable, crusty old sergeant hastily crammed us into three undersized Army buses and transported the Fab 50 to the Honolulu Airport. At 0730, we departed for the eighteen-hour flight to the Republic of Vietnam.

Again, nobody cheered.

Part II

Battle for Warehouse 32

June 1969 - November 1969

Chapter VI

Leaving on a Jet Plane

(Peter, Paul & Mary, 1969)

The grueling eighteen-hour flight to Vietnam mentally drained me. As I sat between Bill Harper and Dave Schrunk, I unsuccessfully attempted to doze. Next, I rationalized my situation, striving desperately to put a positive spin on the reality I faced. Okay, so all my plans and schemes to avoid the Army and Vietnam had failed. Here I was, sitting in a plane with a one-way ticket to the "bush." Once there, I might get shot and killed—or perhaps worse, paralyzed. Then again, I could get only slightly wounded and be sent home a "war hero." Then all the good-looking chicks would surround me at parties and beg to hear some more of my harrowing "Nam" stories.

On a more mature note, I considered responding intellectually to the challenges ahead, welcoming the opportunity for new experiences while embracing Vietnam's cultural differences. After a short mental debate, I decided on a course of action: make the most of a dreadful situation; quit feeling sorry for myself; attempt to stay safe; keep out of trouble; and remain off all "shit-lists." Those resolutions formed the new-and-improved "Whalon Plan."

We made a short, one-hour stop in Osaka, Japan, to refuel and to change flight crews. In the airport gift shop, I purchased a gaudy, multicolored Japanese smoking jacket for my dad and an inexpensive, imitation-pearl necklace for my mom. My poor taste came to light when I found that my mom had buried the "pearls" in the bottom of her jewelry box; they never saw the light of day. My dad wore the smoking jacket one time only—to change the oil of his lime-green 1966 Dodge Dart. After the plane was refueled, we boarded it once again for the remaining six hours of our flight.

Suddenly, the somber, gruff voice of the pilot shook me from my catnap: "Men, we have just crossed the border and are now flying over the Republic of Vietnam. We will be landing at Bien Hoa Air Base in approximately twenty minutes. Please remain seated."

A chill surged through my body. Everybody on the plane moved toward the tiny windows, eager for his first glimpse of Nam. Jungle stretched out before us for as far as the eye could see. No roads, no buildings, no people— nothing but dense, dark-green foliage.

Schrunk, the eternal optimist, offered calming words. "Don't sweat it, kids. We're going to be in Saigon, the capital of Vietnam; we won't even see the jungle after we land, boys. Relax—look on the bright side; this might be a hoot. I hear there are some good lookin' chickadees in Saigon." Schrunk's inane observations made me want to crush his windpipe with my thumbs.

"Dave, shut your wrinkled lips (a reference to his advanced age of twenty-three years)," I retorted. "If I start to have 'fun' in this jungle, you have my permission to blow me away with the nearest gun—please."

Neither Harper nor I was in the mood for optimistic prattle.

"Shit-fire, gramps, y'all just a silly ass," contributed Harper, jumping in. "You'd rather be here than Hawaii, I bet. This is gonna be a world of hurt—no more cheery talk, man!" Harper used his exaggerated Southern drawl in an attempt to irritate Dave.

I sat down as the others gawked at the endless variety of trees, bushes, weeds, and shrubs. I could see no purpose in trying to gather insight at an altitude of two thousand feet. The moment I plopped down, a tidal wave of anxiety consumed me: I'm in Vietnam! I never truly believed I would end up there. In the most remote corners of my mind, I had subconsciously held out a glimmer of hope that something or someone would intervene and spare me from this certainty. Now all hope had been extinguished.

The absolute reality of my situation started my insides churning. "Shit!" I half-screamed to no one in particular. I found it difficult to breathe.

Harper turned from the window. He asked with feigned concern, "Waz up, Whalon—you okay?"

"I just remembered… I left my favorite sunglasses in Hawaii," I joked. I could see no good reason to share my epiphany with Bill or anyone else.

As our plane touched down at Bien Hoa Air Base, Republic of Vietnam, Schrunk, undaunted by our verbal mugging, attempted his misguided brand of historical humor. In what I can only assume was his best Franklin Delano Roosevelt impression, he chimed, "You have nothing to fear but fear itself!" He chuckled like a preteenaged girl.

"Screw you, Skunk! Sit down," Jerry grunted from the row behind.

"Where's your sense of humor, Jerry? That's a classic Roosevelt," Dave gleefully said without turning around.

"Up yours, FDR!" As always, Jerry Judge loved getting in the last remark.

For five minutes, we had to wait in the motionless plane. Finally, the door swung open and we, the "fresh meat," began unloading. By the time I exited, I could see a stream of would-be heroes dragging their duffel bags toward an enormous metallic building about 300 yards away. The procession reminded me of a line of soldier ants advancing on a sugar cube. Inside the hangar, numerous rows of folding chairs faced a small stage at the front. I assumed a plane had arrived before ours, since a large group of rookies all ready sat in about the first ten rows. Standing at the entrance to the building, I glanced back to see another plane landing. Our group jockeyed for some chairs and waited for the third group to join us. A few minutes after the third cluster settled in the chairs, a captain walked to the microphone at center stage and addressed the somber gathering.

"Men, welcome to the Republic of Vietnam. Hotter than hell here, isn't it?" The captain smiled—we didn't.

"Upon completion of your orientation today, you will be transported to your duty stations throughout the country. If your duty station is further away, you will be taken by C-130 transport planes tomorrow morning. All assignments and any information you'll need are on the bulletin board at the rear of the room. Everybody check the boards to make sure your name is there before you exit the building today. This orientation will take approximately three hours. Don't ask anything until the speaker calls for your questions. Listen to every word that is spoken here today because it just might save your cherry ass." After these final words of warning, the captain stepped off stage to talk with the upcoming speakers.

A pause in the program came up, so I considered the captain's final advice. This far in my Army employment, I had never listened very closely to any of the endless, mind-numbing orientations and lectures I'd attended. Making a calculated decision, I concluded this might be the time to start having an open ear. I hoped to gain some small insight into what lay ahead for us.

Meanwhile, I desperately attempted to conceal that I was terrified out of my mind and about to lose the stale box lunch I had consumed on the plane. I diverted my attention from my stomach by observing the room. As we waited for the next presenter, the first thing I noticed was the different green shades of the uniforms the men wore. Everyone wore the same olive-drab jungle fatigues in Vietnam. The difference was that the fatigues all the "new meat" wore were bright OD green. In contrast, the sergeants standing along the walls and the huddle of speakers near the stage wore faded green uniforms. With the intense heat and numerous washings, fatigues quickly and continually faded. The lighter your fatigues, the longer you had been in country. It was an unspoken status symbol to have an very faded uniform, since it signified lots of time in Nam.

The first speaker, Captain Moore, prattled on about malaria, jungle rot, the clap, pubic crab lice, syphilis, gonorrhea, typhoid fever, and encephalitis. He advised us on how to avoid them, how to get rid of them and, if you did contract them, what to tell your wife, girlfriend—or both—if you brought any of them home for a visit. The captain's talk both informed and disgusted us at the same time. I didn't want my friends to think I had no experience in such matters, so I continually nodded my head as if I knew exactly what the captain was talking about. Honestly though, at least half the stuff he covered I'd never even heard of.

A smart-assed lieutenant by the name of Higgs, who distinguished himself by sporting grimy, stringy red hair, delivered the next talk. Higgs tutored us on the "heavy shit." "Men, your asses are in a war zone, and in a war zone, men get wounded, men lose limbs, and men die! Are you prepared to die? Are you prepared to die for your country? You'd better be prepared, 'cause if you're prepared to die, you'll have a better chance to live!"

About twenty guys who apparently knew what Higgs was talking about began clapping. Maybe I had missed something, but his gung-ho declaration made absolutely no sense to me—although I understandingly nodded along with all the other clueless cherries. Glancing left and right, I noticed Harper, Judge and Schrunk all bobbing their heads. Give me a break, I thought, you dudes are as clueless as I am.

The looie (nickname for lieutenant) howled on. "How you react to a hostile situation could make the difference between the life and death of the man next to you." I glanced at Harper sitting to my left, shook my head, and whispered, "You're seriously screwed, Harp!" He elbowed me and muttered, "So are you, Whale."

"You cherries had better learn to sleep with one eye open, to fart silently, to shit in your boots, to piss in your hat, to eat bugs, to crawl on your gut in torrential rain, to smell Charlie comin' five klicks away, and to hear the poisonous snakes crawlin' through the bush, or you will not last one damn day in this godforsaken shit-hole. The 'bush' will eat you alive and spit out your bones if you are a pansy-ass! I shit you not, new meat, I shit you not! Be smart, watch your ass, and listen to the vets—you just might make it back to the world in one piece. Good luck, you're gonna need it, cherries." With that, he did an about-face and marched off the stage. After the lieutenant left, I wasn't quite sure whether to laugh about his presentation or cry at my situation.

Now that was a speech John Wayne and General George Patton would have been mighty proud of—a lecture from a gung-ho lifer who lived for this shit. Higgs loved the Army and he loved the war. Most of all, the lieutenant loved scaring the shit out of new cherries such as the terrified captive audience he'd just freaked out.

The remaining speakers covered subjects pertaining to military life in Vietnam. We learned about the Vietnamese currency and the exchange rate for the U.S. dollar. *Piaster* was the name for the paper currency of Vietnam and *dong* the name for the coins. A frail-looking sergeant with a nervous twitch delivered a brief warning about Vietnam's black market. He also gave us another warning about street whores, tea girls, and the high rate of VD among GIs. That prompted one goofy-looking GI toward the front of the room to yell, "Sarge, how many piasters for a good whore?"

To this the sergeant replied, "I don't know 'bout a good one, boy, but a bad one goes for 'bout one thousand P (the abbreviation used for piasters)." The sergeant's response received a roaring laugh and a loud cheer from the gathering of cherries.

After the orientation, we spent two hours filling out more forms, getting more shots, and then writing a mandatory letter home. The lifers instructed us to inform our loved ones that we were doing just fine after our initial hours in Nam.

Once we completed our letters, the members of the Fab 50 wandered to the back of the hangar to check out our assignments. Schrunk spotted our unit on the board and relayed the information to everyone. The fifty privates from Stratcom (our unit designation in Hawaii) were to meet a Sergeant Cowing in front of Hangar C at 2:30 p.m. to arrange transport to Saigon. After some confusion in finding Hangar C, the weary members of the Fab 50 piled onto three Army trucks for the twenty-five mile ride to Saigon, our new duty station.

Chapter VII

Heartbreak Hotel

(Elvis Presley, 1956)

Fifteen of us sat crammed into the back of the lead truck as it weaved its way through the crowded streets of downtown Saigon. The avenues of this bustling city were jam-packed with bicycles, modified motorized bicycles with two-seater passenger compartments in the back, taxis, cars, motorcycles, and military vehicles, plus a never-ending stream of crossing pedestrians. Vehicles of all sizes zigzagged their way through traffic while horns honked. Vietnamese locals screamed and gestured at us as our truck drove past them. I wasn't sure if they were cheering our arrival or threatening our lives.

The scene reminded me of my drunken high-school excursions to Tijuana, Mexico, where street traffic pulsated in constant chaos. In Saigon, no one obeyed the traffic laws—not the few on the books, anyway. It was truly "survival of the fittest."

For instance, although most of the intersections had traffic signals or stop signs, nobody seemed to pay much attention to them. The chaotic system seemed simple enough. The bigger the vehicle, the more respect and fear it garnered. The Vietnamese papa-sans, usually pedaling two passengers via their modified bicycles, had the slowest and smallest of the vehicles. The Lambrettas, a motorized version of the pedal bikes, and also capable of transporting two passengers at once, were easily able to maneuver past the huffing and puffing papa-san pedalers. The drivers of the small taxis (mostly Volkswagen "Bugs") constantly beeped their horns as they frantically waved their hands out the windows; somehow these VW drivers skillfully dodged the pedestrians, pedalers, and Lambrettas. Military vehicles had road supremacy—a fact that many of the locals did not appreciate.

The Vietnamese citizens crossed the streets at varying speeds as traffic raced around them. I would quickly learn that the key to crossing the hectic streets of Saigon was to keep moving and never stop. As one grizzled, beer-bellied sergeant explained to a group of us: "Keep your dead ass movin' or you'll end up a 'pavement patty'—I shit you not!" (I don't believe the term roadkill had been coined until after 1969.) Actually, in some peculiar and unexplainable way, the street turmoil functioned quite well. Rarely did I witness a serious traffic accident, although there were numerous minor fender (or leg) benders.

Once we passed the official city limits of Saigon, there were Vietnamese people everywhere—old, young, men, women and children. They walked in front of our vehicle, beside it and behind it, some smiling, some waving, and some shouting unknown words and phrases. Many of the children laughed and ran after our truck, holding out their hands. I would quickly learn that they wanted money, food, or cigarettes to bring home to their families. Vietnamese children hustling GIs in Saigon had developed into an art form by 1969.

The hillbilly sergeant riding shotgun in our truck was screaming helpful hints out his window to us cherries in the overloaded back of the pickup. "Keep your eyes on the gooks with their hands in their pockets," the compassionate sergeant up front counseled. "These dinks are well-known for tossin' grenades into the back of military vehicles."

I couldn't help wondering how many guys had actually been killed on their first day in this godforsaken, backwards country. While we kept our eyes peeled for flying grenades, I relayed a scene to Harper from a war movie I had seen years earlier. A grenade had been tossed into a foxhole and one of the guys dove on it. He saved his buddies but lost his own life. I pointed to Dave Schrunk. "Bill, think we can count on him if a grenade lands here?" I said jokingly.

"I dunno; let's ask," replied Harper. "Dave, me and Pete were wonderin.' Will you dive on a grenade to save our asses if one comes in the truck? We're younger and prettier and got more to live for." Harper loved to needle Dave.

"Sure, no problem," Schrunk responded. "Everybody's gotta go sometime, right Harp? Actually, I might just throw you on top of it and sit on you."

Harper started laughing while Judge added fuel to the fire. "Harp, you gonna let him talk to you that way man?"

Judge had barely got the words out before the sergeant up front screamed, "GRENADE—GET DOWN!"

I saw it out of the corner of my eye, floating in the air, heading right for me. Before I had time to shit my pants, I realized that grenades were not orange. The obnoxious sergeant in front had tossed an orange into the back, trying to freak us out.

"Hey ladies, you can change your panties when we get to the hotel." The sergeant pulled his oversized head back into the cab and began laughing hysterically along with the driver.

"Screw you, lifer," Bellotti muttered softly enough so the sergeant couldn't hear him..

"Schrunk, I didn't see your ass on that orange," Harper began again.

"Only grenades, country boy. Only grenades, not fruit." Dave picked up the orange and tossed it to a small boy running alongside our truck.

"That sorry-ass lifer is just screwin' with us 'cuz we're fresh cherries," observed Bellotti.

This seemed to make sense but I still stayed alert.

Soon we pulled into a small gravel parking lot next to the Hung Dao Hotel, our new living quarters for the next six months. The Hung Dao had six floors, with Air Force personnel occupying the first five. The Fab 50 would occupy the entire sixth floor.

Dave Schrunk and I took one of the rooms at the end of the hall. Mark Goodman roomed with Paul Price, Jerry Judge with Bill Harper, and Bill Oswald teamed up with Gene Bellotti. The rooms were furnished with the basics— two small beds, one dresser, and a nightstand. At the end of the hall was a rec room with a pool table and a few chairs.

When we arrived at the Hung Dao, we were told to go to a mandatory meeting at 6:00 p.m. in the sixth-floor rec room. Sergeant Foster—the NCOIC (noncommissioned officer in charge) at the warehouse where we would be working—would meet with us and answer our questions.

Having a little time, Dave and I unpacked our few possessions. I suddenly realized that our situation wasn't anywhere near as bad as I had imagined. We were in a hotel, in the capital of Vietnam, and would be working in a large warehouse far from the insect-infested jungles. Most importantly, no VC bullets would be whizzing around our heads!

At 6:05 p.m., a hefty, broad-shouldered black sergeant with an oversized gut strolled into the rec room. He was followed by another black sergeant who walked with a slight limp. They took the seats facing us in front and introduced themselves.

"Welcome to Vietnam, men. My name is Sergeant Foster and I am the NCOIC of the warehouse at Camp Davis, the place you'll be working at during the next six months. This is Sergeant Aaron, the sergeant responsible for warehouse operations." Foster gestured toward Aaron.

67

Sergeant Aaron nodded but didn't look up. He appeared to be a man who had been beaten down by the system over the years and was quietly putting in his time until retirement.

With little or no information at my disposal, I often made hasty, detailed conclusions about complete strangers. Foster continued. "Every morning at seven, the trucks will leave for Camp Davis from the parking lot across the street at the Imperial Hotel. You will be off on Sundays, and Saturday will be a half-day of work. The trucks will leave Camp Davis at five each afternoon and return you to the same parking lot across the street. On Saturdays, you will leave Camp Davis at noon. I expect everyone to be on those trucks at seven. If you miss the trucks, you are AWOL and better have a damn good reason why you missed the pickup. If you do miss the trucks, get a taxi as fast as you can and get your ass to the warehouse." Sergeant Foster paused to take a swig from the Coke can in his hand. "The Imperial Hotel is the mess hall for military personnel in Saigon. Breakfast begins at six. You will eat lunch at Camp Davis and eat your dinner back here. Since today is Saturday, you will be off tomorrow. However, Monday morning, have your asses on those trucks or you will be in a world of hurt, I shit you not. Early on Monday, we will go over exactly what you'll be doing at the warehouse. Now I'll answer any questions not related to the warehouse."

I decided at that moment, just for shits-and-giggles, to keep a running total, for the remainder of my military career, of the number of times a lifer said, "I shit you not" and "in a world of hurt."

"Can we leave the hotel when we are off work?" Larry Pratt naively asked.

"You may venture out on the streets, but be careful," Foster warned. "There's a lot of bad shit out there. There's also a midnight curfew. Don't get caught on the street after curfew or the MPs will haul your cherry ass to jail!"

"Do we need to change our money over to Vietnamese currency?" Tight-fisted Schrunk was already worrying about his bankroll.

"Actually, we will convert all your money into MPC on Monday," Foster said. "MPC is the military payment currency we use in the service, and it's accepted everywhere in Vietnam. You'll also pay for things with the local currency, piasters, at times. Good question. Bring all your American money with you on Monday."

Schrunk was proud of his question. In an attempt to sour the moment for him, I snidely whispered in his ear, "Kiss ass!" He ignored me. Although I needled Dave unmercifully, I truly did respect his opinion and was well aware of his big heart and his desire to protect me from myself.

"How do we send and get mail, Sergeant Foster?" one of the married guys asked.

"You will send and receive all mail at the warehouse. That will be your address."

Sergeant Foster's body language revealed he was more than ready to leave. We would learn over the next few months that Sergeant Foster was a man of few words; he had little patience for our petty concerns and sophomoric ways.

"Okay men, it was good to meet you. It looks like a good group and I'm sure we won't have any problems during your tour. See you bright and early Monday morning." Sergeants Foster and Aaron stood and began to exit the room.

Since some of the pack had come to expect an intentional "dumb-ass" question from me in these situations, I decided it was time to fulfill my obligation. "Excuse me, Sergeant Foster," I called out.

Foster turned in the doorway and saw me waving at him. "Yes, what is it?" he said, obviously exasperated.

"Private Whalon, sir." I knew he wasn't a "sir," but that always pissed off lifer sergeants. "How hot does it get in the warehouse, 'cuz I tend to freckle easily in extreme heat?" I struggled to keep a straight face.

Foster just shook his head and disappeared into the hall. It wasn't my best work but it would satisfy the wolves for now.

"Well, at least we know who the teacher's pet will be," I taunted, patting Schrunk on the back as I spoke. "Better have a nice shiny apple for Sergeant Foster on Monday or you might have to clean the blackboard, Dave." Why was I such a jerk sometimes?

"You're just irritated because I asked a good question, Whalon. By the way, next time you need a favor— don't ask." Dave's comebacks were rarely witty.

After a few minutes of small talk, most of the guys began drifting to their rooms. A small group of us stayed to shoot some pool and discuss our new residence. Though most of us were still a little nervous, as far as I could see, it was a pretty good gig. My situation appeared much brighter than the nightmarish projections I had envisioned. Maybe Schrunk was correct. This might not be such bad duty.

The Hung Dao Hotel would remain our home for half a year. Its lobby featured a miniature wooden front desk, four prehistoric chairs, a gaudy, yellow-brown plastic couch, and a pale-green palm tree that appeared to be close to death. Usually, two or three Vietnamese employees worked behind the desk, scurrying around and trying to do too much for the GIs that entered the lobby.

After a few weeks, I developed the strategy of moving quickly from the front door to the elevators. It was my attempt to pass the front desk unnoticed and avoid the barrage of broken-English chatter from the overly obsequious employees. I realized that they meant well but it

70

became embarrassing to me. "GI, you numba one—GI, mama-san cwean' woom, ok?" Or, "GI, you buy fo' me soap, Salem?" The locals constantly badgered GIs to purchase items at the PX for them so they could later sell the products on the black market. The Vietnamese coveted cigarettes, fans, and Tide detergent more than any other product.

If I succeeded in reaching the elevator undetected, the odds were an even 50-50 that I'd find it out of order. I enjoyed the exercise of climbing the six flights of stairs, but several of the more portly (okay, obese) guys bitched about it endlessly. It proved especially entertaining listening to the "chubbies" whine about the heat and how weary their fleshy legs became from the lengthy climb. I assumed the guilty pleasure I derived from their suffering was part of my "dark side."

The narrow hallway on the sixth floor, shaped like a horseshoe, had a prehistoric elevator in the center of the "U." Our room, at the end of the hall, had only one window that looked down on the lobby. At the other end of the hallway lay the rec room, with a creaky balcony overlooking Hung Dao Street. The rec room balcony provided the perfect place from which to people watch and occasionally drop water balloons (a bad habit we had picked up while in Hawaii). Of the twenty-two rooms on our floor, six were designed for three guys and the other sixteen for just two. The lifers stayed at another hotel—presumably for their safety—about one mile from the Hung Dao.

Although the street measured only sixty feet, crossing it to reach the mess hall at the Imperial Hotel became the most dangerous obstacle faced during our stay in Saigon. The traffic passing in front of the hotel never stopped and seldom thinned out until the midnight curfew. The key element in crossing to the other side, as we had been informed, was to keep moving. However, our first encounter with the "Saigon Death March" proved unsuccessful for one of the four pioneers in our group.

Bill Harper, Dave Schrunk, Larry Pratt, and I were the earliest members of our group to attempt a crossing. At first, we stood in amazement in front of our hotel, gazing at the never-ending traffic. It reminded me of the old Westerns I loved to watch on television when I was a kid. It resembled a good old-fashioned stampede, only with vehicles. There were no gaps, holes, or breaks in the traffic; it just kept coming in both directions. Drivers and pedalers made no attempts to stop—they just swerved to avoid contact. Horns blasted, people yelled, and GIs in "monster" trucks screamed obscenities out their windows at the smaller vehicles blocking their path.

Larry Pratt, well known for his naiveté, spoke first. "I don't think I can make it across—why aren't they stopping for us?" he asked with a quivering voice.

"In case you haven't noticed, nobody stops for anything. How in the hell can we get over there? There's gotta be another way," Harper reasoned.

"Yeah, Harp, let's call in a chopper to airlift us across," I chided. "Hey guys—from the rec room this morning, I saw some flyboys (Air Force men) cross. Hey, it's like the fat guy said, keep moving. It's attitude, boys—attitude. The flyboys just started walking and looking back and forth and they made it. I'm goin' for it, dudes—see ya on the other side suckers."

I welcomed the role of trailblazer. I'd cross first and lead the way, like Daniel Boone or Lewis and Clark. I waited for an opening. As a panting papa-san pedaled past us on a bicycle carrying two small, naked, crying kids on the handlebars, I made my move, like a puma, into the street. After four small steps, I broke the cardinal rule—I stopped. Horns blared and people screamed things I couldn't understand. Like a frightened rabbit, I scurried back to the safety of the cement-filled barrels in front of the hotel. I didn't have the nerve to look up, but I heard every word hurled at me.

"You big sissy, you're like a little bitch-girl, chicken-shit!" Harper was having a good laugh at my expense. "You are one sorry soldier, Whalon, I shit you not—you got zero guts and no balls." Harper was laughing so hard he could hardly get his words out.

"So that's how it's done, eh Whalon?" Schrunk followed. "Thanks for that valuable lesson. I think we all learned something here today—Whalon's afraid of the big ole cars and trucks. Big man Pete is gonna be the first to cross. Yeah, right—nice try though, Pete." Schrunk's humor was slightly more subtle than Bill's.

Harper wasn't quite finished with me yet. "Y'all pathetic, Whalon," he jabbed. "Big man gonna be the first across. All talk. See you chickenshits at breakfast." Harp stepped into the chaotic street. He kept moving, darting his head from side to side, bobbing and weaving, shuckin' and jivin'. In less than twenty seconds, Harp stood on the other side, shit-eating grin and all, waving and blowing kisses before he disappeared into the Imperial for breakfast.

"That redneck son of a bitch," I cursed. "I'll never hear the end of this—oh man, I can't believe it!"

Before I finished my lament, Schrunk, without warning, made his way across. Twenty seconds later, he was grinning, waving and heading in for a hot breakfast.

I knew that if I wanted to keep what little "manhood" remained, I absolutely had to cross before Larry Pratt. I made my move, determined to cross or die trying—Death before dishonor! I thought. With fear of failure as my sole motivation, I moved swiftly, jerking my head from side to side—this time not stopping. I easily made it to the other side. I followed suit, smiling and waving to Pratt, who looked lost and forlorn on the other side.

Pratt never did make it to breakfast on that first morning, but he did manage to cross the next day in time to catch the last truck pulling out for the warehouse.

Much to my surprise, it became routine for us to cross in traffic, although occasionally one of the group would get bumped by a small car or a puffing, pedaling papa-san.

Chapter VIII
Working My Way Back to You
(Four Seasons, 1966)

On Monday morning, three trucks and a van (the vehicles transporting the Fab 50) pulled up to the gates of the Tan Son Nhut (TSN) Air Base—the location of our new place of business. Located just outside of Saigon, next to the Saigon River, Tan Son Nhut was South Vietnam's International Airport and the major airbase for the U.S. military. The section of TSN with the Army warehouse was known as Camp Davis. Our vehicles slowly passed through TSN's front gates and began weaving their way around helicopters, planes, and Air Force personnel. Eventually we reached a large fenced-in building. Across and along the top of the fence surrounding the brick structure, lay an uneven row of barbed wire, carelessly spiraled. We drove through the oversized entranceway whose gate hung precariously from one gigantic hinge. The four vehicles stopped in front of a crumbling, red-brick structure the size of an airplane hangar. My group of guys began hopping out of the second truck.

"This place is a rat trap!" observed Jerry Judge. "The building looks like it's ready to cave in."

While Judge was shaking his head in amazement, Schrunk offered unsolicited, comforting words to our group from Truck 2. "Geez guys, quit complaining about everything—there's no VC here—no bullets flyin' 'round our heads. This ain't bad, believe me, this ain't half-bad— you guys just like to bitch about everything." As usual, Dave made a valid point but we didn't care.

"Yeah, Dave, it ain't bad to you 'cuz you're from Iowa," Bellotti taunted. "Iowa is just like this pile of crap!"

Bellotti wasn't quite as sarcastic as I was, but he was getting closer.

I shamelessly joined in on the "Schrunk bashing," with the comment, "This place looks like City Hall in Dubuque (Schrunk's hometown), Iowa."

"No, it looks like the 'drunk tank' at the Dubuque City Jail," Harper jeered. "The place where Schrunk's mom and dad spend their Saturday nights." He wasn't about to be left out of this ass-rippin' session.

At that instant, a cluster of sergeants, led by Foster, walked out of the warehouse and into the yard where all of us were now milling around the trucks. I continued the verbal assault on Schrunk. "Dave, I didn't know your whole family was going to be here," I needled, gesturing toward the sergeants standing just outside the warehouse. The assorted group of lifers surveyed the "new meat." A few of the sergeants waved us over to where they were standing. We slowly converged on their location. Sergeant Netton, the shortest one of the lifers, asked for quiet. Apparently unaware that we had met Sergeant Foster the previous evening, Netton introduced him to us.

I observed the faces of our curious gang of soldiers. Many of the guys were whispering to the person next to them, pointing at the building, or squinting from the sun as they observed the Saigon River just behind the warehouse. Some were smiling, but most of the guys looked as if they had just eaten rotten squid. I had the same reaction to this dilapidated brick structure. It looked as if it was on the verge of collapse. Displayed nearby, a large, faded white sign with permanent black letters did nothing to comfort us. It read: "DANGER - THIS BUILDING IS STRUCTURALLY UNSAFE - USE AT YOUR OWN RISK." Below the warning were three or four lines of Vietnamese writing, presumably explaining what to do if the place caved in on top of you. I glanced at Harper and mouthed the words,

"Remind you of home?" Harper responded by scratching his nose with his middle finger.

Sergeant Foster stepped forward and addressed the Fab 50. "Hello again, men." Foster was the spokesman for the lifers. "I know it ain't much but it's where you'll be working for the next few months. Along with these dedicated sergeants," Foster pointed to the five men directly to his left, "you fifty men will be the only ones working at the warehouse. I would like to introduce these sergeants who will be in charge of your daily schedules and routines. This is Sergeant Aaron, whom you have already met; to his left are Sergeants Chester, Macking, Netton, and Otto. When these men tell you something, you do it. If you follow orders, your time will go by quickly here. If you cause trouble, you'll be in a world of hurt." A couple of the sergeants nodded in agreement.

I shot a quick look at Harper and rolled my eyes. Sergeant Foster had no way of knowing that this wasn't a group of privates who responded well to threats. In fact, most of us acknowledged it as a challenge. Whether true or not, most inmates of the "Saigon Zoo" (the collective name soon adopted for the warehouse and those of us working there) believed that we were much smarter than the Army lifers.

Throughout Foster's standard Army sermon, we produced the common, unspoken gestures that signified the lack of respect we held for authority. Bellotti scratched his eyes with middle fingers, moving them back and forth, giving the silent, double "screw-you" sign. Goodman, our rebel leader, coughed loudly at every sign of Army bullshit in the speech.

At one point, an obviously irritated Sergeant Foster asked, "You okay, Goodman?"

"I've been better, Sarge, I've been much better—but thanks for asking man," Mark sarcastically replied.

"So have I, Goodman—and call me sergeant, not Sarge! Do not mess with me, Goodman, or you will be in a world of hurt!" Foster was seething. I couldn't believe it; he used that lame phrase again. I wanted to scream but I settled for a quiet grunt.

Our first hour was going well, I thought to myself. The battle lines had been drawn early between the lifers and the mutineers. Maybe we were in Saigon, far from the "shit" in the "bush," but my sense was that the "Battle for Warehouse 32" (I compulsively created nicknames and slogans for everybody and everything) would prove to be a grueling one—with numerous casualties.

After Foster completed his rant he designated Sergeant Chester to assign each of us a job in the warehouse. Sergeant Chester looked exactly like Popeye, but without the sailor hat and pipe. I hastily decided that Popeye would be his official nickname. In fact, by the end of the week, with a little help from my friends, we had assigned nicknames to all six sergeants: Foster—Papa Bear; Aaron—Uncle Remus; Macking—Barney Fife; Chester—Popeye; Netton—Bulldog; and Otto—Crabs. They were chosen mostly for their physical characteristics, but in Sergeant Otto's case, it was due to the simple fact that he was the crabbiest, sourest man we had ever met.

"How many of you swinging dicks have gone to college?" Sergeant Chester asked with a look of utter disdain. I raised my hand along with about fifteen other guys.

"Fantastic. You intellectuals will be assigned to cleanup, packing, and unpacking; these are the shit details in the warehouse. Since you're so damn smart with all that college shit, maybe a little physical work will help turn you into men, if that's possible." Popeye then laughed like a constipated rooster.

78

I attempted, in vain, to explain that I really shouldn't be considered a college guy, since I had taken only three classes at a junior college and had dropped out halfway through my first semester with two Fs and a D. Unfortunately, Popeye was enjoying getting over on us smart-ass college types too much and refused my request for "dumb-shit" status with a dismissive wave of his weathered hand. I learned another valuable life lesson that day from this proudly uneducated sergeant: when a lifer asked you if you thought yourself smart, just say "No!"

We wasted the next two hours in the yard working out our job assignments with Sergeant Chester. It didn't take long for me to realize the substantial number of fascinating jobs available to our crew. The hundreds of boxes already waiting for us in the warehouse were packed with miscellaneous building supplies. Our jobs would be to unpack them and distribute the contents to the proper departments designated throughout the warehouse. Each member of the Fab 50 was assigned a workstation in the warehouse. Some of the jobs required only one person while others needed four or five workers. The work assignments were nuts and bolts inventory, wire loft, light bulbs and lamps, conduit, tools, assorted materials, forklift drivers, packers, unpackers, runners, and shelf assembly Team Alpha and Team Bravo. Although I'd drift from job to job, much like a common vagrant (due mainly to my conscious lack of effort), I began my warehouse career as a menial unpacker, along with Goodman and two other "college boys."

After everybody was assigned to a boring job he hated, we trudged inside where Foster introduced us to the man in charge, Warrant Officer Edwards. Just beyond the warehouse entrance, to the left, sat his small office, constructed of unpainted sheets of plywood. Two jumbo Plexiglas windows made up the front, and a secure steel door displayed a wooden sign reading "WO Edwards." As we crowded together, I noticed the squat, portly lifer with Coke-bottle glasses sitting behind his desk in the office. When he realized we were there, Edwards came out to the group.

"Hello, men. I am Warrant Officer Edwards and I will be your Commanding Officer for the next six months. I know you've met the sergeants. They're good men and good soldiers. Listen to them and follow their orders and we'll get along just fine here." Before Edwards completed his introduction, I'd mentally assigned him a nickname—Mr. Peepers, after the hit television series starring Wally Cox. "I know you've been told what your job entails at the warehouse. It's not a glamorous one, but is an important one. If you men work hard and keep those boxes moving," he pointed to an enormous wall of wooden crates toward the back of the building, "we can save Uncle Sam some money and build up your muscles in the process." His failed attempt at humor was greeted with fifty sober faces, and a loud, exaggerated grunt from Mark Goodman.

Edwards babbled on: "Your job is simple. You unpack the incoming boxes, then inventory, sort, and shelf the materials. You then repack outgoing boxes with materials requested by other units throughout Vietnam. The grunts in the 'bush' are counting on you." Goodman started laughing and Sergeant Foster moved toward him. "You'll work Monday through Friday and half-day Saturday. If there are no questions, we..."

To our delight, Mark Goodman raised his hand. We had all come to look forward to Goodman's cynical questions and inane observations.

"Yes, Goodman," Edwards said. (All jungle fatigues had name tags over the left pocket with last names to identify the soldier.)

"Why is it necessary to work on Saturday, Sir Edwards? Don't you think troop morale would be much higher if we had two whole days off?" Mark flashed the

80

peace sign to Edwards, cleverly disguised as a reference to his request for "two" days off.

The audience began stirring and mumbling its approval. This was a great suggestion, a real crowd pleaser. We politely applauded. The other sergeants moved in to quell the uprising.

"Private Goodman, you'll work Saturday because the Army wants you to work Saturday," answered Edwards. "If your morale is low, we have other ways to bring it up, like working Sundays!" The WO was setting the tone—he was the man in charge and wanted everyone to know it.

"Thank you, Warrant Officer Edwards," Goodman replied with his well-crafted sardonic tone. Goodman sure knew how to get a day kick-started, I thought.

Next came a guided tour of the facility, conducted by Sergeant (Crabs) Otto. By the time Sergeant Crabs finished walking us around the warehouse, it was almost 1:00 p.m.

"Okay men, time for chow," Sergeant Crabs barked. "The mess hall is out the gate and straight ahead about four hundred yards. Be back here by 2:00 p.m. ladies, and ready to work!" He began a fake laugh that lasted much too long. (I had developed a theory that requirements for Army lifer status didn't include humor and wit.)

The mess hall at Camp Davis was identical to all the Army mess halls I had eaten in: an enormous, square room with dozens of tables, each with four chairs. You grabbed a tray when you walked in, and passed through the food line. As always, three or four greasy-looking cooks, sweat dripping from their heads, slopped overly salted food onto your tray.

While our small group of conspirators sat huddled together eating the army's meal du jour of chewy chicken, soggy green peas, and lumpy mashed potatoes, we discussed the day's events.

"Bullshit! I gotta work with nuts and bolts. How boring is that crap?" Bellotti got pissed off because he would be a "nuts-and-bolts" man. I honestly couldn't see the difference with that or any other job assignments. They all sounded equally meaningless and tiresome to me.

"Gene, what's the big deal?" I asked him. "All these damn jobs are boring. You're working in a warehouse man, a boring warehouse—nuts and bolts, wire, packing, whatever. They're all BOOOORING, dude!"

"Come on, you guys..." Schrunk was cut off in midsentence.

"Don't start with your happy horseshit, Schrunk," remarked Judge. "You could find good news in a pile of poodle shit." Judge knew Dave was about to put a happy face on our pity party and Jerry hadn't had a chance to bitch about his assignment as a forklift driver yet.

"I don't even have a driver's license—got it taken away for drunk driving last summer," Jerry noted. "What's the penalty for driving a forklift drunk anyway?"

Paul Price answered: "If you run over one of us, you get ten years in the U.S. prison, Leavenworth. If you run over one of the lifers, you get the highest Army commendation, the Congressional Medal of Honor!"

Laughing, we started to head back to the warehouse. A sizeable group of us had decided to return ten minutes late, just to test the limits of our new leaders.

As we walked through the gate, Sergeant Crabs was waiting. He looked at his cheap PX Timex watch and freaked out. "Damn, your first day and you're late from lunch. I don't believe this shit. If you shit-birds think you can pull this crap on me, you're in for a world of hurt, I shit you not. If this happens again, you'll be working Sundays! It's your

82

first day, shit; get your asses in there." Crabs looked dangerously close to a major coronary.

Goodman, our unofficial spokesman, answered for the group: "Sarge, the lines were long and that chicken took forever to chew, like chewin' on some Silly Putty. Don't blame us; blame those greasy, sweating cooks in that pigpen they call a mess hall." Wow—Mark was going for the jugular!

"Get your asses inside and report to your work areas NOW!—you don't want to piss me off!" Crabs screamed, spraying those closest to him with a mist of spit when he said the word "piss."

As we rode back to the hotel that evening, I silently reviewed the past nine hours. We'd had some great laughs on Day One. Through our actions, we had served notice to the lifers that this assignment wouldn't be a picnic for them. To the contrary, I envisioned daily confrontations, and we were younger, stronger, and smarter.

Chapter IX
Eight Miles High
(Byrds, 1966)

The "Saigon 7" was the name I coined for our little band of rebels. The S7 consisted of Schrunk, Goodman, Harper, Bellotti, Judge, Oswald and me. I thought the moniker had a nice militant ring to it. Mills and Price wanted to be included in the group but I told them that the "Saigon 9" just didn't sound quite right. They would have to settle for "fringe" membership.

It didn't take long for the Saigon 7 and friends to discover Tu Do Street, the Sodom and Gomorrah of Vietnam. Tu Do was Saigon's most colorful avenue, and a nightly hangout for GIs looking to party and have a good time. It was located in the heart of downtown Saigon, close to the Saigon River. On its northwestern end stood a large Catholic cathedral and two of the finer hotels in Saigon, the Caravelle and the Continental Palace. At the southeastern end of the street sat a string of bars and whorehouses with rock 'n' roll continually blasting from the entrances.

Tu Do resembled Main Street from the Old West movies of the '50s and '60s. Every night of the week, drunken GIs could be seen stumbling from bar to bar, occasionally fighting over a Saigon "tea girl" or local whore. The tea girls stood just outside of every bar, beckoning the guys with sluttish talk in broken English and promises of extraordinary sex acts that only they could perform. Hiking their short skirts up to their asses was their way of offering tempting samples of the merchandise.

The MPs (serving in their traditional role as killjoys) would cruise up and down Tu Do Street in their Jeeps, while MPs on foot patrol weaved their way in and out of the myriad bars. As long as you weren't fighting, breaking up the tacky, inexpensive bar furnishings, or slapping around a tea girl, they usually left you alone to enjoy yourself. Everybody knew not to screw around with the MPs; if you did, you could get your ass kicked in the back alley and wake up the next morning in the military jail, facing assault charges!

The midnight curfew was strictly enforced on Tu Do and everywhere else in Saigon. If you lost track of time and stayed past midnight at one of the bars, you were forced to spend the night there, for a fee of course. (It seemed everything and everybody in Saigon had a price.) The next morning, after curfew was lifted (5:00 a.m.), you had to catch a cab to get to your duty station in time for work. It was a common sight at the warehouse to see one of the guys stumble in, clothes wrinkled, eyes bloodshot, and smelling like stale beer and decaying fish.

The tea girls' primary scam was to get GIs to buy them a "Saigon Tea," which consisted of colored water and a few ice cubes. If a tea girl performed her job well, a GI would buy her "teas" all night, get drunk, and then take her to one of the upstairs rooms for a quick screw, blow job, or "Steam & Cream" (a steam bath and blow job—a favorite among GIs). Hopefully the guy would then pass out so the girl could hurry back down to the bar and hustle another GI. Any one of the three options went for about 2000 piasters (about 16 American dollars in 1969). However, prices varied depending on your bargaining skills or your level of intoxication. In 1969, 130 piasters equaled one American dollar. Bargaining for sex, similar to purchasing a used car, was acceptable and even expected by the tea girls. Group rates were also common for the roving herd of drunken soldiers.

The head mama-san had the last word on every transaction. Most mama-sans spoke excellent English, and exhibited the kind of savvy found on Wall Street, although many often acted as if they didn't understand what you said.

Their primary mission of separating the GI from his MPC (military payment currency) or piasters depended on their exceptional ability to communicate with Americans when necessary.

Venereal disease, as well as crabs and head lice, ran rampant in Vietnam. The "clap" became a generic term for all of these diseases. Most of the youthful, naive GIs didn't know syphilis from heat rash, so calling all problems with the genitalia "clap" made it easier for all concerned.

It was on Tu Do Street, in The California Bar, that I smoked marijuana for the first time in my life. This cataclysmic event occurred on my fourth night in Saigon.

Although I came from California, the undisputed drug capital of the world in the late '60s, and many of my friends smoked weed regularly, I'd never tried it myself for fear of becoming addicted to a harder drug. I had witnessed high school friends and relatives get hooked on hard drugs and devastate their lives, and I was simply terrified of using any street drugs. But that night, a combination of warm beer, intense peer pressure and curiosity overwhelmed my common sense, and I began a habit that would last my entire twenty-two months in Nam.

"Holy shit guys, you ain't gonna believe this!" It was Charlie Hardy, the streetwise black guy from Philly, heading our way. Charlie took a stool at the jam-packed bar where Bellotti, Judge, Oswald, Stuart, and I sat swilling Coors and swapping bullshit stories from the "world."

"Check this out dudes." Hardy held up what appeared to be a pack of cigarettes.

"Wow, that's amazing," I mocked, "a pack of cigs. Unbelievable—Hardy, really cool man, really cool." Charlie never appreciated my sarcasm.

"It's not cigs, you ass, they're joints! Rolled grass, ready to smoke, two dollars a pack."

Hardy stuck his middle finger in my face while the group inspected the pack. Then Charlie told us that a "brother" he encountered from basic training had informed him that packs of sealed joints called "Park Lanes" could be purchased on any street corner. Actually it wouldn't take us long to learn that anyone could acquire drugs of all kinds as easily on the streets of Saigon as he could buy a pack of Wrigley's gum in a liquor store in the states. Take your pick—marijuana, hashish, opium, heroin, Quaaludes, STP, speed, LSD, morphine, BTs, methamphetamines, Ritalin, amyl nitrate (poppers), epinephrine, Lidocaine, and any other substance the locals or military medical personnel could get their hands on. The demand for drugs in Vietnam was tremendous, and the suppliers always had plenty of merchandise.

"Crack it open and let's smoke a doobie," prompted Bellotti, as our group moved to a table in the back of the bar. "Fire one up, Charlie." Gene was anxious to sample the product.

"In here?" I questioned. "What about the MPs?" I wasn't prepared to confess the fact that I had never smoked grass before. During our time together, it had come up in conversation only a few times, and I cleverly gave the impression of being a "head" (one who smokes grass regularly) without actually answering directly.

"Don't be a pussy, Whalon," Stuart interjected. "Whatta they gonna do, send ya to Nam?"

He had a point. Realizing I couldn't preserve my secret any longer, I attempted a clever diversion. "I quit getting high when I joined the Army—I'm gonna wait 'til I get out to smoke again—you boys, go ahead, fire up."

Judge didn't buy it. That's pure cat shit, Whalon," Jerry charged. "You ain't never smoked weed, have you,

Cherry Boy Whalon? Always dodgin' when the subject of getting loaded comes up." He wouldn't let it drop.

"Pete, you never smoked grass?" Bellotti said, taking this in. "Are you kiddin' me?" Bellotti was crushed—his "homey" was a virgin-lunged phony. I thought he was going to shed tears. His pal from Cal had never fired up a doobie— impossible!

"Okay, okay, assholes, I never smoked before," I confessed finally. "Lighten up dudes—don't mean nothin'. I had two friends back on the block who smoked grass every day and they seemed like they got dumber by the day, and they looked old as dirt. A cousin of mine got hooked on grass and he had to be put into a place for addicts where he went bananas and tried to kill himself. I promised my parents I wouldn't get strung out on drugs when I got to Nam. So screw you, guys!"

They were all howling now—the longer I rambled, the more they laughed. I couldn't blame them—it was funny—I was full of crap. Everything I said was bullshit and they knew it. I was busted.

"Just try it, Peter Whalon," Judge urged. "If you don't like it, then don't smoke it. But at these prices, you'd have to be brainless not to smoke this weed." Judge always used both of my names when trying to talk me into something I didn't want to do. Usually it was I who tried to convince others to go along with one of my schemes. But not this time. I decided the moment had arrived; at the tender age of twenty, I was about to smoke some marijuana. Drum roll please!

"Fire it up, assholes," I said, and the impatient group cheered.

Charlie flicked his Bic and lit a joint, then deeply inhaled and passed it to me, Cherry Boy Whalon. I took a tiny puff and began coughing violently and uncontrollably. I had never even smoked a cigarette in my life and my uninitiated lungs now reminded me of that fact. The boys had a wonderful time at my expense, laughing and calling me derogatory girly names. However, I focused so much on inhaling small amounts of oxygen into my collapsing lungs that I wasn't concerned.

My coughing attracted the attention of the mama-san washing glasses behind the bar. Before I could pass the joint to Bellotti, she assaulted our table with a vengeance. "What you do, GI? You no pot smoke heea—MPs no let you smoke dis in heea—mama-san be numba ten—go jail. Dee dee mow numba ten GIs, dee dee GI, you go now or papa-san cock-a-dow GI. Go!" The mama-san screamed and waved her hands in our faces like a mad woman. While the mama-san was freaking out, Hardy took a long, deep toke on the joint he had taken from me. After holding it in as long as possible, he exhaled a massive plume of smoke which hit the mama-san right between the eyes, engulfing her head in a cloud.

Six tea girls, watching the scene from the bar, and some old papa-san, chewing on what looked like a wad of tar, noticed the smoke ball hit the mama-san. They immediately descended on us like a stampeding herd of rhinos, squawking in high-pitched, ear-piercing broken English and Vietnamese. While Hardy laughed as he blew more smoke clouds and cursed at the whacked-out cluster of bar girls, I coughed as if I had a cantaloupe-sized hairball in my throat.

Oswald began pushing Hardy towards the door and yelling at us to get outside. The fact that the mama-san was screaming for someone to call the MPs had gotten Ozzie's attention—MPs meant trouble. Apparently, you couldn't fire up a joint in the bars and smoke at your leisure. We had been in country only four days and were unaware of the taboos.

We stumbled our way outside and retreated to the bar across the street, The Bunny Club. Although my eyes still watered, the hacking had subsided and my breathing returned to 85% capacity.

"Now that was some good shit. How'd ya like that wad of smoke I blew at the mama-san?"

Hardy was proud of the way he had handled the mama-san. Charlie Hardy hailed from Pottsville, Pennsylvania, a tough town outside Philadelphia. It didn't take long for most us to realize that Hardy was a badassed dude. He had a fullback's build and talked like a Mafia hit man. On many occasions, he reminded us: "I don't put up with no puppy-shit from no white boys!" That was Charlie Hardy—take him or leave him. If Hardy got pissed off at you, he'd look you square in the eye and advise you to get away from him pronto before somebody got hurt. It was good advice. I enjoyed going to Tu Do with Charlie for two reasons: Hardy spun hilarious tales of his life in Pottsville when drunk or loaded, and he feared no person on the entire planet.

After a few beers and numerous inquiries into my first "hit" off a joint, our group decided to go back to the hotel and continue the smoking and drinking there. Along the way, Hardy asked our cab driver to stop and buy us a carton of Park Lanes from a papa-san selling black-market items on the corner.

Beyond street drugs, almost any item in Saigon could be acquired through the black market—including weapons, food, medicines, stereos, and the one true necessity in Vietnam, electric fans. GIs could purchase many of these items through the PX (Post Exchange), but just as many couldn't be found there. In Saigon, Le Loi Street made up the heart of the black market. A GI could get a case of Coke for $2 at the PX, which could then sell for $5 on the market.

By the time we all gathered in Hardy and Stuart's room, our band of merry men had grown from six to nine: Goodman, Price, and Harper had joined the party. Joints fired up almost as soon as everyone arrived. The guys got psyched about my getting loaded for the first time. It was equivalent to a virgin having sex, or so Bellotti informed me. That night, I discovered that Schrunk, Goodman, and Harper did not smoke grass and, although pressured by the "heads" (pot smokers) constantly, they wouldn't smoke it during their entire tour in Nam.

Bellotti began describing the scene at The California Bar for the guys who weren't with us. I took my second hit for the night, coughing again, but not so violently this time. Now that my "cherry-boy" status was common knowledge, everybody kept a close eye on me, waiting for my reaction to the cannabis. I attempted to act normal, but the harder I tried, the more obvious the fact became—I was loaded! By all accounts, the grass was powerful and a real ass-kicker.

I noticed everybody looking in my direction, which caused me to grow paranoid. "Quit staring at me man," I demanded. "What's the big deal anyway? Quit laughing at me, bitches." I turned to Harper, who sat closest to the case of Coors. "Give me a beer," I demanded.

"Hey Pete, why don't you just drink the one in your hand?" Goodman asked.

I looked down and realized that I already held a full can of Coors in my left hand. I just stared quietly at the beer can. Normally I'd have had a quick, sarcastic comeback—but I fell silent. There was no rapid retort, no snappy barb, and no words at all coming out of my mouth. The harder I tried to come up with an appropriate response, the louder the eight sadistic vultures laughed. I stared at the Coors can in my hand, not wanting to look into the faces of the jackals who mocked me.

After what seemed like ten minutes but was more like thirty seconds, I unleashed my razor-sharp reply: "Leave me alone!" I blurted out. "Leave me alone!" Had I really uttered such dribble, such nonsense? "Leave me alone!" That's all I had? An avalanche of ridicule and howling laughter now buried me. I couldn't distinguish who said what. I hastily decided that continuing the silence appeared to be my best option. So there I sat, mutely glaring at a Coors can, while eight of my closest friends derided and ridiculed me unmercifully.

"Guess what, Whalon? You're loaded dude," counseled Oswald. "Don't freak out; you're just not used to being high. Drink your beer and enjoy the buzz Whalon."

Somehow Ozzie's words nudged me a little closer to reality. In an attempt to demonstrate my return to the real world, I took a long drink of beer and threw the now-empty can against the back wall of Hardy's room

"Now hand me that beer, Mr. Harper, if you don't mind," I said, pointing to the cooler.

The occupants of Charlie's smoke-filled room honored me with a standing ovation. I stood smiling sheepishly, raising my cold can of beer. Setting the Coors down for just a moment, I then proudly took a deep bow.

Chapter X

Let's Live for Today

(Grass Roots, 1967)

Our homogeneous group of "good-time Charlies" exhibited very little concern or caution when it came to smoking pot, drinking alcohol, or staying out all night. When we reported to work hung over, loaded, or without sleep, many of us knew it would be easy to skate through the day and avoid work. A small band led by Mark Goodman developed an intricate system of cleverly avoiding the lifers when necessary. For instance, I knew that if I reported to the warehouse worn-out, it would be safe to locate a dim corner of the building behind some boxes, to throw down an Army-issue blanket, and to catch some z's for an hour or two. It was crucial to inform at least one reliable buddy where you planned to relax and to advise him when to wake you up. We watched each other's backs religiously, covering for and protecting anyone who came under fire for transgressions. I always had a bullshit story to assist a buddy out of a jam.

"Goodman, where in the hell were you at two today?" Sergeant Macking demanded one afternoon suspiciously. "I searched everywhere for your sorry ass. We need two spools of #16 wire in the packing area now! I will slap an Article 15 on your ass..."

I jumped in before Barney Fife could get any more words out of his slender, sweating lips. "Sarge, he went with me to get gas for the forklift. Ask Judge or Bellotti; they saw us leave together."

Getting gas provided a good alibi for disappearing. The pumps, located across the base, were almost one mile from the warehouse. You could report six or seven vehicles were lined ahead and you were forced to wait your turn to gas up.

"You're full of horseshit, Whalon. Stay outta this!" Barney ordered, agitated.

I stifled a smile, as nothing pleased us more than getting one of the lifers pissed off. It made for an entertaining day and broke the monotony of warehouse work.

"Sarge, it's the truth. Would I lie to you?" Goodman was incapable of ending a sentence without a dagger attached.

"You assholes are driving me loopy with your daily bullshit—it never ends. Keep it up, Goodman, and we're gonna tangle mister, I shit you not! You're gonna be in a world of hurt if you don't go get me the damn wire now!"

Macking stormed into Warrant Officer Edwards's office like the class tattletale to report our latest act of insubordination. Goodman winked at me and I flashed him the peace sign.

Chalk up another triumph for the adolescent boys!

To combat the daily boredom of our jobs, we schemed constantly, trying to outdo each other with our nonsense and lack of production. We created our own world at the warehouse, producing barely enough work to avoid disciplinary action, but not enough to accomplish the modest goals of our leaders. Not a day passed in the warehouse during which someone didn't pull a stunt or verbally mix it up with one of the lifers.

In high school, I had been one of the "class clowns," driving the teachers crazy with my relentless chatter and inane observations. In the Army, I intended to drive the lifers just as insane, applying the same successful formula from my glory days at Redondo Union High School. My favorite little annoying trick was to prepare a sentence for the day, using a "big word" from *30 Days to a More Powerful*

Vocabulary by Wilfred Funk and Norman Lewis. Then, when the opportunity presented itself, I'd spring it on a lifer, attempting to make him look ignorant, because I knew that he didn't know the meaning of my impressive word.

"Hey Sergeant Macking," I loudly asked so those nearby could hear, "do you find Goodman's supercilious comments are irritating and annoying?"

Of course, the sergeants rarely took the bait, realizing that I purposely attempted to aggravate them. These types of stunts kept me and many of the other wise guys mentally sharp (or so we believed) and helped the time pass more quickly.

The decisive confrontation in the "Battle for Warehouse 32" occurred about one month after our arrival in Saigon. It sprung from the behavior of Private Lee Mills, one of our weed-smoking buddies, who continually showed up late to work. Subsequent to a hard night of drinking, smoking, and chasing tea girls around Tu Do Street, Mills usually had a difficult time waking up at 6:00 a.m. After countless days of unsuccessful attempts, we gave up trying to wake him in the morning. We decided to just let Mills sleep and report to work when he felt like it.

Warrant Officer Edwards warned Lee many times about reporting late for work and finally gave him an ultimatum one Monday morning: "The next time you drag your stoned ass in here late Private Mills, you're going to Okinawa for disciplinary action! Do you understand me, soldier?" Since Mills was too loaded at the time to put together a coherent sentence, he just flashed his typical, casual smile, gave Edwards the peace sign, and shrugged his shoulders. The very next day, Lee strolled into the warehouse two hours late and Edwards exploded. The Warrant Officer stormed out of his office and began screaming and gesturing at Mills. Spit flew from Edwards's mouth as he continued to shout while chasing a small group of smirking onlookers away.

The next morning, Lee flew to Okinawa, with Sergeant Macking as an escort. He had an Article 15 hearing scheduled for early Thursday. Saigon didn't conduct disciplinary action hearings, so all Article 15 proceedings were transferred to Okinawa before an Army military court. This provided Warrant Officer Edwards with a golden opportunity to prove not only to us, but also to the lifers under his command, exactly who ran the show at the warehouse. We became fully aware that if Mills returned with an Article 15 conviction, it wouldn't be long before several of us would follow him to Okinawa for the same fate.

On Friday, at 11:00 a.m., Sergeants Netton and Chester set off to pick up Mills and Barney Fife who flew from Okinawa. At 1:20 p.m. I heard their truck pull into the yard.

"Harper, Goodman... Mills is back," I called to my friends. We hustled our way to the front of the building, near Edwards's office. The word spread swiftly throughout the warehouse. The entire Fab 50 anxiously assembled to witness this monumental event. Sergeants Otto and Aaron also appeared, huddling together with sneers on their craggy faces.

I was nervous, excited, and worried all at the same time. There stood a realistic chance this incident would signal the end to the personal nirvana we had created for ourselves. If Mills went down, life in the warehouse would immediately get a great deal tougher.

Mills swaggered in behind Barney, wedged between Bulldog and Popeye, just as the warrant officer emerged from his air-conditioned office. The glorious moment WO Edwards had fantasized about was at hand. This undisciplined collection of infantile militants was going down, he believed, starting with Private Lee Mills. Edwards flashed a confident, childlike smirk when he stopped in front of Lee. As usual, Lee wore dark sunglasses to conceal his bloodshot eyes.

"Take off those hippie sunglasses, soldier!" Edwards demanded.

We remained silent as Lee slowly moved his shades from his eyes to the top of his head, a gesture that infuriated Edwards. This was *High Noon, The Caine Mutiny,* and *Mister Roberts* all rolled into one! The anticipation was clogging my throat.

"I said take them off, not move them!" Edwards's face was now as red as a monkey's ass.

I whispered to Schrunk, standing next to me, and noted, "This is so cool, man—really great!" Dave nodded his head in agreement but didn't look my way. Lee removed the sunglasses from his head, leisurely folded them, and put the spectacles into his fatigue pocket. Mills looked as cool as Steve McQueen, I thought. It reminded me of a classic chess match, each man anticipating the other's move. Lee had, typically, not spoken a word, but I read something in his eyes (other than that he was stoned on weed) which gave me hope. He didn't strike me as a guy who had gotten busted in Okinawa.

I glanced at Sergeant Macking, who was slowly backing up and away from where Edwards and the other toady sergeants stood. I realized that Barney didn't want to be near the warrant officer when he viewed the Article 15 results. I smiled to myself, knowing what would follow.

Then came the critical question that would seriously affect the "joy ride" we had taken advantage of for the past month. "Private Mills, give me your Article 15 disciplinary action papers. What were the terms and conditions of your punishment, son?" Edwards looked as serious as an executioner about to pull the switch.

When Mills handed Edwards the wrinkled papers he had been holding in his hand, I glanced around to check out the other sergeants' reactions. Foster, Aaron, and Otto were huddled off to the side of Edwards and Mills. These cheerful sergeants all grinned, apparently secure in the belief that this meant the death of our "reign of terror" (another one of my euphemisms). They were confident that control of the warehouse and its rebels (us) would soon return to its rightful owners. However, Sergeants Chester and Netton, who had picked up Mills and Macking at the airport, had joined Sergeant Macking at the back of the assembly.

As Edwards scrutinized the crumpled papers, Mills flashed the wry smile we had all grown accustomed to. In big red letters across the top of the first page, he read the painful words, CHARGES DISMISSED.

Edwards glared at Mills. "I don't believe this horseshit, charges dismissed. Sergeant Macking, what in hell is going on here?" Macking slowly began making his way back toward the front of the fifty grinning privates.

"Sergeant Foster, read these now," Edwards ordered, handing the papers to Papa Bear. "This has got to be a mistake." Edwards questioned Mills further, trying desperately to control his anger. "What exactly did they tell you in Okinawa, Mills? There has to be disciplinary action for your insubordination. This is pure bullshit!"

Edwards's face turned crimson and his glasses were moist from the sweat pouring from his head; his eyes bulged and he clenched his fists. I thought for a minute he'd punch Mills in the face—wishful thinking on my part. At that moment, the warrant officer reminded me of a sunburned blowfish about to explode. I had the sudden urge to scream "Up your hairy ass, Edwards!" but remained silent.

Lee Mills was now smiling with a "screw you, lifers" expression on his face. I loved that look. The other sergeants had drifted to the rear of the group and were now in a circle, grumbling to each other. We remained silent but, with all the silly smiles we flashed, the place could have passed for a Miss America Pageant. Edwards looked seconds away from a major coronary. What a historic moment at the Saigon Zoo—the animals had officially taken control!

"You dudes screwed up my paperwork," Mills informed Edwards. "You didn't inform me of your intentions and didn't allow me time to correct the 'actions' I was falsely accused of. I had a cool lawyer, a young dude from Florida—can you believe that shit? We surfed the same beaches before the Army; he's a cool dude. It's over, Mr. Edwards. All charges dropped—sorry sir!" Mills's shit-eating smile grew wider.

That was it—game, set, and match.

We could no longer contain our high spirits. The workers had struck a blow for the common man—long live Private Lee Mills! We simultaneously broke into a cheer and loud applause. The sergeants attempted in vain to silence us, but the mob wouldn't be hushed. The "Battle for Warehouse 32" was effectively over. Edwards and his posse of sergeants had banked on using fear to control us by making an example of Mills; however, things had gone drastically wrong. Rowdy, triumphant privates, 1; dejected, sulking lifers, 0—game over!

The celebration at the Hung Dao that evening was raucous. We drank record amounts of alcohol and smoked lethal quantities of weed. Lee Mills reigned as Champion of the Day. He had single-handedly extinguished the oppressive fires of tyranny. Okay, maybe that's a little overstated, but Mills sure pissed off the lifers and that was good enough for me. Little did we know that the lifers had a get-together of their own that night—not to celebrate, but to plan their retaliation! We'd learn about their plan first thing the next morning when we arrived for work. However, for the moment, the night was ours.

Chapter XI

Kind of a Drag

(Buckinghams, 1967)

The "Mills Victory Jamboree" had carried on until the wee hours of the morning. By sunrise, most of us were nursing severe hangovers and experiencing serious trouble keeping down the contents in our churning stomachs.

We arrived at the warehouse expecting the silent treatment from the lifers. This was one day that we wanted to be left alone, to have time to recover from our self-inflicted wounds from the night before. Unexpectedly, Sergeant "Bulldog" Netton met us at the front entrance.

"Have fun last night, kids?" he rhetorically asked. "I hope so." His phony smile, revealing yellowish teeth, made me queasy. Or maybe the fourteen bottles of Vietnamese beer and five cans of beanie-weenies I had consumed the night before caused my nausea.

Bulldog continued as he peeked at his watch. "There will be a mandatory meeting in the packing area in thirty minutes, at 0830 sharp. Go to your workstations until then and WORK!"

When the sergeant abruptly turned to retreat into the building, he began laughing and shaking his head. This bit of news did not help my pounding headache. A small group of us remained outside in the yard to discuss the sergeant's remarks.

Schrunk, the worrywart, spoke first. "What the hell is that all about? I think we might have gone too far guys. I told you they wouldn't put up with all this stuff for long. We have to pick our battles in the future."

"Quit being a little bitch, Dave," Judge responded. "The lifers won't harm you. I'll protect you little Puss-'n-Boots." Jerry enjoyed firing verbal buckshot.

"Meetings with lifers are never good, never good, man," Bellotti said, adding his two cents' worth. "Maybe Dave's right. Who's got some Anacin? My head is killin' me."

"Quit sweatin' it, you whining babies," urged Goodman. "They can't do jack shit to us. We got 'em by the balls—Mills kicked their ass, dudes. It's probably some work assignment changes to try to punish us for yesterday. Who cares? Relax—don't mean nothin'!" Mark Goodman always had confidence when it came to the lifers versus him. Goodman honestly believed the lifers could do us little or no harm and he was usually right. Plus, Mark appreciated a first-rate challenge from the lifers. It gave him the opportunity to show his superiority to these men who had wasted their lives in the Army.

"I dunno, Mark. Bulldog looked weird..." Before I could finish, a gut-wrenching "whoosh" sound from behind us got our attention. Bill Oswald was skillfully painting the wall of the empty warehouse next to ours with chipped beef, toast, and stale beer.

"Shit, Ozzie, couldn't ya puke outside the gate? That stinks like gook food, man." Judge looked about ready to assist Ozzie with his processed-food paint job.

We started to chant. "Ozzie, Ozzie, Ozzie..." Oswald clutched his stomach with one hand and flipped us the "bird" with the other.

"You're a disgusting piece of rat shit, Oz, you woman," jeered Bellotti, as Harper snapped a picture of Oswald just as his final eruption splashed against the bricks. Bill Harper always carried his Nikon camera with him.

"Can I get a color copy of that, Harp?" I requested as we finally headed for our workstations inside the warehouse.

"I'd like to send it to Ozzie's parents and the imaginary girlfriend he's always bragging about. I think they'd be so proud of their little baby boy. Hey Ozzie, ya got some shit-brown chunks on your moustache—very cool, man."

We spent the thirty minutes prior to our meeting speculating on what the lifers had in store for us. The general consensus was a reorganization of work assignments and stricter enforcement of existing rules. By 8:25, everybody had gathered in the packing area. I stood in the back of the group, as usual, with Harper, Schrunk, and Oswald. Goodman took pleasure in being up front, in striking distance of the lifers. My hangover had subsided, leaving me with a slight headache and cottonmouth.

At 8:33 Edwards joined the assembly, looking all business. "I'll make this brief," he began. "You've been averaging twenty-five boxes a week, which is unacceptable. You'll now produce a quota of weekly boxes. If you don't meet the quota by Saturday at noon, you'll work Saturday afternoon and Sunday until the quota is met. The new quota is sixty boxes a week." Edwards turned and retreated into his office.

So that was their "master plan." Create a quota impossible to meet, which forces the conspirators to work weekends. It sounded like a perfect plan to screw the mutineers and pay us back for the "Mills Revolt." However, as usual with our leaders' strategies, it contained a fatal flaw.

The lifers had drastically underestimated how slowly we actually worked and what little effort most members of the Fab 50 put forth during the course of one week. Most of our time and energy was spent looking for ways to avoid strenuous work and the never-ending nagging from the lifers. Since I was assigned to unpacking boxes, I knew well the effort involved with this work detail at the warehouse. To complete a box, it had to be unpacked, broken down for various departments in the warehouse, and delivered to those areas. When it arrived, the parts got recorded in a log and stored on shelves. We usually unpacked and delivered about five crates (boxes) per day. With zero motivation and ambition, our work pace moved slightly slower than weeds growing. In a nutshell, most of us were young, lazy-assed, goldbricking slackers who resented not being back in the world, guzzling beer, and chasing skirts with the friends who had somehow avoided this horrendous nightmare.

A group of us decided to stay in the warehouse for our lunch break. A few of the "worriers" (not to be confused with "warriors") voiced concern about the quota and working weekends. Goodman and I eased their troubled minds.

"Relax guys," I advised. "We could do twenty boxes a day without breaking a sweat. We can do sixty by Wednesday afternoon. Right, Goodman?"

Mark continued where I had left off. "Shit, sixty crates a week, no sweat GI. Whalon and I debated all the time about who does the least amount of work. Some days, we do nothing at all—and I mean nothing! Ever see me or Whalon break a sweat? Hell, Schrunk can unload ten boxes a day by himself, and he's older then lint. Trust me, we'll never work past noon on Saturday, I guarantee it. It's gonna cut into my siesta time in the wire bin, and Buzz and Oz might have to smoke one less joint a day, but I'll sacrifice for the common good—shit, this is a joke."

Goodman sure knew how to work a crowd and he was right on target. I had learned a simple fact in the Army that I assume most government employees know: if you speak extremely loud and move around swiftly, others assume that you're conscientiously working. If you toss in periodic complaints about your job's difficulty they assume you are working extra hard.

"What about loggin' the box shit after it goes to us? I don't need no lifer in my face making me write fast. Shit!" Willie Stuart worried about having to note all the materials in a log book—more boxes, more writing. He enjoyed working slowly, with no undue pressure. The fact that Willie stayed stoned fifteen hours a day did not aid his productivity.

"Stuart, who's gonna know five thousand nuts and bolts or one thousand #4 screws don't get logged?" Charlie Hardy interjected. "Any lifers ever look at your log book, ever? Shit no. I don't think the lifers can even read your pathetic writing." Hardy always looked out for Stuart. Being the only two black guys in our elite clique of saboteurs made them very protective of each other.

"I dunno if I can work any faster, since I'm loaded all the time." Bellotti was concerned he might have to cut back drastically on his weed smoking. Everybody had his priorities.

"Don't worry, Gene, we'll pick up the slack for your worn-out ass," Oswald offered. "The good thing, Bellotti, is that you couldn't possibly work any slower, Turtle Man." Oswald excelled at pushing Bellotti's buttons.

"Screw you, Ozzie. I work as fast as you losers and you know it," Bellotti whined. "Don't give me a ration of shit, Billy Goat Man."

"That's the point, dick-face," Oswald shot back. "You're a lazy redneck, and brainless as the blocks holding up this prison."

Ozzie flicked a lit cigarette butt at Bellotti, hitting him on the shoulder. Bellotti jumped up and began chasing Ozzie around the warehouse. It reminded me of the sixth grade, when I would slap Susan Gilmore on the head and she would chase me around the playground at Fulton School.

"Fight, fight, fight," Goodman screamed, trying to attract the attention of one of the lifers inside the office. Hearing the commotion, Sergeant "Papa Bear" Foster bolted out of the office with a grimace on his face and marched over to where we sat. He saw the two incorrigible children, Oswald and Bellotti, wrestling between two wooden pallets.

"Maybe they'll kill each other and save me the trouble," the sergeant muttered to no one in particular.

As Papa Bear turned and began stepping away, Goodman couldn't let the opportunity slip by. He fired back: "Thanks, Sarge, for your assistance in breaking up the scuffle." Foster just kept going, shaking his oversized head from side to side. I was sure that if the sergeant had been holding an M16 in his hands, he would've turned around and emptied its entire magazine into our clique, ending the source of his frustration once and for all.

Ozzie and Gene stopped their wrestling match when they heard Foster's voice and returned to our discussion.

"You kids better behave or you'll be staying after school with the lifers," Harper needled.

"Okay, it's this simple..." Goodman began explaining how we'd deal with the latest attempt to get us under control. "We start the week slowly, then each day do a few more boxes until Saturday. We make the lifers believe we're busting ass to meet the quota to avoid working over. Some weeks, we can even go over the sixty boxes to keep them happy. Me and Whalon will keep track of the total and let you guys know where we stand each day. Don't spread this around to the other guys in the Fab 50. The fewer guys who know, the less chance the lifers will find out, okay?"

We all agreed.

The first week of the new quota system, we finished Box number 60 at 11:45 a.m. Saturday morning—fifteen minutes before quitting time. Goodman and I beautifully orchestrated the whole thing. The crew had counted on us and we came through with flying colors.

Our new quota system soon became a running joke among the Fab 50. The weary lifers no longer enforced it when they realized it didn't challenge us any more.

Very soon after the demise of the quota, Foster and his dedicated sergeants ran out of gas in their all-out effort to transform us into productive soldiers. We had effectively broken their spirits. For the remainder of our time in Saigon, the demoralized warrant officer and his disheartened sergeants expended very little energy in their attempts to adjust our attitude or to correct the problems at the warehouse. As long as we reported to work each morning and were somewhat productive, the lifers avoided confrontations with the Fab 50, and especially with the Saigon 7.

Chapter XII

Up on the Roof

(Drifters, 1962)

On Saturdays, we worked from 8:00 a.m. to noon, and returned to our hotel about 12:30 p.m. Usually a group of us would eat lunch together and talk over plans for that night and Sunday. After lunch, we would return to our rooms, change into shorts or swimming trunks, and make our way to the hotel roof. I always looked forward to these Saturday afternoons. It was a great escape time for us heads.

Although I wouldn't call it difficult, getting to the roof wasn't easy either. You had to climb a short set of stairs at the end of the hall on the sixth floor, walk down a narrow corridor, scale a vertical ladder missing two rungs, rotate a heavy latch on a twenty-five-pound steel trapdoor, heave it open, and hoist yourself to the roof. Still, partying there had distinct advantages. You could hear someone climbing the ladder, before he reached the trapdoor. If you wanted to screw with a buddy, or just didn't want visitors, all you had to do was stand on the trapdoor, preventing them from pushing it open. Our group even developed a secret knock to identify visitors, although we rarely used it.

The roof was our sanctuary from the military atmosphere that permeated Saigon. Bellotti dubbed the roof, "The Head Rest." In an attempt to create a "back-in-the-world" feel, we purchased beach chairs at the PX and left them on the roof for our use. We also equipped our getaway with two reel-to-reel tape players, three ice coolers, a pair of binoculars, assorted magazines and books, and a large Army-green umbrella "borrowed" from the warehouse. (The umbrella was a necessity to protect the "white bodies" from the sun.)

The roof offered a breathtaking panoramic view of Saigon. From our vantage point, there was no hint of a war going on except for the occasional explosion off in the distance. Directly below, the hectic streets of the city bustled with Vietnamese and military personnel. Most of the buildings making up the skyline measured fewer than ten stories high. Although Saigon was the most modern city in Vietnam, countless structures stood in dire need of repairs. However, I rarely witnessed improvements made to any of the hotels or restaurants lining Hung Dao Street. I figured that the years of conflict in the country had taken their toll in various ways.

We observed incredible, billowy, snow-white cloud formations from on high. After a few "hits" from one of the many "bongs" (water pipes) available, these massive milky puffs took on an amazing resemblance to famous people or exotic animals. We often wasted hours pointing at clouds and trying to convince others of their likeness to Lyndon Johnson, Raquel Welch, Don Knotts, or a three-legged poodle with two miniature dicks.

To the north flowed the Saigon River, with its rapidly moving current, while to the south one could take in the never-ending layers of corrugated tin that formed the roofs of the dense housing of Saigon's underprivileged citizens. The roof and its picturesque view had a tranquil effect on me. For some unexplainable reason, I felt more at home on the roof of the Hung Dao Hotel than at any other time in country.

When on the roof, we could freely smoke grass, drink beer, and just bullshit about meaningless stuff—and when smoking grass, our little faction of the Fab 50 had volumes of meaningless stuff to talk about.

Our conversations on the roof varied widely. (However, we attempted to keep the banter free from warehouse talk and military jargon.) I'm sure to a casual observer, these discussions would have appeared trite, sophomoric, and often incoherent. Our favorite topics of conversation included chicks, sports, entertainment, sexual exploits, alcohol adventures, the best food to eat when experiencing a "marijuana-munchies moment," and everybody's favorite: "What are you going to do when released from Army incarceration?"

One particularly sweltering Saturday, the entire Saigon 7 gathered on the roof, as well as Charlie Hardy, Paul Price, Willie Stuart, and Lee Mills. It was the first time we had all hung out together for amusement in Saigon. Although Goodman, Harper, and Schrunk never smoked weed, they had still joined us. I sat there, observing this odd collection of American youth, contemplating what truly made these guys tick. I decided to probe deep inside their psyches by posing a profound, provocative question sure to reveal a window into their very souls.

"Okay boys," I soberly asked, "what job do you see yourselves doing ten years from now?"

"Who gives a bat's ass, Whalon?" Goodman shot back. "Don't start bringin' this party down with your moronic questions about nothing."

Mark Goodman was a true provocateur, especially whenever we smoked "dew." His finely honed verbal buckshot usually created heated discussions to which we would continually add fuel. This time, I didn't bite.

"Anyway class," I said, pointing to Paul Price, "you start, Paul, and we'll go around the circle."

In his pronounced New York accent, Paul gladly answered the question. "Well ladies, in ten years, I will be a high-priced, bloodsucking lawyer in New York City." Paul flashed the peace sign at the jeering crowd.

"Just what the world needs," Bellotti sarcastically said. "Another shyster lawyer from New York! Hey Paul, how can you tell when a lawyer is lying to you?" Gene

110

didn't wait for an answer. "His lips are moving! In ten years, I'm gonna have my own construction business in Frisco. I'll be building million-dollar homes in Marin County."

"Yeah, and you'll probably be wearin' shit-stained pants and livin' in a cardboard box at Fisherman's Wharf," Oswald fired back.

I jumped in with my future plans before Bill and Gene began wrestling. "Okay losers, mine is a little more realistic." Price and Bellotti booed my reference to their dreams. "I will be the head coach of the Los Angeles Rams, unless I'm managing the L.A. Dodgers."

"Hey Pete, Judge yelled as I struck the pose of Sandy Kofax hurling a fastball, didn't you get kicked off your Little League team for taking bets on the games?"

That remark brought a hearty laugh from the gang. As was the case with most of our conversations, one person would say something and another would make a sarcastic remark. Soon the conversation would degenerate into an "ass-rippin'" session, with everybody trying to outdo each other. This ingredient, among others, made Saturday afternoons on the roof of the Hung Dao Hotel so memorable.

After everyone had a chance to predict his future, Goodman, Schrunk, Price, and Harper decided to return to their rooms. Seven of us now remained on the roof.

The open section of the roof was a 40' by 40' cement slab. Directly in the middle stood a cement water tank that fed our showers and toilets with non-potable water. The water tank measured five-feet square, with thick cement walls extending four feet above the roof deck. The only opening in the tank was a narrow slit on one side, three feet long and eighteen inches high. It looked like a cement box with one narrow, open window. Through trial and error, we discovered that it was possible to lower one of the "skinny" guys into the tank by holding his legs as he wriggled through

111

the slot. To extract him, two guys had to grab his wrists and very slowly pull him out through the opening. It wasn't a trouble-free process, but it always invigorated me whenever I stood neck deep in the cool water after a few hours under the blistering Saigon sun. I was one of the "skinnies" that could fit through the slender portal.

"Charlie, Jerry...drop me in the tank. It's hotter than hell today," I said. Grumbling, Hardy and Judge dragged themselves over to the tank where I stood. They held my ankles as I twisted and squirmed through the hole. I felt terrific immersed in the invigorating liquid, but felt sorry for the guys who were too large to enjoy this stimulating diversion. I ducked under the cool water. After surfacing, I noticed the guys whispering and laughing as they headed towards the hatch.

"What's so funny, girls?" I sarcastically asked.

"Nothing 'Bubbles'—enjoy your dip," Bellotti said as the group lined up at the hatch and began descending the ladder. They all laughed but refused to look my way.

"Very funny. Now get me outta here. Come on, I've got a cramp in my leg. I just ate and I'm getting stomach cramps." (This myth, perpetuated by our parents, had not been completely dispelled by 1969.) "Stuart, Ozzie, come on, cut the shit. I'm wrinklin' like a prune, man."

Apparently unimpressed by my medical conditions, my six friends had gone. I stood alone, trapped in a water-filled prison. I knew, due to previous attempts, that it was physically impossible to extricate myself from this liquid grave. I remained calm, briefly, secure in the knowledge that my good buddies were just screwing with my head and would return soon. After all, they knew well of my penchant for severe paranoia when I smoked weed.

After fifteen minutes of struggling to remain composed, the paranoia set in, mainly because I had smoked enough dew to stone Sasquatch. The rapid process began with intellectual paranoia, giving way to mild hysteria, and culminating with full-blown panic. My mind raced through the many horrific possibilities as reality blurred.

Then I heard a familiar sound. Four pigeons had landed on the roof, two feet from the open window on the side of my crypt. I'd later lay blame on the "devil weed" for my idiotic, quickly devised plan, although at that moment in time it seemed like a darn good idea. I'd lure a mindless, cooing pigeon within my reach. Then, with lightning speed, I'd grab the bird and snap its neck, killing it instantly. I'd then swiftly tie my brightly colored Hang-10 trunks to its twisted neck and, using a sidearm swing motion, heave it over the roof to the congested street below. When one of the Vietnamese pedestrians would see the lifeless pile of bone and feathers wrapped in bright orange-and-yellow cloth, he'd look up and realize some pathetic unfortunate nut-job was trapped on the roof of the hotel. The person would then report the incident to the authorities and I'd be rescued with an excessive degree of humiliation. Whom was I trying to fool? I got squeamish when I'd accidentally squash a bug on the sidewalk. I knew I could not snap the neck of an innocent, tiny bird.

I hastily made the decision to implement my backup plan—scream like a wounded banshee!

"Help! Help! Help, heeeeeelllllllp!"

Out of breath and growing more desperate by the second, I decided to attempt climbing out through the opening. After four failed attempts, my forearms began to bleed from scrapes received while trying to pull myself through the gap.

Just as I prepared to unleash my primal death scream one more time, the hatch flew open and up came Larry Pratt.

"They weren't lying! You *are* in the tank." Larry was grinning and shaking his head. "Those guys are in your room laughing their butts off and smoking like chimneys. They told me what they did but I didn't believe them, so I came up to see for myself." Good ole reliable Larry Pratt stood there awkwardly smiling and scratching his chin.

"Go get another dude and get me outta here," I ordered. "But don't get one of those assholes who left me here to shrivel. I've been here for over an hour—I thought I was gonna die, Larry."

"It's only been ten minutes, Pete, ten minutes. I was in the hall when they came down from here." Larry pointed to his watch.

"Bullshit, Larry," I said, looking up at him through the opening in the tank. "It's been over an hour, closer to two, I think." I was positive at least an hour had passed.

"Pete, it was ten minutes, honest." Larry again pointed to his watch. "They were going to come back in another five minutes to get you out. You should quit smoking that stuff. I don't think it's good for your overall health. I think it makes time slow down or something."

The last thing I wanted right then was a lecture from Larry Pratt about the evils of smoking pot. He had never even gotten drunk, let alone smoked weed. Larry Pratt was more "clean and sober" than anyone I had ever met, and just the type of person I needed at that moment.

"Go get another guy, but not any of the punks who left me here to die like a rat," I repeated. I wanted to make sure that Larry didn't bring one of my executioners for the extraction. I didn't want to give them the satisfaction.

"Get Goodman. He's in his room writing letters. And Larry, don't mention anything about the one-hour time distortion, okay? Are you sure it was only ten minutes, man?" I knew Pratt didn't lie, but still questioned his declaration.

"Ya know, Pete, you could've just covered the drain at the bottom of the tank, and when somebody didn't get any shower water, a hotel worker would've come up here to check the tank and see what was blocking it." Larry politely laughed.

"Hurry up Pratt; I'm turning into a human prune!" Humiliation can be quite humbling, I concluded.

As Larry closed the hatch, one of the pigeons landed on the edge of the opening in the tank. I swear that the little guy looked me straight in the eye and winked before flying away.

Chapter XIII

Groovin'

(Young Rascals, 1967)

My favorite day of the week in Saigon was Sunday. No warehouse, no lifers, no getting up at 6:00 a.m., and no mess-hall meals unless I chose to eat there. Saigon had some fantastic restaurants in the downtown area. Most Sunday evenings, a group of us would get together and dine at one of the finer places. Although the restaurants offered a wide variety of international dishes, I usually ordered spaghetti or a large-cut T-bone steak. Other activities I enjoyed on Sundays were playing poker, walking the streets to people-watch, and catching a flick after a satisfying spaghetti dinner.

After six weeks in Saigon, I made a crucial declaration to myself: Sunday mornings, I wouldn't smoke weed or drink alcohol before noon, consciously making the intellectual decision that having a clear head for at least six hours a week was probably a healthy choice for my overall well-being.

On that decisive Sunday morning, after self-imposing my weed-smoking, alcohol-consuming ban, I decided to head across the street to the Imperial Hotel and invest a few bucks in the stingy slot machines in the back of the bar area. I looked forward to going it solo that Sunday morning, and this was my usual practice. The time by myself gave me a chance to collect my thoughts and reflect on my past, present, and future. I also derived great pleasure from thinking about home, family, and my good friends back in California. Most days, from the time I got up in the morning to the time I went to bed, I spent in the company of my Fab 50 friends. We ate together, worked together, and partied together. Sunday morning I cherished my "alone time."

Having a room at the end of the hall made it almost impossible for me to sneak out of the hotel unnoticed on Sunday mornings. To reach the elevator undetected, I had to pass six rooms on the left and seven on the right side of the hall. Invariably, someone would be awake with his door open when I walked past. On some Sundays, it could take me up to forty minutes to stealthily complete the 90-foot walk to the elevator. This Sunday morning proved no different.

"Whalon, where the heck you goin' this early? You goin' to chow? Wait for me, I'll go with you." Bellotti had just opened his door as I sneaked by.

"Not breakfast," I half-whispered, not wanting anyone else to hear us talking. "I'm just going to play some slots and have a cup of coffee. Go back to bed, Gene. You look like day-old cat shit." I pushed Bellotti inside his room and quickly closed the door behind him. It swung open immediately.

"No Pete, come in man," Bellotti begged. "I gotta tell you this; it's cool, really mind-blowin' cool. Get in here; this is a real trip. I'll get dressed and go with ya."

Bellotti firmly grabbed my collar and pulled me into his room. I reluctantly went in as Gene began babbling on about some street whore he had argued with the night before, how the MPs came and broke it up, how he flipped them off, how they were going to take him in, and how I should've been there to witness him kicking MP ass.

"Whalon, are you hearin' me? Shit, come on, wait here while I shower and I'll go with ya. Hey, let's go to the Annex tonight after dinner to catch the flick." He reminded me that a group of us had made plans to have dinner together at the Continental Hotel that very night. "They got a skin-3, fuzz-2 flick, *Barbarella,* with that commie bitch Jane Fonda." Bellotti was all smiles.

At some point during the early years of the war, an unknown GI had cleverly created a film-rating guide for the movies shown in Nam. The ratings were: skin 1, skin 2, and skin 3, plus fuzz 1, fuzz 2, and fuzz 3. "Skin" referred to the amount of nudity seen in the film, and "fuzz" referred to the amount of pubic hair visible. The higher the number, the better the film. A GI's dream was a skin-3, fuzz-3 rating, equating to plenty of boobs and plenty of bush.

I had already seen *Barbarella* in Hawaii. However, since it boasted a preferable skin/fuzz rating, I agreed to go watch it again.

"Sounds like a plan to me, Geno," I yelled as Bellotti turned on the bathroom faucet to brush his teeth. "I've seen it but it's outstanding. Very trippy but cool, and that Fonda chick does have a fantastic 'bod'—hey, did you ever see *Twelve Angry Men*? Her dad's in it with Lee J. Cobb and E.G. Marshall. Now that's a brilliant flick. Okay, after dinner at the Continental Hotel, we'll catch a cab to the Annex. The movie starts at 7:30. Hey, let's ask Harp to go; he likes Fonda."

"Now get your ass in gear, Gene, and scrub that infested, shriveled carcass you call a body and let's go to the bar. I got a slot machine whose ass I'm gonna kick for taking me for twenty bucks last Sunday." I paused a moment to consider my getaway options. "Better yet, I'll meet you there," I added quickly.

I hustled out the door, not waiting for Bellotti's response. At least I'd have a few minutes alone before Gene joined me at the bar.

After squandering another $20 on the "one-armed bandit," I decided to take a walk with Bellotti who had arrived five minutes earlier. Strolling the streets of Saigon, day or night, always provided an adventure. Vietnamese pedestrians crowded the sidewalks, moving swiftly, carrying their baby-sans or shopping items, or both. Open markets lined the congested streets. Numerous street hustlers assaulted the GIs unmercifully, from the moment we reached the street to the time we returned to our living quarters. (All military living quarters in Saigon had armed American MPs out front, twenty-four hours a day.) The hustlers sold anything you wanted, including their relatives. It seemed that the average Vietnamese citizen believed every American GI was filthy rich.

As we walked leisurely down Hung Dao Street, toward the Saigon River, the locals surrounded us, attempting to make a sale: "GI want boom-boom from numba one mama-san?" or, "GI want numba one blow job from my sista?" As well as offering family members for sexual acts, the peddlers pleaded for us to buy them valuable PX items that they could resell on the street for a hefty profit. "GI buy me soap and Salem, me gib you boo-coo money," and, "You buy fo me fan from PX, my sista lub you long time, GI Numba One."

During my first month in Saigon, I thought it cool to bullshit and barter with the locals, but I soon tired of the exhausting routine. The quickest way to discourage a hustler was to respond by threatening, "You dee-dee or I call MP." Most of the hustlers were deathly afraid of the MPs for two valid reasons. First, MPs had the legal authority to arrest them and, second, a number of the macho Military Police were sadistic assholes who loved rousting the "gooks," as well as the GIs. There was nothing more futile and exhausting than dealing with an ignorant, macho MP attempting to prove his manhood.

Although the street hustlers could drain me, I looked forward to interacting with the children. The Vietnamese kids never ceased to amaze me with their friendliness. They were always courteous, and usually in high spirits. The kids seemed so completely innocent and unaware of the appalling conditions that surrounded them. I secretly worried about what would ultimately happen to these engaging children when the United States military inevitably pulled out of their country. This unsettling thought troubled me deeply.

Whenever I ate at the Army mess hall across from our hotel, I'd fill my fatigue pockets with apples and oranges just before leaving. Then, when I appeared outside, I'd take out the fruit, one by one, and toss it like a baseball to the awaiting hands of the smiling youngsters. The enthusiastic kids would all scream, "Rau, rau, rau," hoping I would chuck an apple their way. "Rau" in Vietnamese means moustache, and I had a long, thick, black moustache. This interaction became a game I enjoyed as much as the screaming kids did. The sight of those extraordinarily deprived children and other profound experiences in Vietnam helped instill in me a vast and lasting appreciation of just how fortunate I was to have been born in the United States. There, but for the grace of God, go I!

Gene and I reminisced about California and Hawaii during our stroll that cloudy Sunday. Along the way, we also munched on some Vietnamese concoction of vegetables and meat purchased from a cantankerous old papa-san street vendor. Bellotti believed the dish included some chunks of dog meat, but I told him it tasted more like Siamese cat to me. By the time Gene and I returned to the hotel, noon approached. The morning had gone outstanding so far. I was in good spirits and more than ready to indulge in our Sunday afternoon ritual of playing poker.

I had a passion (bordering on obsession) for playing cards—hearts, spades, and especially poker. Judge, Harper, and I were the preeminent poker players in the group. Making personal insults and derogatory references to their manhood, the three of us often teamed up to badger weaker players into a "few hands, just for the fun of it." A first-rate game consisted of Judge, Harper, me, and four or five "born losers" (a name I affectionately called them to their faces repeatedly during the course of a poker session).

When you call a soldier a "loser" during a poker game, it tends to make him more determined to stay in the action and prove you wrong. Nobody likes to be called a "loser," especially a young, macho male dressed in jungle fatigues. The difficult part for us proved to be keeping them in the battle until we had extracted as much money as humanly possible. Unfortunately, many losers discourage easily and require incentives to remain in the game.

"Come on, Price, you puss, just three more deals and if you don't win, you can quit like the girlie bitch that you are, you whining, immature woman," I badgered. "Stay in for a few more hands and be a real man for once in your pathetic, useless, meaningless existence. Don't be a quittin' fairy like Stuart yesterday. You're due to get some good cards, I feel it, man."

This grueling process was necessary for the survival of the weekly game we appropriately dubbed "Sunday Slaughter." A $6 bottle of Jim Beam and $5 worth of Cambodian Red weed (CBR) would usually yield huge dividends. The three of us would shamelessly lie to the clueless suckers about how much better they were playing since their last fleecing. When it came to poker, we had no shame.

And so it went—the bullshit flowed, whiskey poured, smoke filled the room, and the hopeless flock kept right on losing. The big winner in the game would buy dinner for the other players that evening. This wasn't a game about money, but something more primal—bragging rights and machismo.

That evening, as previously planned, Bellotti, Pratt, Schrunk, Mills, Stuart, Hardy, Judge, Ozzie, Goodman, Price, Harper, and I gathered at the Continental Hotel for dinner. The hotel offered the finest restaurant in Saigon, which served magnificent spaghetti—my all-time favorite. The heads in the group huddled in my room, prior to dinner,

121

to get loaded. Nothing satisfied the palate more than getting a good "weed buzz," chowing down a mouthwatering plate of pasta, and drinking an ice-cold Coors. For some peculiar reason, I could eat twice as much when stoned and the food tasted three times as good.

After dinner, some of the guys headed back to our hotel. A few of the cheerful drunks walked the four blocks to Tu Do Street for a late night of drinking and womanizing (okay, whoring). Bellotti and I grabbed a cab to the Annex to see the highly rated flick, *Barbarella*. We had tried to convince some of the group to come with us to see Jane Fonda's tits, but everybody had seen them in Hawaii. I think Bellotti had seen the flick in Hawaii also but had been too stoned to remember the experience. Bellotti and I promised the drinkers that we'd join them in "Dodge City" for some late-night carousing after the flick.

Our cab headed west, and the Annex stood on the east side of the street. Traffic was moving at a snail's pace so Bellotti and I decided to get out of the cab in the middle of the road, to cross to the Annex instead of waiting for the driver to turn around. We overpaid the driver, hopped out, and stood in traffic waiting for a break in the flow. Suddenly there sounded a loud thump and a shriek.

"Asshole!" I heard Bellotti yell. "Slant-eyed slope gook bastard!"

I had been looking to my left at oncoming traffic as Bellotti stood on my right side. A Volkswagen cab had crossed the middle line (a common practice) to pass a slower car and had struck Bellotti in the leg. By the time I turned around, Bellotti was sprawled on the ground staring up at the flabbergasted cab driver, and firing an admirable, rapid verbal assault of profanity and insults. My California buddy's tirade caused the cabbie, a tiny cross-eyed man, to quiver.

I helped Gene to his feet as he raised a fist. Bellotti began hopping towards the wide-eyed driver like a one-legged Muhammad Ali. With a glazed, crazed look in his eyes, Gene chased the terrified, miniature man around his cab. Buzz continued to hop on one leg, while cursing at his prey. The petrified driver rapidly screeched in broken English and Vietnamese, pleading for Bellotti to spare his life.

Cars beeped, people shouted, and I tried desperately to lead Bellotti to the sidewalk and safety for both of us. I knew the three joints and four glasses of Merlot wine Gene had consumed in the past hour may have contributed to his lack of judgment and uncontrollable anger. Bellotti used words I hadn't even heard before.

"I'll kill you, you gook bastard—you rice-eatin' midget, lob-dick, fart-blowing fairy, chop-stick Chink! You'll be maggot chow when I catch your ass-kissin', blow-hole, pickle-suckin' peanut packer!"

Bellotti became exhausted from his one-legged pursuit and verbal barrage. He had to lean against the hood of the cab to catch his breath. I laughed hysterically, but seized the opportunity to grab Bellotti's arm and pull him to the sidewalk while he continued his verbal offensive. Simultaneously, I motioned for the traumatized driver, who was huffing and puffing like a locomotive, to get into his cab and take off.

"Dee-dee papa-san, dee-dee mau!" I screamed at the driver as I tried to control my laughing.

"You numba one GI!" the driver yelled to me. "You numba one!" He jumped into his VW Bug and sped off.

"Get your fairy-fruitcake ass back here, Mr. Moto smack-head!" Bellotti screamed as the car disappeared in traffic. The madder Gene became the more I howled.

I knew if the MPs showed up, Bellotti and his trash-mouth would only get us into more trouble. I helped Gene inside the Annex and onto a narrow bench in the hallway.

"Lighten up dude. Where in the world did you get some of those words you were usin'?" I asked, snickering. "I know 'Frisco' is a far-out place, but man, Gene, that was weird, I mean really bizarre stuff. By the way, what's a 'Mr. Moto smack-head' genius? How's your boney twig anyway?"

Bellotti pulled up the pant leg of his fatigues. There was a microscopic scrape with a little blood and slight swelling.

"You pussy," I taunted. "That's a scratch, you wimp, you girl. Jeez, how fast was he going when he hit you—like a half-mile an hour? You are such a puss, you little bitch, I swear to God. I'm ashamed to call you a Californian, you woman. Are you sure you're not from Mississippi?"

I was hoping to divert Bellotti's attention from the fact that I had encouraged the driver to take off, preventing Gene from kicking the mini-man's ass.

"Not very fast, but it pissed me off, Pete. Why'd you tell him to take off, Whalon?" Gene inquired. "I wanted to kick his scrawny ass and call the MPs."

"The guy weighed like seventy-five pounds soaking wet, Gene. Just lighten up, man. The MPs would've arrested you just for those off-the-wall words you made up, idiot."

We were both cracking up now.

"Don't mean nothing.' Right Whalon? Don't mean shit." Bellotti had suddenly realized it really was no big deal.

"You still want to see *Barbarella*, Merriam-Webster?" I asked.

"Yeah, let's go get a good look at that commie bitch's tits!" Gene replied, with a big smile.

It was the first sensible thing Bellotti had said for some time.

Chapter XIV
Fun, Fun, Fun
(Beach Boys, 1964)

Life at the warehouse was filled with distractions and disruptions on a daily basis. Our unusual clique of malcontents had perfected the age-old practice of "goldbricking" at work. Our primary goal each day consisted of making the time pass quickly, by using a combination of pranks, BS sessions, and the ever-popular ritual of hassling our beleaguered bevy of career soldiers. In a way, it was a lot like high school for me. The lifers played the teachers and we were the incorrigible students. Our small horde of renegades was made up of the class clowns who searched for the next outrageous practical joke that would outdo the last one.

During the course of a day, we'd regularly test the lifers and see how long we could go without doing any work—nothing. Not lift, move, or place one piece of material on a shelf, not help anybody else do a lick of work, or give assistance in any way. Specific rules reigned when we competed in the warehouse 32 "Lazy-Ass Olympics."

The clock started when the designated lazy-ass informed the official timer, "let the games begin," and ended when a lifer forced the slacker du jour back into a work mode. The lazy-ass monitor for the day vigilantly recorded the time. The coveted trophy, an eight-inch piece of lead pipe with the words "Lazy-Ass Champion" roughly etched in the metal, was awarded at the end of the week in a drunken ceremony back at the hotel. No one dared remove the pipe from the hotel for fear a sergeant would discover it and bust our sophomoric competition.

My favorite ploy to avoid work when competing was to carry a piece of conduit in one hand and a crowbar in the other, briskly striding past the "Lifer Lounge" (Edwards's air-conditioned office where his sergeants spent most of their time plotting to squash the rebellion), and feigning a look of insightful concern and purpose. It usually bought me a little time before one of the sergeants realized I had scammed him.

Mark Goodman, master of the game, usually received the trophy at week's end. He keenly understood the true meaning of the word lazy-ass. Many of his trademark maneuvers shone brilliantly in their simplicity.

One of Goodman's most basic tricks (often mimicked by his admirers) consisted of carrying a clipboard with papers and, assuming a look of trepidation, to make checkmarks with a pencil while staring at the endless rows of boxes. Something about a clipboard in hand always conveys, "I'm an essential individual performing a crucial responsibility." Mark would also engage in dialogue with one of us, wildly waving his hands and pointing to various areas of the warehouse. To a lifer out of earshot, it appeared that Mark was having an intense discussion concerning a warehouse problem. Of course, the person listening to him at the time was most likely getting a lesson on how to avoid getting ripped off by a tea girl, or discovering why he believed the Yanks would win the World Series that year.

Mark had a sixth sense when it came to lifers. Instinctively, he generally knew when one was watching him. Occasionally, for dramatic effect, he would slam down his clipboard on the ground and storm out of the warehouse. Lifers rarely followed, assuming he needed time to cool off.

I admired Mark's competitive spirit. I learned from the master numerous valuable lessons on the art of goldbricking that I'd often put to use during the remainder of my stay with Uncle Sam.

The creation of our own Shangri-la in the wire loft, high above the ground-dwellers' view, became the greatest single accomplishment during our six months at the warehouse. The elevated wire-storage area lay at the south end of the warehouse, and reached all the way to the back of the building. Wire spools, some as big as a VW Bug, came into the warehouse in all sizes. The only way to store the spools in the loft was to stack them on top of each other in long rows. This created a solid wall of wire spools 25 feet long and 5 feet high. The spool formation created a private hideaway similar to a den. No one standing below and looking up to the loft could see behind the spool walls.

Due to their enormous size and weight, only a forklift could budge the wire spools, and only a forklift could reach the loft. In effect, the loft resembled a second-story room with no stairs. With only three forklifts in the warehouse and all the drivers members of the Fab 50, no snooping lifer was able to reach the loft without assistance from one of us.

The loft scam got initiated one day while Ozzie nursed a colossal hangover. He brought a chair to the loft so he could catch a catnap and recuperate from the "Saigon Flu," without the sergeants pestering him. Three days later, the loft held four chairs and some magazines behind the spools. By week's end, it contained six chairs, over two dozen magazines, a large Styrofoam cooler, a cassette player, three decks of cards, and Jimi Hendrix, Bob Dylan, and Grand Funk Railroad posters. Within two weeks, the area had been transformed into an entertainment center. Books, board games, music, air mattresses, food, beer, and fans now made up part of the "Commune."

At first, we cautiously took turns, not allowing more than four guys up at any one time. We put into place a simple warning system to alert the loungers whenever an intruder approached. Any time a lifer asked for the use of a forklift, the driver would honk the horn one long time, signaling a possible incursion. With the immensity of the warehouse, the substantial number of workers, and the fact that the lifers had been beaten like a kettledrum by our constant, unrelenting assaults on their authority, we easily remained undetected in our "Paradise of Spools" (Bill Harper's winning entry in a contest held to name the loft). It became the ideal place to catch a few z's, recover from a rough night on Tu Do Street, read, write a letter, chug a quick beer, or avoid strenuous work. As the days passed, we became more relaxed in our security. Sometimes I'd get to the loft and find seven or eight guys crammed in, playing cards, listening to music, and talking much too loud.

Since the Lee Mills rebellion, Sergeants Bulldog Netton and Crabs Otto had taken it upon themselves to bust our asses whenever the opportunity presented itself. Bulldog especially delighted in figuring out one of our schemes and assigning extra work hours for punishment. He correctly believed that keeping us longer at the warehouse was a fate worse than death to most members of the Fab 50.

One morning, I sat in the loft looking for some new words to spring on the lifers, from my favorite book, *30 Days to a More Powerful Vocabulary*. Three others— Bellotti, Harper and Judge—relaxed in the loft with me. When I heard the forklift below, I assumed one of the guys had come up for a visit, so I continued reading my paperback. I glanced up to see which one of my friends came to join us, and there on the forklift blades stood Bulldog. I dropped the Coors can in my hand but Sergeant Netton saw my move.

"Your skinny ass is mine now, Whalon—you long-haired hippie. I got you now boy!" the sergeant bellowed. "I've been watching you punks for a week and..." He stopped in mid-sentence, turning his full attention on Bellotti.

All of us loafers leaped to our feet. Bulldog stormed over to where Bellotti stood and picked up a plastic bag, half-filled with weed, from the floor. While Gene lay on a mat, the bag had slipped from his pocket.

"What have we here, Private Bellotti?" Bulldog dangled the bag in front of Gene's face. The sergeant reminded you of a prosecutor showing a murder weapon to a defendant on the witness stand.

"It's not mine, sergeant Netton. It was on the floor when I got here." Gene shrugged his shoulders. "I never saw that stuff before. I'm not even sure what it is." Bellotti snuck a quick look my way and I shrugged my shoulders also.

"Bullshit! And you know damn well this is marijuana, Bellotti. You been smokin' this shit since the day you got here!" Bulldog was screaming in Bellotti's face. "You faggots finally went too far. Let's see what the man (Warrant Officer Edwards) has to say 'bout this. You women have one hour to dismantle this garbage dump. Take everything out of here and break down those spools. I don't want any spools stacked..." Bulldog was interrupted by a familiar voice from below.

"Hey Sarge, what's goin' on up there? Need any help?" Goodman, standing below, was yelling up at Bulldog and waving his arm like a politician running for office.

"Goodman, get your flat ass outta my sight or you're goin' down with these four drug addicts."

Although I believed Bulldog rather liked me, I knew he hated Mark Goodman with a passion. To Bulldog, Goodman represented the smart-ass college crowd that was ruining our country with its hippie lifestyle and promotion of peace and love.

"Yes sergeant, anything you say, sir. See you later, sergeant Bulldog—see you guys later. Oh Bellotti, bring down my copies of *Playboy*, would ya?" Goodman smiled politely, waved to Sergeant Netton, flashed us the peace sign, and then leisurely walked into the main area.

"Get your asses busy!" Bulldog boomed. He looked down and hollered at Stuart, whom he had ordered to lift him up on the forklift. "Get me down now, Stuart!"

Bulldog took the bag of weed and my can of beer with him. By the time the sergeant reached the ground, about thirty of the guys had gathered below to check out the action. Most of the guys had used the loft at one time or another during the past six weeks and weren't thrilled with Bulldog's discovery.

From the loft in question, Bellotti looked down at the quizzical faces staring up at us and succinctly furnished a final report. "Soldiers, the 'Paradise of Spools' is officially closed." Then, while the onlookers booed and hissed, Bellotti grabbed an armful of Goodman's *Playboy* and *Penthouse* magazines and pitched them to the dejected horde below.

Once we cleared the loft and moved the spools, we dragged ourselves to Edwards's office, prepared to receive our scolding. Warrant Officer Edwards, Papa Bear Foster, and Bulldog took turns calling us lots of derogatory names we had heard many times before. Although the trio unleashed numerous threats, our sentence was rather mild. They assigned us to clean-up detail for two weeks and to stay one hour later each night to tidy up the "Prison Yard." A letter of reprimand would be placed in our files, which would probably prevent us from being promoted any time soon. They also restricted us to our hotel, except to cross the street for meals. I almost laughed out loud when I heard that last one. All things considered, it was a light punishment. I almost felt sorry for the ineptness of our hapless leaders— but not quite.

The most disappointing aspect of the whole ordeal was the loss of our loft. I, along with many others, would certainly miss my time spent in "A Spool's Paradise"—my entry in the contest, which came in second.

Chapter XV
Games People Play
(Joe South, 1969)

One of my favorite activities in the evening was to join Bill Harper at the Victoria Hotel and watch him hustle 9-ball. Harp excelled at it and was a master at hustling unsuspecting hotshots who thought they could "shoot stick" and earn a little cash by taking down Saigon Bill. Vietnamese workers at the hotel bestowed on Harper that nickname out of respect for his prowess with a pool cue. The employees of the Victoria also adored Bill because he tipped them generously, especially after a profitable evening at the tables.

The Victoria Hotel was about a mile down the street from our home base, the Hung Dao. On the third floor of the Victoria was a huge, smoke-filled pool hall with over twenty-five tables. An extra-long bar extended down the entire length of the back wall. Numerous low-hanging florescent lights lit up the smoggy room, recalling the illumination of a night game at the Los Angeles Coliseum. Along the three open walls of the room sat undersized wooden tables with two or three chairs for spectators, and the "young guns" waiting for the next game. Vietnamese drink servers hustled from table to table taking orders, while they smiled and nodded their heads at the GIs.

Although anyone could play in the pool room, rarely did I see any Vietnamese shooting a game. This was a GI hangout for guys who lived for shooting pool. Most of the shooters at the Victoria were deadly serious about their pool-playing and didn't appreciate losing. Often I would hear a challenge to "step outside asshole!" or "you ain't shit, dude, just a lucky ass." Although hustlers commonly made macho threats, seldom did two competitors actually exchange

132

punches. I believe they were fearful of losing their place in line for the next game.

Seven nights a week, the pool room at the Victoria stayed jam-packed with wise-guy hustlers trying to demonstrate they shot the best "stick" in Saigon. I observed hundreds of pool players during my six months in Saigon and, without question, the "top gun" at 9-ball was Saigon Bill Harper.

At least two nights a week, Harper would visit the Victoria to shoot stick and, more importantly, separate over-confident, cocky shooters from their money. Bill Harper liked using his country-boy accent when anyone approached him for a "friendly" game. Calmly waiting for his first victim of the night, Bill would slightly cock his Army cap to one side, order a Coke in a glass with a straw, and shoot around on his own or with me.

One Friday night after an exhausting day of avoiding warehouse work, I joined Bill at the Victoria so I could watch him play pool. As usual, I planned to sit back, drink beer, and observe as Saigon Bill skillfully overwhelmed his competitors. I had told Bellotti earlier in the evening that Harper and I would join their group at The Cal Bar later. I was just finishing my first beer when two grungy-looking dudes smoking cheap cigars approached Bill.

"Hey, country boy, want a game? We'll play doubles for a few bucks if ya ain't chickenshit."

Harper kept shooting, never looking up. The two guys then looked at me. That was my cue (pun intended) to take a seat and witness the inevitable parade of unsuspecting cows enter the slaughterhouse.

"No, not me, I'm a shitty player but Harp might play ya a game or two." I gestured towards Bill.

I then waved to a waitress and pointed at my beer. I wanted a nice cold one for the action. The two dupes were swigging beer between puffs on their cigars and flashing familiar "this-is-gonna-be-as-simple-as-taking-candy-from-a-country-ass-baby" smiles.

"You want a game, Harp? I'm Jimmy Capalitti from the Bronx and this here is 'Speedy' Jones from Brooklyn." (In the service, everybody I met from Brooklyn had a catchy nickname such as Rocket, Bull's-eye, Blackball, Turtle, etc.)

The two New Yorkers shook hands with Bill. Using his thickest, laid-back Southern drawl, Harper gave them the answer they were looking for. "Shoor Jimmy," Harper said, "but I only play 9-ball—how much ya wanna play for, buddy?"

"I'll play ya first," the much-too-cocky Jimmy C said. "Then Speedy can have a piece of ya, if ya got any MPC left." The two New Yorkers both laughed. "How 'bout two bucks a ball and five a game? Is that in your budget, Country Bill?"

Jimmy was beginning to drool with anticipation. Saigon Bill politely accepted the challenge, flashed the Easterners a grin, and racked the balls.

I sat there silently drinking my Coors. I couldn't wait for Harp to shut these wiseasses up. If I were playing, I'd already be in their faces with nasty insults about their appearance and provocative references to their manhood. Bill, who possessed more common sense, remained cool and calm—a necessity for a successful hustler. Playing well and hustling took concentration and rigid discipline—two admirable traits I had not yet acquired in my young life.

The next hour got painfully ugly for the pair of aces from the Big Apple. Harper took the first seven games, lost one, then won five more. I intentionally exaggerated my hyena laugh every time Bill sunk a ball. Predictably, the hot-shots got pissed off at Harp and themselves, drank more brew, and played exceedingly worse. Harper, maintaining his laid-back style throughout the ordeal, would smile and wink at me when he was about to run the table and take another game from the city slickers.

I used my Vin Scully voice impersonation to announce the final results. "Ladies and gentlemen, the score now stands—Saigon Bill Harper, 12 games; wiseass New York Boys, 1!" I had gotten under their skin. Speedy flipped me off and threw his cigar butt at my head. It missed and hit the wall behind me.

As they stormed away, I couldn't resist one parting shot. "Hey Speedy Boy," I yelled, "that cigar was high and outside, ball 4, take a walk, loser!" I forced a high-pitched laugh, almost straining my vocal chords.

Harp never drank alcohol when he played pool—his sole purpose was to win money. Playing 9-ball was a side job to him. Bill had honed his exceptional stick skills in the scores of smoke-filled pool halls that peppered the downtown area of Rocky Mount, North Carolina. He often tried to tutor me on my game, to transform me into the West Coast version of Saigon Bill. Unfortunately, my lack of patience, desire, sobriety, and understanding of the subtleties of the game doomed me to the sidelines. By choice, I became Saigon Bill's designated heckler—a role I lived for and excelled at.

It didn't take very long for Harper's ability with a cue to become common knowledge in the pool hall. To my surprise, instead of wannabes being frightened away, Harper had more challengers than he could handle. As in the Old West, everybody wanted to go up against the quickest draw in town. At the Victoria pool hall, in 1969, that distinction belonged to Private Bill Harper, United States Army. The more Bill won, the more he played, and the more I heckled.

That night, after three hours of some serious stick, Harper walked away up $565 and was primed for a night on Tu Do Street and some good, old-fashioned barhopping.

After we climbed in a cab heading downtown, Bill reminded me about not letting the other guys know how much he had won. With the easy access to drugs, booze, and women, getting through the month on an Army private's pay was a real challenge for the military consumer in Vietnam. Many of the GIs went broke by the tenth of the month and looked to float a loan from anyone with a little cash in his pocket. Those who had the stomach for loan-sharking made lots of extra cash from this financially challenged group of GIs. I was considered a soft touch, naively believing any far-out tale concerning someone's lack of funds.

The first stop in Dodge City was always The California Bar. Any time after 5:00 p.m., you could bet there would be at least one member of the Fab 50 sitting at the bar, getting smashed and perhaps hassling some savvy tea girl. This night was no exception.

"Whalon, Harp, over here!" Bellotti waved his hand and whistled to get our attention. In the back corner gathered around two tables were Bellotti, Judge, Stuart, Hardy, Schrunk, Oswald, Mills, and Price. At the bar sat three other guys from the warehouse, deeply immersed in an intellectual conversation about who was the best black female singer— Diana Ross, Little Eva, or Fontella Bass.

"How much cash you win tonight, Saigon Bill?" Stuart asked, curious. He was broke and as usual looking for a loan.

"Not much, fifty bucks," Bill lied. He knew Stuart wanted to hit him up for another handout.

"Can I borrow ten until payday? I need some weed and I'm busted, man. Come on, just ten for the Stuman. Bill, help a brother in need." Willie Stuart always had dire need of some Mary Jane.

"Yeah, okay Willie," Harper said, "but that's it for this month. No more loans. Got it? How much you owe me now?" Bill calculated that it was well over $300 but wanted to see if Stuart had any clue of his total.

"'Bout one hundred, I think, Bill...maybe one hundred and fifty. Shit, I dunno." Stuart began laughing as he always did when pressured or facing a problem. Harper just shook his head and threw Willie a 10-spot, knowing there was a good chance he'd never see any of the debt returned.

At that moment, an unexpected warm feeling came over me as I looked around at my group of friends sitting, drinking, and bullshitting with each other. A little over a year ago, I didn't even know these guys and now they felt like lifelong friends—like family. I wasn't quite sure if it was the amount of beer I had consumed or a flash of mental clarity, but at that exact moment in time, I wouldn't have traded places with anybody in the world. Here I sat, in a bar in downtown Saigon, during the height of the Vietnam War, and perfectly content. I silently joked to myself that I should pay a visit to the clinic next week to have my head examined.

I was just finishing my first beer when I heard screaming coming from outside. We all rushed for the door at the same time, not wanting to miss any action. There, in the middle of the street, stood a tall, lanky black guy with a huge afro and dark sunglasses. He was squeezing the top of a broken beer bottle in one hand and slowly staggering forward. Standing twenty feet in front of him stood an obese white dude with no shirt on; the white dude's impressive beerbelly hid his belt buckle.

Within seconds, two hundred cheering GIs lined the sidewalks, egging on the combatants and hoping to witness a bloody street brawl. There were predominately black guys on the other side of the street and all white guys on our side. The absence of the MPs amazed me. They usually patrolled around Tu Do Street and especially The Melody Bar (the only exclusive black bar on Tu Do and the scene of some of the greatest slugfests and all-out brawls in Dodge). I figured there must have been something significant happening somewhere else in Saigon to take the MPs' attention away from Tu Do.

The black guy started taunting the white dude: "You dumbshit, white, honky asshole—I'll cut your heart out with my razor and shit in the bloody hole, redneck. Keep your country ass outta the Melody; that's a brothers' bar." While working the crowd of his black brothers into a frenzy, he slowly advanced towards the white lard ass.

I got amused and a little excited by the scene. I loved watching drunks fight because they seldom quit, even when getting their asses kicked.

Disappointingly, before a single blow was exchanged, the MPs abruptly crashed our party. "Okay ladies, break it up!" a stocky MP ordered as he approached the white guy. "The sheriff is back in town—Matt Dillon has arrived, so get your dead asses back into the bars or go to jail!" At the end of the street, three MP jeeps had appeared and eight MPs gazed at the scene with their helmets on and their nightsticks out.

Just before I turned to go back to The Cal Bar, I noticed objects in the air, coming towards me from the other side of the street. Over fifty beer bottles started crashing on the buildings and striking the retreating GIs in different parts of their bodies. I ducked as a bottle whizzed past my ear. The guy standing next to me caught one on his shoulder and started screaming in pain and anger. I dropped down on all fours and low-crawled back into the bar as dozens of others scrambled for safety from the air assault.

The MPs, seeing the bottles flying, sprinted down the middle of the street yelling and waving their hands for everybody to get inside. In what seemed like minutes but was only about thirty seconds, the street was emptied except for two drunks—one Black and one White— passed out in the gutter.

"Whalon, what you doin' crawlin' on the ground like a bitch, you pussy?" Judge had approached me just inside the door and began questioning my exit strategy and manhood.

"Up your ass, Jerry," I fired back. "I didn't want a Coors bottle tattooing my head—you turned and ran like a chickenshit schoolgirl when it got rough out there, ass-face, so don't jump in my shit, fool."

I laughed as I jumped to my feet and returned to our table. Somehow none of my friends had gotten whacked by a bottle. Recalling a close call, Bellotti told us that a flying Budweiser can had just missed his head and hit the dude behind him square in the nose.

"Shit, Gene, I saw you haul ass back inside the second you saw a fight break out," I joked. "You're a pussy with a capital P. I'd hate to have your San Francisco, queer ass backin' me up if we were in the bush." I always seized the opportunity to bag on Gene Bellotti. I simply enjoyed watching him get all serious.

"Hey guys, be extra careful messing with those black guys," Schrunk warned. "There's a lot of tension these days between black and white, especially in the Army."

The last thing we wanted right then was a lecture from Grandpa Schrunk.

"Thanks Professor Schrunk," Harper chided. "Will there be a pop quiz tomorrow on black-white relations in the military, Professor?"

Mills joined in. "Professor Schrunk, where did you get your BS degree again? 'Cuz you're really full of BS this fine evening." Lee wasn't the funniest clown in the circus, but he had his moments.

Hardy and Stuart had not returned to The Cal Bar with us, so we felt comfortable doing the black-white humor thing.

"Well ladies," I declared, "I'm goin' to the Continental for some spaghetti and meatballs—anybody want to join me?" I was in a euphoric mood and especially hungry.

Bellotti, Judge, Schrunk, and I caught a cab and headed for the Continental Hotel. I sat in the back of the cab in silence, smiling. It had been one of those magical nights in one's life when, for whatever reason, everything was simply perfect.

Chapter XVI

Wild Thing

(Troggs, 1966)

When we had received our orders in Hawaii for Vietnam, they stated that we'd be sent on TDY (temporary duty) to Nam for six months. After half a year, we were scheduled to return to our PCS (permanent change of station), Hawaii. Although the lifers at the warehouse intended not to advise us of our status, we understood that, in twenty-one days, the Fab 50 would make its triumphant return to the sunny shores of Waikiki Beach—hopefully, for the duration of our military service.

We had done our homework and our group clearly understood the Army regulations pertaining to TDY and PCS. The limitations were crystal clear: the longest period of time a GI could spend on TDY was 180 days. We assumed our vindictive leaders' silence on the matter was because they didn't want to grant us the satisfaction of hearing about our imminent return to Paradise. The collective mood of our mutinous swarm was one of euphoria. Together we decided not to bring up the subject of our TDY until one of the party poopers mentioned it first.

However, in hindsight, we should've recognized by then that the Army could pretty much do what it wanted, when it wanted. We were guilty of a very common miscalculation, made by youth throughout the course of civilization—we underestimated our elders. Our youthful rebellion had been nothing new to the military. These men, who had lost countless battles to us over the past six months, wouldn't let an irreverent gang of young malcontents win the war.

One humid Saturday evening in early November 1969, with only three short weeks remaining in our Nam tour, a small group of friends gathered in my room to drink booze, smoke weed, and hang out together.

Raising a beer over his head, Ozzie asked for quiet. "Guys, a toast to the Fab 50, and especially to our modest, militant pack of wolves. This six-month stint was actually a lot of fun, but the next year in Hawaii is gonna kick ass—I shit you not, my brothers—I shit you not!"

All present raised their glasses, cheering and hooting for the Wizard of Oz.

That Saturday evening before anyone arrived, I had come up with an idea for our little get-together. (During our frequent gatherings, I'd often feign spontaneity, although my spur-of-the-moment inspirations had often been planned at an earlier time.) "Guys, I've got a cool idea since we're getting out of here soon—let's go 'round the room and describe the most outrageous or defiant incident you remember over the past six months." I could sense by the blank stares that some of my buddies didn't appreciate just how brilliant my idea was.

"Come on, man. It'll be cool to hear what everybody remembers," I urged, attempting to pump up the guys. I was quite proud of myself, even if everybody else thought it a harebrained idea.

"That's sissy bullshit, Whalon," Bellotti protested. "Sounds like something they do at Girl Scout meetings. Hey Pete, can we have a secret handshake too?" Apparently, Mr. Gene Bellotti didn't agree with such an awe-inspiring suggestion.

"No, wait a minute Buzz—that sounds cool, Pete," Ozzie said, jumping in. "You go first, Whalon."

The unsuspected support from Oswald started the ball rolling. Of course, I came well prepared to relate my most memorable experience from the warehouse. "Okay lob-dicks, grab a frosty one. I call this *'Harper's Revenge'!*"

It was a sweltering day, even for Vietnam, with temperatures inside the warehouse reaching 115. For some mysterious reason, the sergeants had ridden us particularly hard that week and many of the guys were short-tempered and irritable. Harper had been grudgingly reassigned to separate lamps and bulbs in the back corner of the warehouse, away from all the action. A tedious job, it required long hours of sitting on your ass and organizing hundreds of tiny light bulbs by serial numbers. Next to the thought-provoking nuts-and-bolts assignment, bulbing was the most dreaded duty in the brick-shithouse.

Bulldog, whose primary assignment was to "keep those dope-smoking hippies functioning as soldiers," liked nothing better than to roust members of the Saigon 7. That scorching day, Harper returned ten minutes late from lunch. When Bill reported to his work area, he found Bulldog waiting for him at the bulb table.

"Where have you been, Private Harper? You're ten minutes late to work and that shit don't fly with me. Tomorrow you take a half hour for lunch—that's thirty minutes, missy—do you comprendo, Private Harper?"

Harper casually shook his head and returned to the table where thousands of fragile bulbs rested, neatly lined up and placed in their proper sections. Bulldog closely followed, barking at Harper's back, trying as hard as he could to provoke Bill.

As I kneeled in the wire loft unpacking some crates, Bulldog started yelling at Harp. I had a bird's-eye view of the entire debacle. From my perch, I noticed that ten to twelve other guys had gathered a short distance from Harp and Bulldog, and they also intently observed the confrontation.

143

"Hippie, lazy-ass. You're all the same—lazy, dope-smokin' fairies, incapable of working on..."

Harper interrupted the sergeant in mid-sentence. "Sarge, I've told you before—I do NOT smoke dope and I ain't no fairy!"

"You look like a fairy," Bulldog hollered, "and you act like Tinkerbell—and all you hippies smoke dope—hippie!"

The sergeant could see that he had worked his way under Harp's skin. Bill despised being called a fairy, and since he didn't smoke dope, he hated to be labeled a dope-smokin' hippie. In fact, Harper was the furthest thing from a "dope-smoking hippie" in our elite coalition.

"Sarge, don't call me a fairy or a hippie, please—I do NOT smoke dicks or dope!"

Then the sergeant got pissed and turned blood-red. Bulldog moved closer to Bill and soon stood only two feet from Harper's clammy face.

"You had better show me some respect, private, and watch how you talk to me, soldier, or I will Arty 15 your ass, you dope-smokin' hippie asshole—do you get it, soldier?" Bulldog glared at Harper.

That was it. The volatile combination of extreme heat, verbal assaults, and having a sweaty-faced lifer call him a dope smoker three times in a matter of minutes proved too much for the normally cool Bill Harper to take.

Harper lost it. He moved one step closer to Bulldog. "I ain't no goddammed soldier!"

With his emphatic declaration, Bill stretched his arm across the table and, in one quick move, swept thousands of bulbs and lamps off the table and onto the floor. It was Chinese New Year in the warehouse! Bulbs exploded and popped everywhere. The shattering sound of glass breaking echoed throughout the entire warehouse.

144

Harp heaved his cap across the room and stormed past Bulldog without saying another word. He hurried out of the warehouse and disappeared around the building.

Bulldog's eyes bulged from his contorted, crimson face. He attempted to speak, but the shell-shocked sergeant could find no words to say. Those of us fortunate enough to have witnessed Harper's ultimate act of defiance broke into raucous, spontaneous applause and cheering. Bill Harper had made a bold statement that day for young military men everywhere. It was a defining moment, summing up the feelings of our collective gang in one concise, impulsive declaration—"I ain't no goddammed soldier!" In a fit of rage, Bill Harper had coined a simple phrase that thousands of young men, forced into military service, were feeling every day in this bug-infested inferno of a country!

When I finished my recollection of *"Harper's Revenge,"* everyone cheered wildly again for Bill Harper. Harp stood, saluted, took a bow, and blew kisses to the rowdy crowd gathered in the room.

"Yeah, that was a classic, Pete—a great moment in warehouse folklore—I'll go next if nobody cares," Jerry Judge said. He was now sufficiently loaded and anxious to share a story he dubbed *"Fork You."*

Okay guys, you know I love the forklift races we had on Saturday mornings in the empty Warehouse 33. The championship race a few months ago was another classic. The competition consisted of three legs. Whoever won two of the three was the undisputed champ.

As you know, on Saturdays, only two lifers are scheduled to work. They usually stay inside Edwards's office eating Twinkies and looking at "Penthouse" magazines, rarely coming out before noon. Nothing short of an all-out assault on Saigon by the VC would get the two sergeants to vacate their air-conditioned retreat.

On this particular Saturday, a grudge-match race had been scheduled between the two best drivers in the warehouse—Jesse Roth, a fiercely competitive, six-foot seven-inch ex-football player from the University of Florida with a trick knee, and Chester "The Molester" Seacord, a quiet loner from Texarkana who loved drinking chocolate milk and passing the time reading Zane Grey paperback Westerns. Seacord wasn't really a molester, but the word did rhyme with Chester and we thought the phrase had a cool ring to it. Chester had raced stockcars back in the world before joining the Army. Both Roth and Seacord belonged to the family wing of the Fab 50, and rarely engaged in our warehouse antics.

The odds on the race, scheduled for 10:00 a.m., were even money. And, of course, why would we hold races if we couldn't bet on them? Whalon was designated to hold all bets. When the bets were placed Hardy, the official starter, locked the massive wood-and-tin doors from the inside. Hardy was the perfect person for this job since everybody feared to dispute anything he said or did.

"On three, white boys," Charlie Hardy boomed. "Ready—one-two-three!" Hardy waved his towel to start the first leg of the much-anticipated championship race. In the first lap, Chester stalled his lift, which allowed Jesse to win easily. Leg two went to Chester by six forklift lengths—a huge margin of victory for these two evenly matched competitors.

In lap three of the final race, Jesse began pulling ahead. In the far turn, he blew a tire, sending his lift careening out of control. Fearing the top-heavy lift would tip over, he jumped to the ground, leaving the runaway machine on a collision course with the solid brick wall at the south end of the building. We all stood frozen as the blades of the runaway lift struck the bricks with a tremendous thud. Many *of the chickens bolted for the door, not wanting to be caught in this situation. The other half rushed to the lift, eager to see the damage created. Nothing attracts more rubberneckers than a good runaway forklift crash!*

Paul Price shut off the racing motor while the rest of us surveyed the wreck. The force of the impact had pushed the blades through the solid brick wall. A few of us rolled the lift back, exposing two basketball-sized holes in the side of the building. After a brief discussion, we made the decision to push the lift back to our warehouse and hide it in the far corner of the building. That way, the flat tire would probably not be discovered until Monday—and in the meantime, we would all play dumb (a skill most of us had perfected). Luckily for us, the two openings created by the forklift blades faced away from Warehouse 32 and would likely not be noticed by any of the lifers for quite some time. When it was discovered, we'd—once again—play dumb. Unfortunately, this event marked the demise of our forklift races.

In a raucous ceremony later that evening, we crowned Chester the Molester the "Fab 50 Forker Champion," and awarded him the "Fork-You" Trophy—a gearshift knob from a forklift with the words "Fork You" sloppily scratched into the plastic. Chester quietly thanked us and hastily returned to his room to finish his latest Zane Grey novel.

The following Monday, Sergeant Aaron discovered the flat tire and had it repaired without inquiry. Three weeks after the race, Sergeant Foster began asking around about the two gaping holes he discovered in a wall on the other side of Warehouse 33. We all reported a lack of knowledge on the subject.

"God, I miss those races, Jerry," Bellotti said smiling. "Chester was a real trip when he raced the lifts. He's super competitive too. I'm glad he won. I've got a freaky one for ya. Whalon and Pratt will remember this. They were in the truck with me."

Bellotti grabbed a cold Schlitz and stood so everybody in the room could see him. "I'll call my story—*"Bicycle Built for One!"*

Back in September, Sergeant Aaron had been assigned to take a van to a warehouse, located on the other end of Saigon, to pick up two crates. Aaron was riding shotgun in a van driven by Wayne Malloy. Whalon, Pratt, and I rode in the back. Uncle Remus had selected us to lift the crates. As you all know, Malloy is, by far, the absolute worst driver of the ten guys authorized to drive the vans and trucks. He wears Coke-bottle glasses and has zero peripheral vision. He also hates "gooks" and gets pissed off at every "frickin dink" and "low-life asshole" that honks at him or cuts his vehicle off. As we usually do when riding in the van, we had the sliding side door open in back that day to stay cool. Whalon, Pratt, and I sat just bullshitting and yellin' stupid shit at locals riding bikes and motor scooters.

As we drove, Malloy came dangerously close to the papa-sans riding their crappy bikes. Pratt warned him two or three times about it. Just when Malloy sniped at Pratt to keep his trap shut and mind his own business, the open edge of the van caught the handlebars of a bike ridden by a young Vietnamese man. He instantly slammed against our van with a dull thud, then fell to the ground where his body bounced forward like a rubber ball rolling down a hill. We all screamed at once for Malloy to stop the van.

"Wayne, you hit a guy, idiot!" I yelled. "Stop the van, you moron—stop, stop, he's on the ground and all bloody and shit!"

Whalon was frantically waving his arms and pointing back toward the downed man. Sergeant Aaron instructed Malloy to bring the van to a halt. Once Malloy stopped,

Whalon, Pratt, and I jumped out of the van and rushed back to check out the poor dude we had just thrown to the pavement. The teenager was bleeding from his head and both legs. He screamed in Vietnamese to the gathering crowd of irate onlookers.

Seconds later, two MP jeeps arrived on the scene and attempted to get the enraged crowd that had encircled our van to go away. The first thing the MPs did was order all of us to get back in the van. The mob was yelling at us and pointing at the injured, bloody bike rider.

Malloy displayed his compassion. "Stupid-shit gooks ridin' their bikes all over this shit-hole. Get a car, ass-holes—shit. Hey, let's go, Sergeant Aaron—the MPs can handle this mess—that's what they get paid for, ya know. Geez, you dudes act like I ran over your dog—it's just a gook! Let's go—we're late!"

Sergeant Aaron is a very soft-spoken man and the favorite sergeant among our group. But on that day, Malloy's obnoxious remarks pushed the mild-mannered sergeant's button.

"Shut your filthy mouth now," Aaron barked at Malloy, "or I will shut it for you—I shit you not, soldier!" Aaron shook his massive black fist in Wayne's twisted face.

Malloy, startled by the sergeant's harsh tone, scrunched his nose and nodded his head.

"Yes sir," Malloy whimpered, "I'm sorry."

Malloy had fear in his eyes. At the same time, in the back seat, Whalon, Pratt, and I quietly giggled at Malloy's reprimand, just loud enough for Wayne to hear us. When Malloy peeked back at us, I mouthed the word "pussy."

One of the MPs advised Sergeant Aaron that we should follow his jeep until we drove out of the area. He said the MPs would handle the situation from there and would *contact the sergeant if they needed any more information. Aaron growled at Malloy to move his ass over—the sergeant was going to drive us back to the warehouse. That gave me and Whalon another golden opportunity to snicker at Wayne. We knew our schoolgirl giggling was pissing him off.*

When we pulled away from the scene, the rowdy crowd shouted and jeered at us. The last thing I saw out of the back window was the ambulance attendants loading the injured guy into the back of their vehicle while a group of frightened kids stood by crying. We never did find out what happened to that poor guy.

"I wish Sergeant Aaron had decked Malloy," Ozzie remarked. "Now that would've been somethin' worth seeing. Wayne is a genuine asshole! Is he retarded or somethin'?"

Since our stories had begun, an hour had passed. Now it came time to go get some chow. As the group began discussing where we'd go to eat, Willie Stuart spoke up.

"Wait a minute, guys...it's my turn," Stuart insisted. "I'll make it short, I promise. Give a brother a chance to tell his tale." Stuart loved using the phrase—"Give a brother a chance."

A few guys grumbled but everybody stayed put. "Hurry up, Willie," Judge prodded. "You've got five minutes." He tapped his watch with an index finger.

"Okay, mine's a short one, but a real trippy one," remarked Stuart. "I'm sure you'll all remember this." Willie was excited about the opportunity to share a story he called *"Puppies."*

You guys remember our first week at the Hung Dao? We were still getting acquainted with the traditions and language of the Vietnamese people. Some of us were in the rec room late one night shooting pool. I went out on the balcony to have a smoke. It was just past midnight and the curfew was in effect. The streets were empty—no traffic at all except for an occasional MP jeep.

I was watchin' the MPs race up and down the street, when suddenly a small dog darted down the sidewalk. Then I saw two more. Soon, between ten and twenty small dogs zipped in and out of the alleys and back and forth across the street. It was like the dog catcher had opened his truck at midnight and released hundreds of dogs to roam the streets in search of food or a bitch in heat. It was a real trip, man. I was amazed at the number of dogs running around since I hadn't seen one dog during the daytime our first week in country.

The next morning at breakfast, I talked to a dude from the Air Force who sat at my table. I told him about the dozens of dogs we had seen roaming the streets the night before and how we were surprised that there were no really big dogs like Collies or German shepherds—they all looked like puppies. He gave me this weird look and started laughing and nodding his head.

"Got a news flash for ya, man; those weren't dogs, they were rats. Saigon's full of 'em—giant, disease-infested, stinkin' rats. If you see a dog that's a pet in Nam, it's probably owned by military guys. More bad news, dude—gooks eat dog for breakfast, lunch and dinner. It's like our hamburger, dude." The flyboy was laughing his ass off by then, enjoying the look of shock and disgust on my face.

At the conclusion of his story, Stuart began laughing hysterically.

"Now that was nice and short, Willie," Judge complimented. "And a great just-before-supper tale." Jerry was now laughing also.

"All right, women and children," Hardy said as he stood to leave the room, "I could listen to this shit all night, but I ain't gonna—I'm goin' to Tu Do to check up on my whores. Anybody gonna join me?"

Hardy, not a big fan of bullshit sessions, was always ready for barhoppin' and boozin'. He loved the tea girls and the tea girls loved his money.

Everybody agreed that it was time to move this get-together to Dodge City and get some decent food. After all, we had only two more Saturday nights in Nam.

Chapter XVII

It's My Party

(Lesley Gore, 1963)

We planned a Fab 50 going-away party for the Saturday night before our scheduled departure from Saigon. The bash was to take place on the top floor of the Victoria Hotel, two floors above Saigon Bill's "Hustler's Graveyard." For sheer spite, we supposed, none of the lifers had discussed the details of our return to Hawaii. One of the guys in the office had seen a "secret" memo referring to the "vacating of the warehouse by December 12." Our 180th day in country would fall on December 9, just six days after our party. We figured Warrant Officer Edwards was reluctantly going to spring the good news on us at the party on Saturday. He had to inform us sometime.

One hour before the party, Schrunk, Goodman, Price, Mills, Bellotti, Pratt, Judge, Stuart, Hardy, Oswald, Harper, and I met on the roof to gaze over the city. It was dusk, and the orange-and-blue sky reminded me of looking out from the end of the Redondo Pier on a warm summer night back in California. We had brought two bottles of inexpensive PX champagne and a pack of Park Lanes up to the roof.

"With a little luck, next week at this time we might be on our way home to Hawaii," Goodman profoundly stated. "As a dedicated lifer would say, 'I shit you not.'"

Goodman appeared to be in a festive mood, as we all were. We were looking forward to the party and anticipated the overdue explanation on our return to the world. Still, I had a peculiar, hollow, uneasy feeling, much as I had experienced in Hawaii. However, I didn't share it with the other guys. Somehow it didn't make sense to me that the lifers hadn't told us *anything* concerning our status. Why had Edwards waited this long? I eventually wrote my feelings off as a bad case of anxiety. Surely someone would clear it all up at the celebration.

By the time our jubilant group got to the Victoria, everybody else had arrived. It was an unbelievable turnout with all of the Fab 50 and every lifer in attendance. Mountains of food and an open bar with hard liquor and beer kept us in high spirits. Music was provided by the hotel in the form of a Vietnamese DJ, who somehow owned a record of every rock 'n' roll song ever recorded. But like all parties in Vietnam, it lacked one key element that all gatherings of young, horny men required: chicks. More specifically, round-eyed chicks. Of course, very few American women lived in Nam and the Victoria was a respectable hotel and did not employ tea girls (okay, whores).

The top-floor room where the party was held had a half-roof that provided relief from the sun. It stood only five floors up, so a person could lean over the four-foot retaining wall and watch the Vietnamese people below as they hurriedly moved up and down Hung Dao Street. Along the back wall, an open bar and buffet tables with a wide variety of steaming food beckoned us. The Vietnamese servers stood motionless behind the tables prepared to serve our ravenous mob. The open-roof portion of the sizeable terrace offered an astonishing, panoramic view of the Saigon River and the Presidential Palace.

To my delight, the fifth floor also contained an undersized swimming pool in the open patio off to the left of the party room. The size of a typical backyard pool, it lay surrounded by bamboo lounge chairs and miniature green-plastic tables. There were also a dozen or so inflatable "donuts" in and around the pool, to provide aid in deep-water survival. The water looked surprisingly sanitary, but I made a mental note not to swallow any of it. Not only did I fear getting violently ill from the liquid, I also knew most of the guys would be consuming gallons of beer that night and would probably turn the pool into a giant urinal.

At some point early in the evening, the merrymaking degenerated into a macho-man drinking contest. The more we drank, the more out of control the party became. Goodman, Judge, Price, and I drank shots of Johnny Walker and Jim Beam as if it was Kool-Aid.

After his sixth whisky shooter, Mark Goodman decided it was time to harass the "Warehouse Wonders"— Warrant Officer Edwards and Sergeant Foster. As Mark so eloquently stated, "Shit's hittin' the fan, boys—shit's hittin' the fan now baby!" Then Goodman dug up an ancient Army classic I hadn't heard since Georgia: "Drop your socks and grab your cocks, boys," he loudly proclaimed. "I'm goin' in!"

"Hey Sargie Fostie," Mark said, slurring his words, "when we goin' back to the Isle? Time's come to clue us in on your little lifer camouflage. Come on; let the kids know what's up—you owe us that much."

Had Mark really said, "You owe us that much?" I was pretty buzzed, but still realized his emphatic statement was a colossal mistake. By now, everybody had gathered around the table where Edwards and Foster sat. We intently waited for the reply. Our cards now lay on the table.

A combination of booze, jumbo shrimp, and paranoia started my stomach churning. Sergeant Foster coldly stared into Goodman's bloodshot eyes, casually shook his head no, and replied, "Not now Goodie." Foster then chugged his remaining beer and slammed the bottle back on the table.

I cherished the occasions when Goodman and Foster confronted each other. It was always high drama, like Ali vs. Liston; North vs. South; good vs. evil; right vs. wrong; rebel vs. authority. These were unforgettable confrontations. I stuffed two more shrimp into my mouth and nervously chewed, waiting for the reply.

"Come on Sarge, my battalion wants an answer," Goodman insisted. "Quit treatin' us like babies and playin' these reindeer games. We deserve to know—we need an answer." Had Goodman gone completely mad?

Edwards, who sat two chairs away from Foster, coolly responded to Goodman's drunken demands. "Private Goodman, that question will not be answered here tonight, so you can just cool down and have a good time. This is a party for the men." Edwards then banged the table with his fist, sending Foster's beer bottle crashing to the floor. "We're NOT going to discuss work or anything related to work at this party. That's the last word on the subject!" Edwards banged the table again after finishing his declaration.

You'd think that Edwards would've learned by now that no one got the last word on Goodman—no one! Goodman egged Edwards on. "Mr. Edwards, that ain't work talk, it's about our goin' back to Hawaii—come on, let us know when we leave. We have plans to make and we can't do it without knowing—what's the big secret anyway?"

The crowd of intoxicated privates politely clapped and grumbled their approval, hoping to encourage Edwards to break the news.

Edwards slowly stood and sternly addressed the entire group. "Men, you'll get all the details regarding your next assignment on Monday morning. That *is* the last word on this subject—and I mean the LAST word!" Edwards glared at Goodman, grabbed a drink from the table, and stomped to the pool area.

An ice-cold chill shot down my spine—this wasn't good. What did he mean "next assignment"? Oh no—why hadn't he said, "return trip," "return to Hawaii," "flight out of Saigon," or anything that would give us a glimmer of hope and comfort? I looked in the faces of those closest to me, searching for telltale signs of panic or confusion—but all I saw was intoxication. I concluded that the marijuana, alcohol, shrimp, and assorted cold cuts were somehow combining to make me overly suspicious. I decided to ask Goodman what he thought about the secrecy of Edwards's declarations.

"Mark, what did he mean by 'next assignment'? I don't like the sound of that at all man."

"He just wants to screw with us—mess with our heads. Don't mean nothin'—you know how these lifers are, Whalon—relax. On Monday, he has gotta tell us whether he wants to or not. Don't sweat the small shit, Whalon." Goodman didn't seem the least bit bothered by Edwards's choice of words.

"No, I mean why didn't he say 'Hawaii'? Next assignment could be anywhere—maybe we're stayin' in Nam. Oh shit, maybe we're not leavin' this shit-hole." I was scaring the crap out of myself.

"Whalon, you're just paranoid. You need to quit smokin' that wacky tobacky," Mark advised. "Relax and eat some shrimp, have a drink, and continue getting drunk. That's a direct order, Private Peter-Piper Whalon." Mark saluted me and stumbled away, spilling half of his drink on a potted plant.

I was already smashed, but another drink sounded like an excellent idea. Maybe it would ease my increasing suspicion.

"Whalon, get over here," Bellotti called out. I walked over. "Check it out," Bellotti urged. "Foster is standin' by the edge of the pool—he's asking for it, man. Just cruise by and act like you slipped or tripped and push his fat ass in."

Bellotti had been egging me on all night to push one of the lifers into the pool. I'd resisted his taunts until now. The alcohol had sufficiently dulled that portion of my brain responsible for common sense and good judgment. I knew that nailing "Papa Bear" Foster would be the coup de grace to my six months in Saigon and provide for me on-the-spot legend status. I couldn't resist the opportunity to become an instant superstar.

"Come on, Whalon," Bellotti pressed, "this is your only chance. Get your ass over there before he leaves—don't puss out on me, you're a Californian. Make me proud brother." Buzz flashed the peace sign.

Without answering Bellotti or thinking, I handed Gene my cocktail and strolled into the pool area. Papa Bear Foster stood about eight inches from the pool's edge, casually talking to Sergeant Aaron. I leisurely walked the long way around the pool, making my final approach on Foster's left. When I got within striking distance, I intentionally hooked my left foot behind my right calf, which caused me to stumble into Sergeant Foster. If there had been a stumble move in the Olympic gymnastic competitions, mine would've received a perfect "10." My shoulder caught Sergeant Foster chest high, sending him staggering backwards and into the water. I fell to the ground and began my cover-up maneuver. Foster, who weighed more than most NFL nose tackles, made a huge splash, drawing everyone's attention to the pool area. While he bobbed up and down in the water like a baby sperm whale, I acted as if I had hit my head on the pavement.

Everybody came charging poolside to watch Papa Bear dog-paddle his way to the pool stairs. Sergeant Foster was not smiling. A handful of snickering drunks helped him from the pool. I stood up with one hand on my head and an agonizing, pained expression on my face.

In his soaking-wet fatigues, Papa Bear walked over to where I was feigning a mild concussion. "You okay, Whalon?" Sergeant Foster dubiously asked. He didn't wait for an answer before adding, "I'm going to assume, for your physical safety, that you actually tripped by accident—but there had better NOT be any more accidents tonight or you will be going home to your mama in a body bag. Got it, Private Whale-on?" The sergeant knew I was faking.

158

Foster turned, fists clenched, and stormed inside to cool down and dry off. Bellotti helped me to a chair. He then provided cover by examining my head, like a brain surgeon preparing to make a diagnosis.

Bellotti was struggling to control his laughter. He winked and whispered in my ear, "That was perfect—perfect man. I shit you not—perfect—wow! You numba one GI, me lub you long time."

I winked back while rubbing the nonexistent bump on my head. Bellotti helped me to my feet and I limped to the bar for an adult beverage. Gene was correct—it had been perfect.

By 10:00 p.m., everybody was either drunk or gone. Shortly after Sergeant Foster's cannonball, the lifers disappeared. Only the rowdies and hard-core partiers remained. The shindig quickly got out of control and degenerated into a macho game of "throw-somebody's-ass-into-the-pool."

Inevitably, lounge chairs started flying into the cement pond. A courageous hotel employee came scurrying up to Chris Hansen, an overweight guy from Nebraska with severe acne, and pleaded with him to stop the destruction of hotel property. Before the pint-sized Vietnamese man could get the words out of his mouth, Chris grabbed him around the waist, let out a bloodcurdling scream, and jumped into the pool. Struggling for air, the employee stumbled up the pool stairs, only to be pushed back into the water by Ozzie. When the disoriented man surfaced, Chris picked him up and gently placed him lying down on the deck. Coughing and spitting up water, the tiny local jumped to his feet and sprinted through the doors back into the hotel.

Hotel reinforcements arrived minutes later. Five or six excited, pocket-sized employees babbled in Vietnamese and tried to restore order despite the quickly worsening situation. One by one, we tossed them into the pool like a collection of Raggedy Ann dolls. As they scrambled from the pool, more reinforcements rushed to their aid and promptly got thrown in. Watching the chaos unfold, I fondly remembered the classic *Keystone Kops* episodes I had watched on TV with my dad during my childhood. This was the Vietnamese version of the *Keystone Kops*. Like lemmings, employees appeared and were instantly tossed into the water. When they quit appearing (after about the eleventh worker got dunked), I assumed that the entire night shift had taken its turn in the pool. Surprisingly, none of the employees knew how to swim correctly.

Goodman and Price attempted to gain control of the few maulers still throwing everything in sight into the pool. Mark began telling the instigators that the MPs were on their way. That appeared to sink in and soon relative order returned. The dripping employees began returning to the pool area. They started shaking the hands of their assaulters, laughing and telling everybody in sight, "GI numba one." The drenched staff turned out to be surprisingly good sports, gladly accepting the $250 we collected for a tip and coverage of any damaged property.

I got up from my lounge chair at the far corner of the patio and walked around the party area to survey the damage. Judge lay passed out in a lounge chair, naked, with a glazed donut placed around his penis like a mini-life preserver. Bellotti was straddling the pool diving board, holding a cloth napkin over his left eye. He had sustained a small gash from an ashtray that I had seen strike him. The bottom of the pool lay littered with chairs, trash cans, bottles, various articles of clothing, and ashtrays. Floating on top was a wide variety of food items, one slightly stained pair of underwear, an Afro comb, and hundreds of cigarette butts. I smiled proudly. This had been one hell of a going-away party!

The upper floor of the Victoria resembled the aftermath of a Florida hurricane. While we gathered up the pieces of clothing not attached to our bodies (no one claimed the floating skid-marked undies), a team of five mama-sans scurried past us, brooms in hand, and began restoring order to the disaster zone. They spoke Vietnamese and flashed us disapproving looks.

"Mama-san numba one," I slurred to the group of energetic ladies as Bellotti pushed me towards the elevator.

We grabbed five taxies in front of the hotel and caravanned back to the Hung Dao for some much-needed drying out. In the cab I was riding in, the five of us drunkenly serenaded the nervous driver with our off-key rendition of Joe South's nostalgic hit, "Don't It Make You Want to Go Home?"

Chapter XVIII
Na Na Hey Hey, Kiss Him Good-bye
(Steam, 1969)

After recuperating all day Sunday from severe alcohol poisoning (affectionately known as the Saigon Flu), I began looking forward to my final week at the warehouse. I was also nervously awaiting the Monday briefing when we'd learn about the plans for our departure.

On Monday morning, Popeye informed us that there would be a short meeting in front of Warrant Officer Edwards's office at 0830. This was it!—we were finally going to get information on our return to Paradise. The entire group bubbled over with anticipation. The twenty minutes I nervously paced the warehouse floor seemed like twenty days.

Edwards came out of his office precisely at 0830. The Fab 50 all crowded together in a semicircle, anxiously awaiting the news. All the sergeants, except Sergeant Foster, clustered behind our group. He stood stiffly next to Edwards with the facial expression of a presidential bodyguard. Our group had assembled at this spot many times over the past six months but this was the first time we fully expected good news.

The warrant officer was all business as he addressed us. "Men, I know you've been waiting for orders to return to your PCS in Hawaii. I also know you've done everything within your power to disrupt this project and to harass the dedicated career men under my command. You might be happy to learn that this project has been a failure, and that the warehouse will shut down as of this coming Saturday."

A slight murmur rose from our gang, but we humbly refrained from cheering.

"Now I have some outstanding news to report. Your orders have all been changed from TDY to PCS—you will all be staying in country for another six months." He paused briefly, savoring the moment, then continued. "You will all be sent to other stations in Vietnam..."

Edwards continued talking but I had gone deaf. Utter shock and devastation replaced our ecstasy. I glanced around in vain, looking for comfort on the faces of my close friends. It slowly sank in—my worst fear had become a reality—we were to stay in Vietnam! I hadn't been paranoid—everybody else had been naive.

WO Edwards had gleefully extracted his "pound of flesh." With one brief statement, Edwards and his posse got their retribution for the days, weeks, and months they had endured our lack of respect and puerile disruptions. I couldn't begin to imagine how gratifying it must have felt, deep down in their souls, for this collection of career soldiers to witness our absolute dejection. We had totally discounted the possibility that this uneducated herd of lifers would or could retaliate, in any meaningful way, for our lack of production. We had fallen prey to the Army machine and been violently devoured by the ones we foolishly believed were no match for our wit and cunning. While our "fearless leaders" had plotted behind the scenes, we vicariously dreamed of sun-filled days on the Hawaiian sand. As a group, we stood speechless—as one might expect from a crowd witnessing a horrific disaster.

When the warrant officer concluded his cheerful eulogy and retreated into his sanctuary, Sergeant Foster, beaming from ear to ear, stepped forward to continue the pummeling. The other sergeants had moved forward and now stood just behind him, smiling and giggling like high school girls at a slumber party. A scene that had played out so many times in the past six months had been reversed—the lifers were laughing and enjoying themselves at our expense.

The thought came to my mind that this would make a terrific *Twilight Zone* episode.

"Well, ladies and gentlemen," Papa Bear boomed, "you'll now have the opportunity to complete a full tour in Vietnam, like real men—something I'm sure you'll be proud of someday." Then, in a much-too-jovial tone, he added, "Men, say hello to your mommy and daddy for me when you write home, on tear-stained stationary, explaining why you are serving six more months in Nam." His broad smile exposed a mouth of perfectly formed white teeth. I realized it was the first time I had seen Sergeant Foster fully smile in my six months at the warehouse. The thought dropped my depression one more level.

"Bullshit!" a garbled voice from the back screamed out.

Foster continued, unfazed by the anonymous declaration. "Your transfer orders will arrive here on Thursday. The first batch of hippies will ship out on Saturday. Groups of between ten and twenty of you will go to four different locations in Nam. That's all the information I have for now—any questions from the Flat 50, I mean the Fab 50, today?" It was the first time Sergeant Foster had ever referred to us as the Fab 50.

As if all this wasn't enough, Sergeant "Papa Bear" Foster concluded by flashing our crestfallen congregation the peace sign—a gesture no lifer ever dared perform in front of enlisted men. However, in this circumstance, his timing was perfect. I had to smile at the irony of our situation—it was truly poetic justice.

Mark Goodman asked the only question. "Can I borrow your gun for a minute, Sarge?" Goodman wasn't about to let a little catastrophe keep him from being the class smart-ass.

"Only if you promise to use it on yourself, Private Goodwoman!" Sergeant Foster was having a grand ole time.

164

I got the strong feeling he didn't want this victory celebration to end.

"Can't make that promise, Sergeant Bear—sorry." Goodman, as always, got the last word in.

"If there are no more questions, get back to work," Foster ordered. "And *do* enjoy your last week here at the warehouse." The five beaming sergeants behind Foster began clapping—another first—at the conclusion of his address.

Papa Bear Foster, followed by his toady band of grinning sergeants, joined Edwards in the comfortable confines of the warrant officer's air-conditioned office—I assumed for a serious gloating party.

Most of us retreated outside to the "prison yard." We huddled in packs, pondering our fate and seeking strength in our numbers. It was another black day in my short Army career. It wasn't the first time, nor would it be the last, that the Army sucker punched me with my back turned.

Next came an exhausting week filled with the effort of writing gloomy letters home, mood swings, insomnia, useless rationalizations, bouts of whining, feelings of despair and hopelessness, alcohol abuse, and long sessions of smoking grass and reminiscing with members of our vanquished bunch of lost souls.

On Thursday morning, as promised, we received our new orders for PCS. Along with Schrunk, Harper, Goodman, Price, Judge, Stuart, and Hardy, I would be sent to Long Binh the following Tuesday. This base lay only twenty-two miles from Saigon. We'd be working in the Vietnam Headquarters Communication Center (apparently doing work we had actually trained for) as teletype operators. Bellotti, Pratt, Oswald, and Mills were headed for Que Chi, further north and closer to the "shit." The remaining members of the Fab 50 got divided into two groups. One group would be sent to Bien Hoa, considered a relatively safe base; the other, to Phu Bai, a little further north but not in an overly dangerous area.

Later that day, the lifers released us at noon so we could return to our hotel and begin preparing for the transfer. They informed us that two trucks would return to the warehouse the following morning for those who needed to gather up any personal items they had there. Only Sergeant Aaron would accompany the group, just to let the men in and lock up when they finished.

That night, at a beer-swilling party in my room, we drunkenly planned our final and most spectacular defiant act—to be carried out at the warehouse the following day.

During our trip to the warehouse the next morning, the conspirators all rode in the same truck. We were finalizing plans for our covert operation, "Give Peace a Chance," named after John Lennon's classic song released early that year. This simple plan would allow us to make a statement, hopefully without getting busted. Since it was our last trip to the warehouse, we figured nobody would go into the building again for five or six days. By then, our crew would be spread throughout Vietnam.

Phase One required keeping Sergeant Aaron occupied, away from the warehouse. Hardy, Stuart, and Mills would invite Aaron to play the card game, hearts, with them while the others finished getting their things. Aaron loved hearts and fancied himself an exceptional player. I told the guys to make sure to let Aaron win so he wouldn't get pissed off. Bellotti, Judge, Harper, Oswald, and I would carry out the "Give Peace a Chance" operation and exit the warehouse within fifteen minutes.

Five minutes after our arrival at the warehouse, Aaron sat in the back of one of the trucks playing cards with the three shills. Inside the warehouse, Harper and Judge each fired up a forklift and met Bellotti, Oswald, and me in front of the office. The blades of both forklifts carried a wooden pallet. On each pallet sat ten one-gallon cans of different colored paints. Equipped with a warehouse paint sprayer filled with bright red paint, I jumped on one pallet with Oswald. Bellotti stood alone on the other pallet.

In seconds, we made our way up. My assignment: to spray-paint the words of our chosen aphorism on the wall. Oswald and Bellotti were to open the remaining gallons of paint and, one by one, splatter the contents against the wall surrounding my spray-painted declaration. A combination of fear and excitement had my heart racing. I feverously began spraying while Bellotti and Oswald haphazardly splashed gallon after gallon against the walls. It wasn't pretty but it achieved our desired effect.

As I finished spraying, I screamed for Harper and Judge to get us down. When we reached the ground, Bellotti, Oswald, and I grabbed the twenty empty paint cans and tossed them, along with the sprayer, into the large Dumpster in the rear of the warehouse. Harper and Judge quickly returned the forklifts to their stalls and ran back to the office where Bellotti, Oswald, and I nervously waited. We looked up together, proudly gazing at our legacy.

On the thirty-foot-high brick wall over the office, in extra-large, bright red letters, were the words "GIVE PEACE A CHANCE FAB 50 1969," surrounded by giant, running paint splotches, in a rainbow of colors. It was one of the most hideous paint jobs imaginable, but spectacular!

We hustled outside and jumped on the first truck. I waved to Sergeant Aaron, still playing cards in the other vehicle.

167

"Anytime you're ready, Sarge," I said, smiling. Stuart, Mills, and Hardy gave the excuse of having to use the latrine so they could go inside and check out the wall. When the three guys came running out of the warehouse, they were laughing and flashing us the peace sign. Aaron, without going inside, then locked the tin doors. They all jumped in the second truck, which then followed ours through the gate. The five of us in the lead truck looked back at the warehouse.

"Whalon, you gonna miss this dump?" Harper asked, pointing to Warehouse 32.

"Depends on where we end up I guess, Harp—no, that's bullshit. I'll miss this pile of bricks, and especially all you dudes!" I turned my head to prevent Bill from seeing my eyes tearing up. I impulsively started singing one of my favorite songs, "Homeward Bound." As soon as I began my spirited rendition, Bellotti, Oswald, Harper, and Judge joined in.

Simon and Garfunkel would have been proud!

Pete's Photo Album

Jerry Judge (left) and I on the balcony of a Motel 6 in Hawaii. We're psyching up for the walk across the street to Waikiki Beach to talk to some local chicks.

Dave Schrunk (left) and I on the porch of our rented apartment in Honolulu, Hawaii. I'm just finishing a can of Colt 45 Malt Liquor while Dave catches up on his reading *(Playboy)*.

The Hung Dao Hotel in Saigon, where we lived for six months. If you look closely on the balcony ledge of the sixth floor, you can see my Army-green boxers drying.

Looking down from a sixth-floor balcony of the Hung Dao Hotel. Traffic was very light that day.

Some of the boys and I, standing in front of the Army mess hall across the street from our hotel in Saigon. We're trying to decide if we want to eat the meatloaf offered for lunch that day—and risk food poisoning!

My hotel mama-san ironing my uniforms. She called me "boo-coo rau" because of my thick moustache.

Looking down from the Hung Dao Hotel at a Vietnamese funeral. Those are my jungle boots, waiting for my mama-san to shine them.

The nightly party, with all the usual suspects, just getting started in my hotel room. What's that Bellotti is rolling with his fingers?

The traditional Sunday poker game in my room. Lee Mills (across from yours truly) is preparing to try to bluff me.

Dave Schrunk (left) showing me how they wear their pants in Iowa.

Entrance to Warehouse 32. I know it looks upscale, but it wasn't so plush inside.

Sign on outside wall of Warehouse 32. This did nothing to calm our fears as we drove up to the warehouse the first time in June, 1969. Vietnamese words below translate to: "Good luck, GI!"

Dave Schrunk (left) and I playing "soldier." Don't panic, the guns weren't loaded.

"Saigon Bill" Harper relaxing inside the warehouse and offering his *GQ* pose.

Gene "Buzz" Bellotti taking a break, with the Saigon River in the background. Gene was way ahead of his time with his "muscle shirt."

Bill "Ozzie" Oswald looking for a light. Nice "stash" Oz, but not so long as mine—sorry!

Jerry "The Judge" Judge smoking his first cigarette of the day (at least I think it was a cigarette).

Lee Mills a few days after his return from Okinawa. Doesn't look much like a "hero," does he?

Here I am (left), with Schrunk (center), Goodman (right), and another GI at our going-away party in Saigon. It's hard to tell who's had more to drink—Goodman or I.

Larry Pratt logging nuts and bolts at the warehouse. He perfected the art of sleeping with his eyes open.

Here I take a break on some cockroach-infested sandbags stacked behind Warehouse 32. I'm looking for a new word in *30 Days to a More Powerful Vocabulary* to spring on the lifers.

Shelves of warehouse boxes waiting for inventory. Yes, it was as boring as it looks!

Here's Mark Goodman actually attempting to push down Warehouse 32 with one hand!

Here I relax next to a spray-painted beam featuring my name and home state. I sprayed my name on every beam in the warehouse, although I told everybody Bellotti did it in an attempt to frame me.

Jerry Judge (left) and Gene Bellotti taking a "smoke" break. Nothing like a Park Lane for lunch.

Bill Oswald (left) and I showing off our moustaches. You decide: who has the best stash?

Here I stroll on the street in Company C, heading down to take a shower. I'm smiling because I move into the pool house the next day.

John Soranno (seated left) and I outside the Sugar Shack at the Bayou (Long Binh pool). Montecalvo (back) is looking for the football we hid in the outhouse.

John and I preparing to defend our title of "Horse Fight Champions" of the Bayou.

The Sugar Shack. That's Monte in the doorway, screaming at me to get more beer at the PX.

The aboveground pool where I worked as a lifeguard in Vietnam. Note: You were considered a wimp if you sat under the umbrella.

Here I sit on the pool deck, holding my dog Princess. The speakers behind me blasted music fifteen hours a day, seven days a week. If anyone ever asked us to turn it down, we cranked it up.

Here I demonstrate my unique lifeguarding style of turning my back to the pool and guarding with my ears. The technique never seemed to catch on.

In this photo, I'm making the greatest catch in the history of pool-football. Eat your heart out, Jerry Rice!

Profiles in courage at the Bayou. I'm preparing for my morning inspection of the lifeguards. Everybody got his bottle of Coppertone?

My Bayou water-volleyball team. We had a record of 78-1. Our only loss was to three round-eyed nurses from the 24th Evac Hospital. They told us before the game that if they won, they'd have a beer with us at the NCO club that night. We lost 3 games: 0-15, 0-15, 0-15!

Cleaning the pool is part of the job of a first-class lifeguard. Actually, I was looking for change on the bottom of the pool to buy some Coors.

Got Weed?

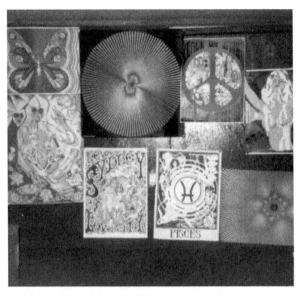

Love & Peace wall inside the Sugar Shack. These weren't Army-issue posters.

Church in the distance, near the Bayou. This is where Schrunk and I spent our first night in Long Binh. That night, it served as our "roach motel."

This was taken the day after my nose operation at the 24th Evac Hospital. Nice professional tape job on my face, don't ya think?

Same day, three hours later. I'm not giving the peace sign. I'm begging John for two more Valium because my buzz is wearing off.

C Company "hooches." This place gave skid row a bad name.

Here I pretend to be a grunt (the picture was taken to impress chicks back home). I know it looks like a Thompson submachine gun, but it's actually a bong.

Part III

Doin' Hard Time at the Long Binh "Bayou"

December 1969 - March 1971

Chapter XIX

Travelin' Man

(Ricky Nelson, 1961)

On Day One in Long Binh, our truck from Saigon pulled in front of C Company, 44th Signal Battalion, around 8:00 a.m. The 44th consisted of five separate companies. Each company was responsible for a different section of communications on the Long Binh base. In the Army, if you fell under the general designation of "Signal," it meant you were somehow involved in communications.

A Corporal Haskell instructed us to wait in front of a certain building for the NCOIC to arrive. The corporal politely asked what unit we had come from and then returned to an office. There we stood—eight dejected members of the disbanded Fab 50, checking out our new surroundings and arriving at the same stark conclusion. This dump was no Saigon.

In 1969, Long Binh was the largest military base in Vietnam. Geographically larger than my hometown of Redondo Beach, it housed over 35,000 military personnel within its perimeter. Long Binh was home for the U.S. Army Headquarters for the Republic of Vietnam, the infamous Long Binh Jail (LBJ, the military stockade), and the 90th Replacement Center—the departure point for most Army personnel in Vietnam when their time came to go home.

Dozens of Army battalions peppered the landscape of Long Binh. It functioned like a small city. The hundreds of individual companies at Long Binh had responsibility for various military operations throughout the post. Each battalion had rows of "hooches" that housed the men in their companies. The battalion sectors scattered on the post were separated by large open areas consisting of dirt, gravel, and dense underbrush. It reminded me of individual neighborhoods within a city; each company went about its business.

There appeared one striking difference between Saigon and Long Binh: Long Binh was all military. The only Vietnamese permitted within the barbed-wire compound were the daily hires that cleaned the GIs' rooms and washed laundry for the men, plus the numerous locals working in the on-site Post Exchange and the clubs for officers. Many of the mama-sans doubled as prostitutes during the course of their day—between loads of laundry. Most of the locals arrived at the front gate to Long Binh early in the morning, where the MPs body-searched them and closely inspected their bags. In the evening, the process was repeated at the gate before the Vietnamese could return to their homes.

My first impression of Long Binh sobered me. As far as the eye could see, the landscape was a combination of wooden buildings with corrugated tin roofs, sandbag bunkers, and exposed patches of dirt, gravel, and brush. One could see few, if any, visible signs of the outside world. For the first time in my brief military service, I sensed the Army had finally and totally engulfed me. The Army was everywhere—Army people, Army vehicles, Army buildings, Army talk, and Army clothes. A wave of hopelessness (a sensation I had unfortunately become semi-familiar with in the past year) rushed over me.

I sat, arms crossed, leaning back on my duffel bag, and hastily evaluated my situation. Here I was, starting over again, in another unfamiliar place with a new set of strangers controlling my life. I found little solace in knowing that I had survived the rigid structure of basic training, the indoctrination to Army life in Georgia, a brief stop at a Hawaiian paradise, and a rebellious six months in the capital of Vietnam—all in the span of sixteen months. In contrast to my momentary state of melancholy, I noticed that Dave Schrunk looked amused. I instinctively sensed that he was about to subject us to one of his patented Pollyanna pabulum-puke speeches. I was correct.

"This place is pretty cool," Schrunk said with an insipid grin. "I didn't realize it would be this big. I think it will be a hoot working at the Comm Center in the Headquarters Building. No more filthy warehouse work for us—cool, man, really cool—very groovy." Schrunk was delusional.

It was up to me to set gramps straight once again. "First of all, David," I began, "no normal person has used the word 'groovy' since the last Gidget flick. So, Moon Doggie, don't say it again or I'll mix rat poison in your oatmeal. Next, please, for the sake of what little sanity I have left, don't act like this military camp is anything other than a human wasteland. I swear, the worse things turn out for us, the happier you are, man—I mean really, what's wrong with you? Really Dave, shit. Maybe we can get sent to Hanoi and really make your day. Dave, it's quite simple, even for you. This shit-hole is not better than Saigon and Saigon was not better than Hawaii, got it?" I knew it would do absolutely no good to criticize Schrunk's most recent "everything-is-beautiful" sermon, but it made me feel better for a few seconds. We all knew Schrunk meant well and was just trying to keep up the spirits of us youngbloods.

"On your feet, men!" screamed an overweight sergeant who had just lumbered out of the building. "Whalon, cut that hippie hair and trim that caterpillar over your lip to comply with Army standards—today Private Whalon, today! You look like Hitler's bastard child! Stuart, untuck that shirt, take that comb out of your Afro, and get your hair cut like a white man! Where did you guys come from—San Francisco? Goodman, put that cover (cap) on your head and tuck your fatigues in your boots! You're in the Army now and you're gonna act like it, dammit!" The corpulent sergeant ran out of breath from hollering at us. "I am First Sergeant Lloyd and I have been in this man's Army for thirty-eight years," the pompous sergeant proclaimed proudly.

I never understood why most lifers insisted on telling us how long they had served in the Army. To me, the longer a lifer stayed in the Army, the more dimwitted he became.

Sergeant Lloyd continued his rant. "I talked with Warrant Officer Edwards yesterday and he informed me of your conduct at the warehouse in Saigon. Do not, for one second, think you can get away with any of that bullshit here at C Company. You screw up here and your ass will be on the first chopper to the Delta, I shit you not new meat. I shit clueless 'cherries' bigger than you every morning before breakfast. Screw with me and I will drop down in your shit with the wrath of almighty God." This blowhard had seen *The Caine Mutiny* one too many times, I thought. "I run this company and there is no room for tit-suckin' pussies and crybaby assholes here. Do what you're told and I'll treat you like the plague—mess with me and you'll be doing some hard time in LBJ—I shit you not, new meat! The company commander is Captain Fuller. Corporal Haskell, whom you have already met, will take you to your hooches. Get your shit squared away tonight. Tomorrow at 0900 we will meet in the dayroom for orientation—save your questions 'til then. Carry on, Corporal Haskell." Sergeant Lloyd turned and lumbered his wide body into the office.

"We're not in Kansas anymore, Toto!" Harper noted.

"You got that shit right, Kemo Sabe!" Hardy shot back.

Each of the five company areas in the 44th Signal had ten hooches lined next to each other, resembling low-income tract housing (or as my New York City buddies called them, the "projects"). Asphalt roads running the length of the ten hooches separated the companies. The hooches were constructed of plywood walls and tin roofs. In between every hooch stood a sandbag bunker for protection from incoming enemy fire. The hooches were built on downhill grades, and they had deep tin gutters on the sides to carry the water down during monsoons (the Vietnamese rainy season). There was very little vegetation in and around the company areas, although many of the open, spacious sections between battalions were overgrown with shrubs, weeds, and small plants of all kinds.

"Okay guys, we have two rooms in H-2, one in H-5, and one in H-9," the corporal said as he pointed to the different hooches. "Who wants what?" Schrunk and I took the H-9 room. Price and Goodman and Stuart and Hardy took the two in H-2, and Harper and Judge roomed together in H-5.

All hooches had entrances on both ends, with a narrow walkway straight down the middle. On each side of the walkway lay eight rooms. The rooms measured 12' x 8' and had bunk beds for two GIs. The plywood walls stopped eight inches from the corrugated tin roof, leaving an opening to the outside air. The outhouses—which we affectionately called the "latrines," "shitters," "poopers," "honey pots," or "assholes"—and the shower rooms stood at the end of the street, below the last hooch. This pigsty environment made the Hung Dao look like the Taj Mahal.

When Schrunk and I stepped through the narrow wooden door to our room in hooch 9, my misery hit a new low. It was bigger than a bread box, barely. The closet-like room was furnished in early "military-crap" style. At that moment, I envied death-row inmates in San Quentin. In the room I beheld a narrow set of bunk beds, an army-green storage box with the instructive phrase "Do NOT store explosives" stenciled on top, and two Army footlockers with what I swore was Alamo hero Jim Bowie's name scratched on one of the lids. The pungent, stale smell reminded me of buttermilk and cat urine.

While I shook my head in absolute despair, Dave attempted to speak. "Pete, you know…"

I abruptly cut him off. "Dave," I slowly said, measuring my words, "don't utter another sound or I'll strangle you while you sleep! I swear to God!"

Chapter XX

The Night Has a Thousand Eyes

(Bobby Vee, 1963)

After the shock wore off, Dave and I quickly unpacked our duffle bags and took a stroll around the company area to survey just how dreadful our situation really was. Of course, Dave was much more optimistic than I.

First, we decided to check on the other guys. Schrunk wanted to examine their rooms, but I just needed to talk to someone who appreciated my negative attitude and cynical commentary. For the most part, the majority of us remained openly bitter about being kept in Vietnam. The eight of us decided that the next day, after our orientation, we'd explore the surrounding area in hopes of finding an upside to our depressing new residence. I knew there had to be more to Long Binh than the shit-hole Schrunk and I would be living in.

Physically exhausted and mentally fatigued, Dave and I turned out the lights fairly early. I silently prayed that a good night's sleep would somehow brighten my mood. However, that night, for the first time since arriving in Vietnam, I'd experience the "horrors of war."

I had just started to doze off when I felt something crawling on the side of my face. I pulled the string dangling from the light above me just in time to see a giant cockroach scurry under a gap between the floor and the wall.

"Ahhhhhhhh, shit!" I screamed.

"What the hell are you doin', Whalon?" Dave demanded as he tried to adjust his eyes to the sudden light. I was on my feet, boot in hand, searching for the leggy monster that had tread on my face. I was prepared to crush the life out of it with my size-9, Army-issue, jungle-fatigue combat boot.

"Did you see that filthy creature run under the wall?" I asked Dave, horrified. "It's like ten inches long, I shit you not. That cockroach looked like a small lobster. God, I hate roaches; they make my skin crawl. That sucker crawled on my face—oh man." I then got on my hands and knees, with my boot raised above the creature's escape crack, waiting for it to peak its flat head out.

Dave began laughing and calling me names. "You sissy, Whalon. One bug and you freak like a baby," Dave needled. "Go back to sleep—it's groovy." Dave had been intentionally overusing the word "groovy" ever since I had called him Moon Doggie earlier in the day. "Hey, I saw mosquito nets in that box; put one over your head to protect you from Roachzilla. Go to sleep, Pete. I'll protect you, you little crybaby." Dave was still laughing at me as he lay back down and turned away from the light. I opened the box and pulled out a dusty net, checking it closely for any of my attacker's relatives. I knew these things traveled in large, creeping packs. I jumped back in bed, covered my entire body with the net, scanned the room for intruders, and then shut off the light.

A few minutes later, I felt something moving across the net covering my legs. He's back! I thought. I sat up and quickly switched on the light, hoping to catch the creepy-crawler off guard and turn the creature into a brown stain on the cement floor.

"Ahhhhhhhhhh, Ahhhh, no, shit!" My bloodcurdling squeal sent Dave leaping out of his bed. On the net covering my body, about twenty-five roaches crawled, searching for a way under my protective cover. The floor was thick with the repulsive pests, scurrying back and forth. Peering down from the gaps between the walls and the roof, another fifty or so invaders surveyed the action below, checking to see if their roaches-in-arms were in need of reinforcements. We had come under full attack—"Code Red." When Dave finally realized that our compound was being overrun, he bolted out the door like a man with his hair on fire.

"Ahhhhhhhhh, Ahhhhhh." Schrunk's high-pitched scream pierced my ears. I darted right behind him, trying desperately to breathe through my longtime-malfunctioning nose. I feared that if I had left my mouth open, one or more of the roaches somehow might have crawled in!

We dashed out of the hooch, across the large gravel rocks surrounding the building, and into the street. Unfortunately, the sharp, jagged edges of the rocks beneath our bare feet sliced the flesh like a Ginzu knife. For the first time that night, we synchronized our squeals. We now stood in the street, 20 yards from our hooch. It was so dark I couldn't make out Dave's face, though he stood only a foot from me. The only visible light came from one bulb hanging in the hallway of our wretched new home, hooch 9. We gingerly ambled back across the rocks, using the hallway light as our beacon.

Arriving, I glanced at the soles of my feet. Both soles bled. Dave's feet were also bloody yet there we stood for a time—two fools huddled in the narrow hallway, wearing only our boxer shorts. Our feet continued to ooze blood and soon began to bloat. I couldn't believe that the two of us were homeless because a horde of filthy, mindless roaches had driven us from our room. We started to talk aimlessly to calm our nerves.

"Shut your damn mouths or I'll shut 'em for ya, assholes—damn cherry fags!" a voice cried out. Somebody was trying to sleep in one of the nearby rooms. I pointed outside. Dave and I, using the asphalt path this time, delicately and painfully limped down to the showers below hooch 10 to discuss our predicament. On the way, I looked skyward and silently asked my Creator: "What are You doing to me?" It was pitch-black outside, my feet ached, and

I felt exhausted. I also had the creepy, uneasy sensation of bugs crawling on my skin.

"What's the matter, tough guy?—afraid of a few tiny roaches?" I ridiculed Dave. "You shot outta that room like Jesse Owens on speed, man. Schrunk, just go back and put the net over your head. You'll be okay, Dave." I loved mocking people. "Shit! Whatta we do now, Einstein? There were like ten thousand of those suckers in there—I'm not goin' back in that bug-ridden hole. Where are we gonna sleep, Professor Schrunk? I'm dead tired but I ain't goin' back to that infested room—ahhhh, is there a roach on my back?"

I limped to one of the showers and began washing off the blood on my feet and checking the damage. I sat down on the floor to get a better look at the soles of my feet and sat in a puddle of what I prayed was only water. Now it looked as though I had taken a massive piss in my boxers.

"Great—just great," I whined. "I'm gonna go roll in a pile of dog shit to finish the job—unbelievable!" I was losing it fast. It was times like these when it was very helpful to have a "steady hand" like Dave Schrunk around.

"Let's go to the dayroom," Dave advised. "There are a couple sofas inside. We can sleep on them tonight. Tomorrow we'll figure out how to get rid of the roaches. It's cool, Pete—it's okay." Schrunk had always been an excellent problem solver. No matter how hard I drilled Schrunk with my acerbic words, he was always there when I needed assistance. I benevolently decided to grant Dave a forty-eight hour, self-imposed ban on any sarcastic comments directed toward him. Besides, I could use the time to get a firmer grip on my sanity. I wondered if Schrunk would tell anybody if I began to cry.

Every company had a dayroom equipped with magazines, board games, and a Ping-Pong table for the troops to use during their off time. Staying at ours sounded like a sensible plan to me. I needed sleep desperately.

I emphatically refused to return to the room and retrieve my uniform. I knew the creatures would be waiting, with their little antennas twitching, to finish the final assault. Dave, seizing his opportunity for heroism, charged in, grabbed our boots, pants, and shirts, and rushed out. We quietly sat down in the hallway and laced up our boots. God, I was a wimp sometimes.

As we walked toward the dayroom, located above the mess hall, I complained to Dave, "Can you believe this shit? I saw one cockroach in Saigon—one! There must have been thousands in our room tonight. God, I hate those creepy things. And they were gigantic, like in the movie *Them*—the giant ants, ever see that one, Schrunk? How come the rats and roaches are so damn huge in this country and the people are so damn tiny? God, I hate this place."

I tried to open the door to the dayroom, then turned grimacing at Schrunk. "I don't believe this shit! Dave, it's locked," I reported. I pounded the door with my fist. "What now, Sherlock?" I muttered. It sure hadn't taken me long to break my forty-eight hour oath. Dave wasn't sympathetic to my pessimistic attitude.

"Damn, Whalon, you're actin' like a baby. Get your shit together. I noticed a chapel around the corner from the PX on our way in. Churches always stay open. Let's go sleep in the pews." Dave was on a roll tonight. I made another mental note to lighten up on Schrunk in the future, although I knew I wouldn't follow through. He appeared as frustrated as I, but handled the offensive with much more class. I had to hand it to Dave. He'd come up with another exceptional plan. I decided to quit acting like a little bitch and help us get through the night together.

"Sounds groovy to me, Gidget" I said, trying to project a cheerful mood. "Tomorrow, let's find some sheets and cardboard and make that room airtight—roach proof. How do these other dudes sleep at night with those disgusting cocksuckers crawlin' all over them? I swear to God—I'd give my right arm (I was left-handed) and three toes to be back in Hawaii right now, gulping down an ice-cold Colt 45 on the beach and talkin' shit to some brain-dead blonde in a bikini. Between the roaches and that fat-assed Sergeant Lloyd, I ain't gonna make it through this shit." Feeling sorry for myself had drained what little energy I still had.

"Cockroaches, Pete, not cocksuckers," Dave corrected me, laughing.

I'm not sure if it was my lack of sleep or my appreciation of Dave's solution to our predicament, but I did something I rarely did—I laughed at one of Dave's lame jokes. Even when Dave was funny, I tried not to give him the satisfaction of a chuckle. I made another promise to myself—that I'd always express amusement at Dave's jokes in the future, whether funny or not.

We found the church open and vacant. I quickly circled the interior of the building looking for possible openings for an attack. The construction of the church proved far superior to our hut. The walls were solid from floor to ceiling. I curled up on a bench and silently recited the Lord's Prayer.

"Thanks Dave," I said sincerely after finishing my invocation. "Let's not mention this to the other guys, okay?"

Steadfast Dave was already sleeping and beginning to snore. I grabbed a book of hymns for my pillow, closed my eyes, and strained to conjure up images of a sunny summer day on the sand near Second Street in Hermosa Beach, California.

Chapter XXI
Ring of Fire
(Johnny Cash, 1963)

I didn't sleep well that first night in Long Binh. The combination of lying on a narrow wood slab and visions of thousands of hideous creatures carrying my body off to the jungle made for some squirmy, restless nocturnal hours. We woke up early and immediately headed back to our room. On the way, Dave and I made a pact: we would tell no one about our ordeal and take to the grave our cowardly acts of the night before.

As the two of us cautiously entered our hooch 9 room, the sunlight pierced through the slat windows. Undoubtedly the light had sent the army of roaches retreating to their darkened fortress below ground. I knew these relentless mercenaries would diligently work all day on their invasion plans for that night. This time we'd be prepared!

I heard someone in the room next to ours opening the door. I rushed out to intercept him in the hallway, hoping to obtain valuable information on how to best combat our roach crisis.

"Hey, what's happening?" I said, smiling and extending my hand to shake his. "I'm Pete, just came up from Saigon yesterday."

The disheveled soldier wore dingy boxers and two left-footed flip-flops. He had that death look you get coming off a three-day binge of cheap wine and warm beer. My neighbor turned to see who had interrupted his morning routine. With eyes half-squinted closed and left hand scratching his balls, he responded, "Was that you makin' all that racket last night—mudsuckin' cherry?" He turned away, slogged out of the hooch, and headed for the showers. Schrunk, standing in our doorway, just shrugged his shoulders.

"I hate this shit-hole, Dave. What a stuck-up asshole! That dude looks like he'll have a heart attack before he reaches the shitter. Hey Dave, you ever see that movie, *Death Takes a Holiday*, where this creepy man...?"

A hoarse voice drifted out of the room the asshole had just exited, interrupting my insightful synopsis. "He's only an asshole in the morning. Come on in, guys."

I slowly pushed open the narrow door and saw another strange-looking, scruffy GI in boxers, taking hits from a marijuana joint as he lounged in a stained canvas chair. A set of Pioneer headphones rested around his neck, and they were plugged into an extra-large reel-to-reel tape player. He removed his headphones, stood up, and shook my hand. His moist palm caused me to pull back from the handshake too quickly.

"Hey guys, new meat, eh? Don't mind Bullwinkle. It takes him three hours to get his peepers open. I'm Rocky— want a hit?"

He handed me the joint in his hand. Before smoking it, I noticed some white powder at the tip.

"What's that white stuff, Rocky?" I asked, pointing at the joint. I thought he might have spilled some talcum powder on it. I was about to receive my first sobering lesson on the heavier drugs used in Vietnam.

"It's smack, dude. Most of these brainless junkies around here think this shit is cocaine, but this shit is pure heroin—bad shit—very bad. Unfortunately I'm beyond hope—been strung out on the shit for six months." At this point in Rocky's crash course on smoking heroin, I decided to hand him back the joint. He displayed a twisted smile,

208

shook his head, and then continued. "Bull's monkey is worse than mine. He tries to kick it by taking speed. All that does is make him lose weight and talk shit all night about stuff he don't even understand. That's why he looks like a walking corpse—got the 'cocaine blues'—he's bad, man—but he's cool." In between sentences, Rocky continued to take hits from his heroin joint. "You cherries came from Saigon and don't know about smack, right? Far-out, man. Missin' some fine shit."

Rocky looked to be in slightly better physical condition than Bullwinkle, but not by much. He was gaunt, with ashen-white skin and dilated pupils. He twitched his neck and continually rubbed his left leg with his left palm. Just watching him made me nervous.

As I hastily tried to come up with an exit strategy, Bullwinkle walked in. His bloodshot eyes had opened slightly more.

"Sorry 'bout before, dude. I had to take a massive shit. If I'da shook your paw, I woulda' shit on your feet, dude—no shit. I'm Bullwinkle." The GI grinned, revealing crooked banana-yellow teeth. Pointing to Rocky, he added, "Rocky and Bullwinkle, get it?—the cartoon freaks."

I forced a grin, realizing for the first time they were nicknamed after the popular cartoon duo. It then struck me like a lightning bolt that the names truly fit; they looked exactly like the cartoon characters. This really freaked me out. Meanwhile, Dave had already slithered back to our room, not wanting to deal with these two cranked-out head cases.

"I gotta go to an orientation at nine," I nervously said. "I'll see you guys later. Thanks. Nice meeting you fellows." I had actually used the word "fellows" for the first time in my life, like some Ivy League geek. I quickly turned to leave.

Rocky shouted at me as I closed the door. "Hey cherry, don't let that fat cow Sergeant Lloyd give ya any bullshit. Tell him Rocky already gave you an orientation." Rocky and Bullwinkle started laughing hysterically.

I returned to my room, but with the low, open ceilings and wafer-thin walls, it was like being separated by two-ply toilet paper. Rocky continued chattering to me. "Hey dude, come over tonight, do some crank—we'll coke up together—maybe drop some speed or BTs and listen to some tapes. That French speed is an ass-kicker, man—a real ass-kicker!" Again the two cartoon characters laughed at Rocky's statement.

I wanted to scream, "Not funny, you creepy carney buffoons!" but I didn't. "Sounds cool, Rocky" was all I could manage. I hoped this would shut him up.

Sitting on his bunk, Dave silently laughed while pointing to his head—letting me know they were both nuts. I shook my head in agreement.

We attended the orientation with the other members of our crew from Saigon. Corporal Haskell proved extremely helpful with our roach problem and quietly gave us very specific and useful information on how to combat the pests. We also learned about our work assignments.

I was always amused by and got a huge kick out of the endless Army orientations. The Army loved "shoveling shit" to new arrivals at every change in duty stations. They always treated us "new meat" as if we were ten years old— apparently assuming that not one piece of usable, valuable information had remained in our heads from our last duty station. After my first year in the military, I developed a theory on the necessity for orientations. Since there were so many screw-ups and dumbshits in the Army, lifers realized there'd be numerous occasions when idiots would do something stupid. Orientations provided cover in the event the Army got blamed later for not instructing the GIs on proper military procedures. When a GI used the "I-didn't-know-you-couldn't-do-that" defense, the Army would counter with the "we-covered-that-in-your-orientation" rebuttal. Since nobody really paid close attention to these talks and they were never recorded, the GI had no recourse but to take the fall. And if it was your word against a sergeant's or officer's, guess what?—you lose! The Army creed "Cover your ass!" was sound advice.

We did receive, however, what I considered some moderately good and valuable news from First Sergeant Lloyd. Apparently C Company had too many Comm Center workers at their disposal. Consequently, no jobs existed for us at the time. When the Army had no jobs for GIs to perform, the soldiers usually got assigned to "shit" details. The next morning, eight once-proud members of the Fab 50 met Corporal Haskell at 0800 hours, in the dayroom, for our initial shit-detail assignment.

After the meeting, Haskell released us for the remainder of day to get our rooms in order and familiarize ourselves with the battalion area. For Dave and me that meant one critically important task—prepare defenses and countermeasures for the impending invasion—Operation Roach-Proof was on!

Haskell had given us easy-to-follow instructions to make our room hostile to roaches. He directed us first to a small gift shop on post where we purchased a large piece of thick pink silk. (We hoped pink might repulse the macho bugs.) We used this silk as a ceiling, tightly stapling and taping it to the top of our walls, creating an inside cover. The roaches would be able to crawl on the top from the outside, but couldn't squeeze in under the heavily stapled and taped material. Next, we visited the post PX to purchase sizeable quantities of rat poison and powdered insecticide. Using generous amounts of the powder, we then circled the entire hooch and our room, inside and out. After that, we strategically placed the rat poison in the walls, on top of our silk ceiling, and under our bunks. I think I'd have even eaten some of the poison if I believed it would've helped repel the sinister creatures! We also purchased ten cans of Raid, just in case one of the resilient pests broke our perimeter and somehow ended up inside the walls. With a deadly combination of poison spray and Army-issue boot heels, the few "soldiers" penetrating our defenses would be quickly exterminated—sending a clear message to roaches in and around hooch 9: *You do NOT want a piece of these two warriors!* (Not to be confused with worriers.)

By 7:00 p.m., Dave and I were exhausted. I felt confident that we had adequately prepared for any impending assault. The next battle would go down in the cockroach annals of history as their Armageddon! We conducted one final check of our defenses, then slipped below our mosquito nets and crawled under the covers for a good night's sleep. As a final assurance, I placed a can of Raid at my side.

Our preparation and hard work paid off. Not one roach slipped inside our room that night. The only interruption to our sleep was the continual playing of Johnny Cash's song, *Ring of Fire,* coming from Rocky and Bull's room next door. I would've yelled at them to turn it down but feared they'd come over and explain to me why it was such a fantastic song when smoking junk. I drifted off with the Man in Black's words ringing in my ears.

Chapter XXII

Surfin' U.S.A.

(Beach Boys, 1963)

The next morning, the eight of us met Corporal Cody Benjamin Haskell at 8:00 in front of the dayroom. He called out our names from a clipboard, checking us off one by one. The corporal then clued us in on his plans regarding our details.

"Okay guys, here's the deal." He glanced around, making sure no lifers were in earshot. "I ain't no lifer but I play the game 'cuz I got a good gig here. Lloyd wants me to work your asses off. He thinks you're a bunch of Communist hippies. Anyway, most of the lifers are at the Comm Center by nine. Top—the first sergeant—stays in his air-conditioned office all day trying to keep his rolls of lard dry. So you guys meet me at eight and we'll do a few bullshit things around the company to make it look like we're workin'. At about eleven or so, I'll let you go but you gotta leave the company area until four, okay?"

The more he talked, the more I liked Corporal Haskell. He would've made a solid member of the Fab 50, I thought.

Haskell continued. "There's an aboveground swimming pool just a quarter of a mile down the road. It's a cool place to hang out and catch some rays—and lifers rarely go there 'cuz they don't like being around the regulars. You guys got any questions?" he asked in conclusion.

Schrunk shot up his hand like a precocious grade-schooler. I prayed Dave wouldn't blow what sounded like a perfect plan for us.

"Corporal," Schrunk said, "do you know how long it will be until we get assigned to the Comm Center?" Safe question, Dave, I thought. That shouldn't hurt us.

Haskell said he had no idea. Everybody else kept quiet, not wanting to take the chance of screwing up Haskell's outstanding strategy.

Cody Haskell turned out to be a really cool guy. It didn't take me long to realize that he was a master at wasting time and scamming lifers. In fact, at one point during that first day, I jokingly asked Goodman, "Hey Mark, is this guy related to you?"

At 11:00 a.m. sharp, Corporal Haskell instructed us to hustle to our rooms, put trunks on under our uniforms, and return to the dayroom. We returned in less than ten minutes.

"Listen guys," Haskell warned, "don't blow this. Stay at the pool 'til four or stay in your room. If a C Company lifer sees you walking around and questions you, tell him you weren't feelin' good and Haskell told you to go to your room and rest. And make damn sure you let me know about the encounter the next day, okay? Say hi to Randy O'Toole for me. He's the head lifeguard at the pool."

Haskell flashed us the peace sign and headed off. We followed the route he had told us to take to the pool, stopping at the EM Club first to pick up a couple of six-packs of Coors beer. By 11:30, we were lounging on the pool deck, drinking beer and reminiscing about our eventful days back at the warehouse in Saigon.

Haskell had informed us that there were twelve aboveground pools scattered around Long Binh. Two or three battalions used each pool on post, although GIs could swim at any of the pools if they chose. Our little oasis was mainly for the Signal and the Military Police Battalions. The MP hooches stood just across the street. The MPs at Long Binh pulled duty mainly as prison guards and security details

214

for the infamous Long Binh Jail. Our pool sat in a vast dirt valley, just below the barbed-wire walls of LBJ.

All soldiers in Nam knew the Long Binh Jail, since it was the stockade for prisoners from the US military. Most inmates in LBJ served time for drugs, desertion, or lifer fraggings. The jail had a nasty reputation for guard cruelty and racially motivated beatings and stabbings. Inside its walls, prisoner riots happened often. Any soldier serving in Nam soon learned that LBJ was *not* a place where you wanted to do time.

Our new swimming hole rose five feet above ground and measured only four feet at its deepest end. To enter the pool, we had to climb a short stairway on the south side. A five-foot-wide, wood-planked deck completely bordered the exceptionally large rectangular pool. The deck planks were alternately painted white and blue. On three sides of the pool, at ground level, thick plywood sheets covered the 2x4 framework, which created a smooth walking surface for the patrons. Also on the ground level, about twenty-five yards from the pool on one side, sat a small house the size of a one-bedroom apartment; it served as the living quarters for the lifeguards. The plywood walking surface surrounded the entire pool house, making it possible to circle the living quarters without ever having to walk on the jagged gravel ground.

Next to the house stood a tiny plywood room that did duty as a snack bar. During operating hours, it offered cold drinks, snacks, and suntan lotion. At the east end of the pool stood two outdoor showers and a metal storage container that we used as a changing room.

The entire pool area reminded me of the small western towns I had seen so often on my favorite television shows such as *Have Gun Will Travel, Rawhide, Yancy Derringer, Sugarfoot, The Lawman,* and *Wagon Train.* I soon knew that I'd be spending a major portion of my free time poolside.

While popping my second beer, I noticed one of the lifeguards playing cards with three other guys under an umbrella at the far end of the pool. Anytime I saw someone playing cards, I began to salivate (not unlike Pavlov's dog)—it brought out the gambling demons in me. A few minutes later, the card-playing group broke up, and two of the players jumped into the pool to cool off. One of the guys swimming by me looked familiar. I couldn't believe it. I had gone to high school with him! He had a couple of years on me and wasn't anybody I had hung out with, but I recognized him.

I approached my California "buddy" when he climbed out of the pool. "Hey man, didn't you go to Redondo High?" I called out from behind him.

He turned and squinted at me, then smiled. "Shit yeah, I know you. I can't believe this. I forgot your name. I'm Steve St. Charles. I graduated in '64—unbelievable!" He grinned and shook his head in disbelief.

"I'm Pete Whalon, class of '67. I saw you swimmin' and thought you looked familiar. This is far-out, man. Unbelievable is right—what are you guys playin' down there?" I pointed to the corner where his three buddies had resumed the card game.

"Hearts. You play?" he asked, then waved for me to follow him.

Do I play hearts?—is he kidding?—does a stray dog sniff ass? Actually I thought of myself as one of the world's ten best hearts players.

"Yeah, I play a little. You guys play for money?" I asked optimistically. He didn't answer my question.

"This is so cool. I can't believe it," he said, shooting me another grin. "Hey dudes," he called out, pointing at me,

216

"I went to high school with this guy—can you believe that shit? Pete, this is Henry, Jake, and Randy."

I exchanged handshakes with all the card players. "Hey Randy," I said as I took his hand, "Cody Haskell said to say hi."

Randy nodded and continued to play cards. I sat down to watch the game and talk to my fellow Redondo High grad.

During the conversation over the next hour, I learned that Randy O'Toole, the head lifeguard, was leaving Nam in two weeks—his tour of duty was up. Randy informed me that at the time only two lifeguards worked at this pool. The other lifeguard stationed there, Neil Wallace, acted as more of a pool-maintenance man. The head lifeguard had lighter caretaker duties. Since the water stood only four feet deep, there proved little need for rescues (unless a midget or double amputee began drowning in the shallow water). I grew curious, wondering how Randy had gotten such an unbelievable assignment, and who planned to take his place at the pool after he left. To my surprise, Randy informed me that to his knowledge no one had been assigned yet. A slight rush of adrenaline shot through my body.

"Randy, how would I go about trying to get your gig? Whose ass needs to be kissed to be a guard?—I'm a strong swimmer and a first-rate hearts player," I joked.

"You gotta talk to Lieutenant Wicker in Company B; he's the one who oversees the pool operation. He's pretty cool for a lifer, but I'm sure he already has somebody in mind. This is a kick-ass assignment most dudes would kill for, I shit you not!"

Randy didn't have to tell me that! I thanked him, told Steve I'd see him the next day at the pool, and returned to Goodman, Harper, and the other guys sitting close by.

217

"I gotta go, Harp. There's a job for a lifeguard open here—Randy, the guy in the red trunks, is going back to the world and they need someone to work at the pool. I gotta go see a 'looey' in Company B to apply or whatever I need to do—I wonder if he'd take a bribe? Can you believe this shit?" I got a little too excited at the thought of serving my country poolside. I realized it was a long shot but true gamblers loved "shots."

"Whalon, are you that full of shit?" Mark asked. "You're assigned to the Comm Center—you ain't even in Company B, dude. That fat-ass Sergeant Lloyd would never let you transfer here. Dump that hallucination in the honey-pot man."

Goodman had released his usual dark cloud over my picnic, but it had no effect on my highly motivated state. Even Goodman, the grand master of cynicism, couldn't suppress the unlikely daydream I harbored—sitting poolside, yelling at some pink-skinned cherry boy to stop running on deck, or explaining to some round-eyed nurse the finer aspects of the breaststroke. I grew light-headed at the prospect.

"I gotta go get a clean uniform on and trim my stash for my job interview—I can't believe this, man. Harp, can I borrow your boots?" I begged. "Mine look like crap and you always keep yours spit-shined. Shit, should I get a haircut first?"

Harp nodded affirmatively in my direction. I grabbed my towel and two cans of beer for the walk back to the company. I tended to communicate with lifers better with a slight buzz on.

"Catch you deadbeats later—gotta go."

I began with a brisk walk that turned into a slow jog back to the company. I wanted to go see Lieutenant Wicker immediately, before he could give my job to someone else. This would be the perfect fit for the Army—a beach guy

218

from California as head lifeguard at the pool. That was what I'd tell Lieutenant Wicker anyway. I was nervous and energized at the same time.

By the time I reached my room and began putting on my uniform, reality had calmed my mood. I was, unfortunately, a realist at heart. No matter how excited I became about the possibilities in any given situation, little time passed before I viewed the circumstances with cold, hard realism. A million things could go wrong and prevent me from being assigned to the pool for my remaining six months in country. However, I figured it was worth an effort. I dressed quickly, wet and combed my hair back to make it appear shorter, and headed for Company B.

When I arrived, I saw a weathered, grumpy-looking sergeant at the desk in the CO's office.

"Excuse me, Sergeant. Is Lieutenant Wicker in?" I asked politely.

"Who wants to know, boy?" He grumbled, playing the tough Army sergeant.

"Randy O'toole told me I needed to talk to him about the lifeguard job down at the pool. Is he in?"

I attempted to be respectful but this lard-ass lifer quickly pissed me off. I constantly marveled how so many lifer losers tried to verbally prove how tough they were. I wanted to scream in his wrinkled face, "Get off your lumpy ass and just tell him his next head lifeguard is here, ass-face!" But I remained silent.

The sergeant slowly pulled his oversized butt from the chair, exposing a huge gut and nauseating sweat rings on the underarms of his fatigues. He disappeared down a short hall, returning in less than a minute.

"You got two minutes, boy—so make it brief," he tersely informed me. "He's down the hall on your left, sunshine." He plopped back in the weather-beaten chair, making the sound my old "whoopee cushion" often made back in high school.

"Thank you, sergeant. You've been very helpful." I struggled to keep my sarcasm to a minimum, not wanting to jeopardize my chances of getting this fantasy assignment. I walked down the hall to an open door on the left. The lieutenant waved me in and asked me to sit down.

"What can I do for you, private?" Lt. Wicker was all business.

"I visited the pool earlier today, sir," I began in a humble tone. "I met Randy O'Toole, the lifeguard. He told me that he was going home in a few weeks and maybe there'd be an opening for a new lifeguard. I'm a very good swimmer, sir." Like an idiot, I made a swimming motion with my arms.

"Do you have a WSI card?" Wicker asked.

Oh shit! I didn't even know what a WSI card was. I later learned it was a Red Cross certification for lifeguarding and instructing. It stood for Water Safety Instructor.

"No sir, but like I said, I am a very good swimmer."

That's all the ammo I had. It was like applying for a job as a head chef at a four-star establishment, with your only qualification being that you once ate at a French restaurant. I realized how foolish I must have sounded. At least I had refrained from repeating the retarded swimming motion with my arms.

"What company are you assigned to?" More trouble—this was going poorly.

"C Company, sir." What *was* I doing here? I thought to myself. My earlier "high" began spiraling down the crapper.

"Let's see," the lieutenant said in a semi-mocking voice, "no WSI card and you're not assigned to B Company—not a lot going for you, private." He politely laughed. "I don't think this will work but thanks for stopping by. Sorry. I've got someone else who has been waiting for this assignment."

Silently I rose to leave as the lieutenant casually asked me one glorious, life-changing, orgasmic question. It was one of those rare moments in life when the stars aligned, the seas parted, and a miracle was born.

"Where are you from, private?" he inquired.

"From Redondo Beach, California, sir." I turned to leave.

"No shit!" Lieutenant Wicker blurted out. "You're from Redondo—the city in the song 'Surfin' U.S.A.'? Are you shittin' me, dude? That's my favorite song! Do you surf?—do you know surfers Dewey Weber or Bing Copeland?—are the broads all tan in Cal, like in the movies?"

His sudden bout of schizophrenia frightened me for a moment. Wicker now acted like a schoolyard kid talking to his favorite sports hero. The words "Redondo Beach, California" had mystically transformed him from a no-nonsense second lieutenant into a starstruck schoolgirl meeting Elvis Presley for the first time. Incredibly weird.

He continued without a response. "Have you ever surfed Surf City, Huntington Beach? How 'bout Malibu?" The lieutenant grew more animated as he talked. "I'm moving to California as soon as I get out of the Army—it's so damn cool there—hey, maybe I can visit you in Redondo when I get out?" he said, slightly hyperventilating.

This was unbelievable! He had transformed from Lieutenant Wicker, lifer asshole, into a Little Leaguer shaking hands with Mickey Mantle. He wanted to be my best friend and I hadn't spoken one word in two minutes. My mind raced, searching for the correct approach. I realized this opened the door for me and I sought desperately for the perfect response that would get me back into the game. The one thing I knew not to say was "I'm a good swimmer."

"Sit down, Whalon," Lieutenant Wicker said. He had calmed down slightly and his breathing had returned to normal. The last thing I needed right now was for him to have a heart attack. "Tell me about Redondo Beach. Is it near San Diego? Shit, this is sooooo cool—what's the biggest wave you ever surfed?"

Lieutenant Wicker laughed and shook his head like a restless child. I decided my best approach was to stay with the California theme for the moment and ride it as long as possible.

"Yeah, I surfed with Weber and Bing," I lied. "Malibu is an ass-kicker. If you come to Redondo, I'll set you up with some bitchin' beach chicks—you dig blondes?—my sister is twenty-one and surfs her ass off. (I didn't have a sister, but pimping her seemed like a smart move at the time.) You'd love it there. The weather is great and the chicks wear bikinis all year round. Lieutenant Wicker..."

He interrupted me. "Shit, you call me Jimmy," Wicker demanded in a goofy voice. "What's your first name, dude?" He stood and shook my hand. "Pete."

I decided to go for the kill. "Jimmy, this is so cool. Is there any possible way I could get the lifeguard job at the pool, any way at all? I'll do a great job, I swear to God—can you give the other guy a different job or have both of us be guards?" I crossed my fingers, legs, arms, and eyes.

"Are you shittin' me, Pete?" the lieutenant boomed. "There's no other guy, dude. I was BS'n you to get rid of your cherry ass. The job is yours—under one condition: I can come down to the pool and smoke a little 'doobie' with you once in a while and bullshit about California." He now talked

222

in a whisper, making sure the flabby sergeant up front couldn't hear him. "I can't smoke around here being an officer and all that shit. Also, you'll have to talk to your CO and get reassigned to B Company. If they release you, I can transfer you here and you can start immediately. Want the job, Pete?" He leaned forward and began laughing, waiting for my reply.

I wasn't sure what had just happened. I couldn't process fast enough the bizarre events that had unfolded over the past five minutes. Once again I expected to see chubby Allen Funt pop out from behind the wall and crush my dream by chirping, "Smile, you're on *Candid Camera!*" One thing was crystal clear—I wanted that job!

"Yes sir, Jimmy, that gig was made for me—great! What's the best way to get reassigned? What do I say?" I knew that would be the tricky part, but hoped my surf buddy, Jimmy, could help me out.

"No sweat, GI. I'm good friends with Captain Frank Fuller," Wicker confidently remarked. "Ask him to call me right away. Go see him today; he owes me one. Shit, Redondo Beach, surfin' U.S.A., dude—surfin' U.S.A."

I had never seen anyone so ecstatic over the mention of a city before. It creeped me out a little, but it brought me a tremendous reward. As I left the office, Jimmy enthusiastically began singing "Surfin' U.S.A."

During my jog back to C Company, I silently thanked my parents for having the foresight to move from Connecticut to Redondo Beach, California in 1955.

Chapter XXIII
Sunshine Superman
(Donovan, 1966)

Over the course of the next two days, the pieces to my improbable puzzle fell neatly into place. Captain Fuller called Lieutenant Wicker and released me to Company B. With the overflow of Communication Center workers assigned to Company C at that time, the loss of one private with a bad reputation and no experience in Comm Center work had no consequence. All concerned personnel signed the necessary papers for my transfer, with no Army snags—a small miracle in itself. The following day, I'd begin my training with Randy O'Toole, the outgoing lifeguard. When Randy returned to the states after ten days, I'd move into the lifeguard house at the pool with Neil Wallace, the other guard.

The night before the lifeguard training started, I sat with my Saigon buddies in beach chairs outside hooch 9 and filled them in on the glorious details of my good fortune.

"You are the luckiest shit-bird in Nam, Whalon," Goodman lamented. "How'd you pull that shit off? I thought I was the best scammer in the Army." Goodman was letting his jealousy show. I couldn't blame him.

"Guess I'll have a room to myself for a while," Schrunk remarked, with a little too much glee in his voice. "You are a lucky SOB, Pete. I swear to God—a lifeguard at the pool." Schrunk seemed happy for me but, along with the others, a little resentful of my good fortune—and understandably so. Duly humble, I mocked:

"Kiss my ass, lifers," then laughed at the somber group. "I'll be livin' poolside in ten days. Guess what my duty uniform is, dudes?"

I didn't wait for a response. "Swim trunks or shorts and a T-shirt. That's right, future lifers—you guys will be wearin' fatigues, sweatin' your asses off digging holes to shit in, and I'll be in a tank top and competition-stripe Hang-10s—how cool is that? Life is good boys, life is good—I shit you not. Life is actually too good right now!" I knew the smug look on my face pissed them off.

Harper shook his bottle of beer and sprayed me with foam. "That feels like a cool summer mist coming from the pool in the evening—thanks, Harp," I quipped.

My obnoxious behavior began making even me a little queasy. I decided to lighten up and show some sincere humility—not usually one of my strong points.

"Hey guys," I said in a more serious tone, "you can come down any time and swim or stay at the pool house. It'll be like Saigon again. Maybe I can get some of you guys on as lifeguards. Neil has only forty-seven days left in country. I'll tell Wicker we need four or five lifeguards at the pool— too bad you're not from Redondo." I thought I had sounded well-meaning and genuine.

"Shut up, asshole," Price countered. "You'll get tired of sittin' in the sun all day doin' nothin' but drinking beer and swimming in the pool. It'll get old after a few weeks." Even he started laughing, along with the others, at the absurdity of this declaration.

"Yeah, you're right, Paul," I said, grinning at him widely. "I'll go tell Lieutenant Wicker tomorrow that I don't want the job. I'll tell him I'd rather pull twelve-hour shifts six days a week at the Comm Center, typing Army shit to Army shit-birds. Yeah, you're makin' good sense, Price— thanks. I'm goin' to bed. I gotta go to the pool at nine and begin my first grueling training session. See you dudes tomorrow."

A vicious barrage of verbal insults followed me to the room. I did feel a little guilty at my good luck. I recalled an old saying my dad used on me a few times when he had experienced some good fortune: "Pete, remember—luck is the residue of design!" I could never figure out exactly what he meant; I still had no clue.

The next morning, I put on my trunks and tank top and headed down to the pool. When I got there, Neil was hosing the pool deck. I waved at Neil and yelled for Randy at the same time. Randy emerged from the pool house rubbing his eyes. Seeing me, my new trainer strolled over in my direction. I could tell by the way Randy began smiling and shaking his head that he'd received the news of my assignment.

"How in the hell did you pull this off, Whalon?" Randy asked in disbelief as he approached me. "I didn't think you had a Chinaman's chance to get assigned here. You didn't give him a blow job, did you?" he asked baffled by my stunning success.

Instead of trying to explain the details, I opted for the *Reader's Digest* version: "Right place, right time, dude." It couldn't get any simpler than that.

"Lucky shit, Whalon," Randy responded, as he slapped my shoulder. "Don't blow this gig, man. Okay, training will take about ten minutes if you're a retard. Follow me… I'll show you how to backwash the pump, clean the filters, and add chlorine. That's all there is to it, unless I need to show you how to turn on the hose to wash off the deck. Open at 9:00 a.m. every day; close at 7:00 p.m. Do a daily attendance count and log it in the book and you'll be done. In case you haven't figured it out by now, this is *the* killer job in Nam! It sure beats humpin' the bush or typin' Army crap at the CC." He pointed toward the Comm Center located about one-half mile from the pool.

We walked to the pump on the far side of the pool, where he tutored me on the uncomplicated tasks of backwashing, cleaning filters, and adding chlorine. Next, he explained the intricacies of the sophisticated attendance log (a notebook with handwritten numbers placed by the days of the month) and how to operate the snack bar.

Then came one last aspect of my initial training with Randy. He covered what to do if someone got into trouble in the pool and started going under or yelling for help. The proper procedure was to scream at the top of your lungs, "Stand up, STUPID!" He smilingly confessed that this usually did the trick.

"Dude, you are now officially trained," he proudly proclaimed. "Time to catch some rays and put some beer on ice."

For the next nine days, I reported to the pool at 9:00 a.m. I easily mastered the effortless tasks of backwashing and chlorination. Attendance was a snap: at the end of the day make up a number between 75 and 250 (depending on the day's temperature) and write it in the book. If you forgot to enter attendance for a day or two, or three, no problem: just make up numbers and add them the next time you remembered to take attendance.

Most of my "work" time during this transition period I squandered on frivolous pursuits—playing cards and water football, getting tanned, listening to music, participating in bull sessions with pool patrons, and drinking beer. Apparently, no Army regulations prevented a lifeguard from drinking on duty.

In the evening, when the pool technically closed, the real action began. Randy's friends and mine, who had been typing all day at the Comm Center, were more than ready for a little rest and relaxation. The after-hours regulars would drop by for a session of cards, football, and drinking. By popular demand, I added weed-smoking to the evening activities. We never smoked grass during official pool hours. It didn't matter to me if I stayed up all night and felt exhausted the next day—I could take a nap on the pool deck.

The day soon arrived for Randy O'Toole to return home. That morning, I purchased his reel-to-reel tape player and fifty tapes of recorded music. I was truly sorry to see him go but anxious to move out of hooch 9 and into my new poolside home. We quickly said our good-byes, with the obligatory "look-me-up-when-you-get-out" line.

After stowing his gear, Randy jumped into the jeep waiting to drive him to the Processing Center. In a few minutes, the jeep disappeared over the dirt hill leading to Long Binh's main highway. When the vehicle drove out of sight, I told Neil I was going back to the company to get my belongings. The time came to pack my few worldly possessions and move into the pool house.

That evening after closing time, Neil and I sat outside my new home and listened to one of my newly acquired tapes. The front door of the house faced the aboveground pool. Even from ground level, you could see the pool water shimmering as the sun set in the distance. The tranquil view was calming. I was excited about spending my first night in the pool house.

Neil then informed me that he planned to stay in a buddy's room at Company B. The next day, he'd be moving out of the pool house completely. He said he preferred to stay at Company B for the remainder of his time in country.

I had learned earlier in the evening that Neil was a devout Mormon and didn't approve of drinking alcohol and smoking marijuana. Neil had gleaned from my conversations over the past ten days that those two activities were very important to me and would now be a prominent part of life at the pool. I told him that I understood and hoped he had no resentment.

I had mixed feelings about living at the pool by myself. I enjoyed having my friends around to talk to and play cards with. The pool house stood at least 500 yards from the nearest building. At night, in the valley, it was pitch dark. Although the pool and deck had lighting, Wicker had instructed me to turn the lights off no later than 10:00 p.m.

Neil also informed me that he'd receive an "early out" from Vietnam and in eight days he'd be going home. That left me as the only lifeguard working at the pool. I decided to go see Lieutenant Wicker the first thing the next morning to attempt to parlay my "SoCal" status into lifeguard jobs for Harper, Goodman, and Judge. I definitely didn't want to live and work at the pool by myself. That would take all the fun out of this gravy train. I needed somebody to party with. After informing me of his plans, Neil Wallace nervously finished his can of Orange Crush soda and headed to Company B.

Sitting by myself in the dead of night, I couldn't recall the last time I had been completely alone in the Army. An eerie feeling shivered through me. I tossed an empty can of beer into the trash barrel and went inside the pool house, hoping to get a good night's sleep.

I drifted off to sleep sometime after 10:00 p.m. About an hour later, the sound of a vehicle skidding to a stop near the pool area awakened me. I heard yelling and what I thought sounded like a guy sobbing. I turned on the ground-level lights, opened the front door, and saw an MP jeep and two MPs in uniform dragging a guy in Army-green boxer shorts and a white T-shirt up the steps to the pool deck. The guy in boxers coughed and cried at the same time. When the two MPs heard the door open, they turned and saw me standing in the doorway.

"Who the hell are you—where's O'Toole?" one MP demanded.

"Uh…I'm the new lifeguard, Pete," I stuttered. "Randy went home today—he's out."

I wasn't sure what to do. The two MPs had guns and looked deadly serious. I nervously waited for a response. The two cops whispered to each other while their prisoner, on all fours at the top of the pool stairs, continued to whimper.

The taller MP then made my next move crystal clear. "Get your cherry ass back in the shack, Pat." I didn't correct him on getting my name wrong. "Turn out the lights and go back to sleep—this never happened—got it, cherry boy?" He gestured me back inside the house.

They turned away unconcerned, as I closed the door and turned off the lights. I ducked down and crept to the window to peek outside. They dragged the whimperer from the stairs and pushed him into the pool. I quickly ducked below the window and slithered back into my bunk like a garden snake. My mind raced. I momentarily considered bolting out the back door into the dead of night; however, I quickly realized that these guys could hunt me down any time they wanted. I decided to lie there, keep as quiet as Helen Keller, and hope the uninvited trio would soon leave. I could hear one of the MPs yelling something about his "whore" and "your ass is grass" and "LBJ faggots." The poor sobbing guy in the boxers never spoke a word. The more the MPs yelled, the more he sniveled.

After about five minutes, I heard the MPs' footsteps on the deck, followed shortly by the start of an engine and tires peeling out on dirt. Ten seconds later, it fell dead silent again. I stayed in bed for another ten minutes, then quietly crawled back to the window and peeked out, without turning on the pool lights. I couldn't see anything unusual.

I was tempted to turn on the upper and lower pool lights to see if I could spot a body lying on the walkway or floating in the pool. Instead, selfishly thinking only of my own safety, I decided to wait until morning. If I found a body in the pool, I would tell the MPs investigating the death that I was sound asleep the night before and didn't hear anything. You idiot, I thought—they won't believe you slept through that! For all I knew, the MPs they would send to investigate would be the killers. I remembered seeing a *Perry Mason* episode like that once. Why in the hell did this happen on my first day staying in the pool house? I wondered. I quelled my extreme guilt feelings with one of my favorite quotes: *Discretion is the better part of valor!* It seemed easier than calling myself a chickenshit coward.

After an hour or so of tossing and turning, the overwhelming guilt drove me from my bed. This time, I turned on all the lights before I peeked through the window. I saw no signs of life and, mercifully, no bloated body floating in the pool.

I slowly opened the door and peeked around the corner. It looked clear so I cautiously ventured outside. At the foot of the stairs I saw a fresh blood stain and droplets on every stair leading to the pool deck. At a snail's pace I climbed the six stairs. "Thank God," I then blurted aloud. There was no stiff lying on the bottom of the pool. I looked up to the heavens, exclaiming, "Thank you, Lord!" I wouldn't have to concoct some half-baked alibi, explaining how a dead dude in boxers ended up in the pool on my very first night. Growing up Catholic (a religion based primarily on guilt), I experienced severe regret even if I had only *accidentally* eaten meat on a Friday. I couldn't fathom how bad my guilty feelings would've been if I had let some pitiful slob float facedown in the pool while I lay in bed, hiding under my covers, like a little bitch. "Thank you God and all your wonderful saints!" I proclaimed as I stared skyward.

Now I was positive. I needed more guards at the pool—for companionship *and* protection. I hoped that Lieutenant Wicker was still "high" on California, my imaginary sister, and Redondo Beach. I decided to go see the lieutenant first thing in the morning. I'd begin my request for more guards with a small white lie: I'd tell him that when he came to California after his Army service, I'd introduce him to Greg Noll (a surfing legend in the '60s). I thought I might even quietly hum the melody of "Surfin' U.S.A."

Chapter XXIV

Sugar Shack

(Jimmy Gilmer & the Fireballs, 1963)

The next morning, my meeting with Lieutenant Wicker started out well. We talked casually about my training and first overnight at the pool (Of course, I failed to mention the incident with the two psycho MPs). I planned to convince the lieutenant of the immediate need for more lifeguards, then suggest some perfect candidates—Bill Harper, Jerry Judge, and Mark Goodman.

Before I could set my scheme in motion, the lieutenant stuck a sharp pin in my balloon. "There's another thing I wanted to tell you..." He stopped talking momentarily to light a cigarette and then resumed. "I have three new guys who are going to join you as lifeguards at the pool, Pete. I always intended to have four guards working there but O'Toole didn't want anyone else. Now that he's gone, I'm going to get us up to full strength. Besides, Pete, it'll give you someone to party with." He flashed me a smile, then added, "They'll all report to you next Monday morning."

I decided to keep quiet and not take the chance of jeopardizing my job by saying the wrong thing. I really didn't truly believe that I could have gotten my friends jobs there anyway.

The truth came out during the remainder of my conversation with Lieutenant Wicker. The three cherries had gotten on Captain Fuller's shit-list, and the captain now called on Wicker to return the favor for letting me transfer to Company B.

I was satisfied with the results of our meeting when I walked out of the lieutenant's office. Although I couldn't get my friends assigned to the pool, I'd now have some "new meat" to party and play cards with there. I could only hope they were cool dudes and poor card players.

The following Monday morning, Frank "Monte" Montecalvo, Wade "Sleepy" Fossett, and Buddy Beard reported to the pool dressed in full fatigues and combat boots. Although I didn't recognize any one of them, they knew me. I assumed Lieutenant Wicker had given me a fairly impressive buildup. I asked Goodman (he still had not been assigned to the Comm Center, and spent most days at the pool with me) to keep an eye on the pool while I took the fresh cherries inside to give them an orientation. I wondered if they'd act like me at orientations and not listen to a word.

I spent the next half hour informing them of their duties, providing a little background on my time in Nam, and going over the basic rules for water football. I received my first laugh of the day when I explained the importance of the "Stand up, STUPID!" command. We then walked outdoors to the far side of the pool, where I demonstrated how to backwash and clean the filters and chlorinate the water. "Training" ended in less than ten minutes.

By the time I had completed my spiel and the pump demonstration, all three cherries were sweating like sumo wrestlers. We retreated to the pool house, where I popped my first beer of the day. It hadn't taken me long to realize that these three wide-eyed rookies were clueless to all aspects of life in Vietnam.

"Okay Monte, Sleepy, and Buddy, here's what you do. Go back to the company and pack your shit." I spoke slowly to make sure they understood what I said. "Next, you need to go to the motor pool and check out a truck to get your crap down here. Reserve the truck for tomorrow, not today. As soon as you're done, get your white cherry asses to the PX and buy three or four swim suits each. And don't even think about comin' back here wearing those queer 'bun-hugger' trunks. Get something cool, like Hang-10s, okay? Do everything you gotta do today and come back tomorrow with all your stuff." I tossed my empty beer can into the trash and grabbed a cold Coors from my cooler. "Oh, get sunglasses, Coppertone, and a case of beer each." The last item brought smiles to their faces. "I'd give you one of these," I held up the can in my hand, "but I have only ten left. Go guys, now." I waved them out the door. "And make sure you get Coors, not Bud."

It felt really weird standing there in the doorway watching the three giggling baby-faced soldiers jog up the hill toward the company. There I was, head lifeguard Private Pete Whalon—with three inexperienced lifeguards under my command—very strange!

The next day at 3:00 p.m., I sat on the pool deck involved in a deadly serious game of "cutthroat" hearts. I heard a vehicle approaching and turned to see a large Army deuce-and-a-half truck roaring up to the back of the pool house. My three employees, all sporting new swimming trunks, jumped from the cab, flashed me the peace sign, and began unloading their belongings and carrying them into the house. To my relief, none of them sported "bun-huggers."

That evening after the pool closed, the four of us sat on the deck, drinking beer and exchanging more detailed introductions. The three new guards—Monte, from Oshkosh, Wisconsin; Buddy, from Milwaukee, Wisconsin; and Sleepy, from Santa Fe, New Mexico—and I took turns describing the journey that had brought us to this point in our young lives.

The previous night, I had mentally prepared a few things I wanted to pass on to my crew. It was important to my lifestyle that they understood where I was coming from. The last thing I needed was to be saddled with some lifer wanna-be or pansy-assed crybaby.

"Okay guys, before I start, there are a couple things I want to run by you." I glanced at the clipboard in my hand like a foreman at a construction site, although I had only four words written down. "I thought the words 'pool house' and 'pool area' too boring, so I came up with some cooler names. Our house here will now be known as the 'Sugar Shack,' and the whole pool area we'll call 'The Bayou.' That gives it a little personality, eh?"

I had agonized most of the night trying to come up with the perfect names for the house and pool area. I felt exceedingly proud of my creativity and fully expected accolades from my cherries. Instead, I got greeted with blank stares—as if from three zombies.

I continued, assuming that they had missed the connection to Creedence Clearwater Revival. "The whole valley—including the pool, house, gravel, and hills—will be called the 'Bayou,' after the CCR song. You know, 'Born on the Bayou'—pretty cool, huh? They *do* play CCR in Wisconsin, don't they?" I asked as sarcastically as humanly possible.

In a barely audible voice, Monte responded, "That's cool, I guess." Buddy and Sleepy stoically maintained their android stares. I was bombing big time.

I quickly moved on to my grand finale. "You guys have heard the song 'Sugar Shack,' right?" I inquired in my characteristic mocking tone.

No one said a word.

"Do you dudes even listen to music, shit?"

I was getting a little pissed off at their lack of appreciation and they could now see this. The silent trio made the correct move—they instantly began kissing my ass.

"Hey Pete, those are cool. I dig the 'Sugar Shack' name." Monte was the first to pucker up.

"Hey Pete, who sings that cool song?" Sleepy asked. "That's a far-out name, really cool, Pete—I mean it, really cool and far-out, really."

Buddy didn't speak, but he shook his head in agreement and smiled at me like a homecoming queen.

Generally, I wasn't a person who appreciated false accolades or bullshit compliments. However, this time it felt right and prevented me from kicking their new-meat asses back to Company B. I quickly thanked Monte and Sleepy for their appreciative comments, and moved on to my awe-inspiring war record. I briefly related my journey from Hawaii to Saigon to Long Binh and ultimately to the pool—er, I mean Bayou. When I finished, I asked Sleepy to give us his story.

Wade "Sleepy" Fossett had been in country for thirteen days—this made him a bona fide cherry boy. He received his nickname "Sleepy" from some guy in basic training, who said Wade always looked as if he'd just gotten out of bed. Sleepy Fossett had been placed on Sergeant Lloyd's shit-list by responding, "That's cool, Sarge," when the sergeant informed him that he had an uncle living in New Mexico. Apparently, Lloyd believed everybody using the word "cool," unless referring to the weather, was a "sissy-hippie-commie-punk." The simple use of the word instantly moved Sleepy to the top of First Sergeant Lloyd's shit-list.

Actually, Wade *was* a card-carrying hippie. In the "world," he had fully embraced the hippie lifestyle. Wade had experimented with a wide variety of drugs and couldn't wait to try some of the "good shit" in Nam that he had heard so much about. For some unexplainable reason, Wade wasn't that thrilled with the assignment to the pool; still, this wayward soldier liked that he could wear shorts all day and didn't need to keep his boots shined. Wade stood a very thin 5' 8"—admittedly from "taking a shitload of 'whites'" (the most popular form of speed in the U.S.) back in the world and drinkin' that liquid French speed since he had landed in

Nam. I got the impression that Sleepy would fit in just fine at the Bayou, but might need some serious monitoring of his drug intake. He had a definite edge and was a little quirky, but he appeared honest, funny, and sincere.

Frank "Monte" Montecalvo proudly informed us that he would one day be a wide receiver for the Green Bay Packers. He was 6' 2" and wiry strong. He looked and talked like an athlete. Monte, like Sleepy, had been in country only a short time.

Monte reported that he and Buddy had ticked off Sergeant Lloyd together during the same incident. They were in the company area, tossing around the football Monte carried with him at all times, when the sergeant walked close by. Monte yelled, "Sarge, catch," as he tossed him the pigskin. Unfortunately, Lloyd didn't hear the call and was looking in the other direction when the ball struck him on the side of his head. Buddy Beard made the fatal mistake of applauding at the accuracy of the pass and remarking, "Nice hands, Sarge." Sergeant Lloyd put them both on KP duty for one week. Before the week had ended, they got dumped on B Company and reassigned to the pool.

I loved sports—especially football—so it thrilled me to have this aspiring NFL wide receiver assigned to the pool. I was in the process of forming a water-football league and made a mental note to make sure I put Monte on my team. I informed Monte that I believed I could play for the Los Angeles Rams except that I was turtle slow, had hands the size of a fifth-grade girl, and didn't like sweaty dudes patting my ass.

While Buddy Beard mesmerized us with his descriptions of the Wisconsin farm he grew up on and how he discovered the best way to milk their three-legged cow named Tripod, I decided to make it a personal project to transform him into a "cool dude'—somewhat like a military version of *My Fair Lady.* The truth? Buddy was a skinny, awkward kid who badly needed to shed his square-looking image. The transformation would require some patience, but I had lots of time on my tiny hands.

Also, as Buddy talked, it became clear that he and Monte had become fast friends in the two weeks since they met. Since both of them hailed from Wisconsin, it created an instant bond that would last for their entire Nam tour.

After a few hours of drinking beer and BS'n with the three cherry guards, I came to a hasty conclusion: these three new arrivals were pretty cool. We differed in many ways, but with the common bond of being stuck in this South- eastern inferno, I felt confident that we'd have a great time down on the Bayou.

Over the next three weeks, the four of us became comfortable with each other's quirks and foibles. For the most part, we enjoyed the same types of activities. We each had different groups of friends who would visit the pool at night or on their days off, but everything flowed smoothly. The Bayou became the primary battalion hangout for those who wanted to escape the Army routine and the ever-present lifers. It sat as an island oasis in a sea of sharks.

We also made friends with dozens of guys from other companies throughout Long Binh. Word quickly spread that the Bayou was the coolest pool (of the twelve on the base) to party at. The biggest selling points? Cold beer, loud music, no lifers, and very few rules. Among our collection of new friends were four maverick MPs who assured us that we'd never get busted for smoking weed while they remained in country. My conditions couldn't have been better if I had planned them myself! I wanted desperately to send a poolside picture of myself, with a cold Coors in hand, to Warrant Officer Edwards and all the toady sergeants. Unfortunately, I had no idea where they were stationed.

If you had stopped by the Bayou on a typical evening during this period, you'd have seen twenty-five to thirty drunks in and around the pool. You'd have heard music blasting from the Sugar Shack, seen a rowdy water-football game in progress, and endured a raging marathon session of Monopoly (the Bayou's official game) in the Shack. You'd have smelled marijuana permeating the air and tripped over empty beer cans and wine bottles littering the ground. Every night we had an open-pool party, with very few restrictions and all the "fixins" except one—American chicks, affectionately referred to by all GIs in Nam as "round-eyes." The Bayou was a veritable cuckoo's nest, overflowing with peculiar, eccentric birds.

Since I was the person in charge and ultimately responsible for all activities at the pool, paranoia always kept me a little on edge. I knew if we *did* get busted for one of the many Army regulations we abused daily, I'd lose this cushy assignment. Depending on the infraction, I could also wind up in the barbed-wire compound—LBJ—a stone's throw from the pool. I rarely shared these concerns with friends, for fear they'd ridicule and dub me a sissy, bitch, fairy, or worse, a lifer.

Occasionally, I needed to get away from the nonstop partying for some peace and quiet, and to clear my head. I often felt as though I was hosting a perpetual, out-of-control frat party—seven nights a week. Once or twice a week, I would go to one of the companies on post and watch a movie or go visit my Saigon buddies in C Company.

Surprisingly, the members of the Fab 50 now stationed at Long Binh rarely visited the Bayou in the evening. The combination of heavier drug users and obnoxious, spaced-out GIs proved enough to keep most "normal" guys away. On many nights the Bayou resembled a three-ring circus, with me as the ring leader, attempting to keep the animals caged and the freaks from inflicting pain on themselves or someone else. It was definitely the greatest show on Long Binh, and often a source of severe mental stress for me.

One evening soon after the arrival of my new housemates, Monte, Buddy, and I decided to see a flick at the 24th Evac Hospital, just up the road from the pool. For one simple reason, the 24th Evac was the best place on Long Binh to watch movies—dozens of round-eyes always attended. Army nurses worked the various wards of the hospital and their presence created the only place on Long Binh where you could see real live American chicks—and believe me, that was a big deal for most homesick GIs. Sleepy, coked up on crank and in a foul mood, decided to stay in the Bayou and play Monopoly with two emaciated "speed freaks" from Company D.

One of my new friends from a transportation division about a mile from the pool had asked me earlier in the day if he could have a party for some lifer about to return stateside. Since parties were an everyday event at the Bayou, I didn't ask him a lot of questions and just approved it. I assumed this would be like any other night at the Bayou—a little crazy, but relatively under control.

That night, the 24th Evac showed one of my favorite movies, *Cat Ballou*, with Lee Marvin and Jane Fonda (good ole "Hanoi Jane," the great-looking bitch who betrayed every GI in Nam). After the movie, Monte, Buddy, and I grabbed a beer from the NCO club and headed back to the Bayou. As we approached the hill leading down to the Bayou, I heard Janis Joplin screeching out her Mercedes Benz song. The music played louder than usual, and the magnitude of the background noise coming from the pool area momentarily confused me. When we reached the edge of the road overlooking the Bayou and got our first glimpse of the valley, I froze in my tracks.

"Holy shit!—what the hell is goin' on, shit!" Monte offered as commentary. Montecalvo rarely used profanity but this mind-blowing scene justified it. A horde of drunken insurgents had overrun the Bayou. We saw over 800 GIs wildly partying in the valley, at least a hundred more thrashing in the pool, and another twenty or so dancing like fools in the back of a deuce-and-a-half truck.

The three of us started down the slope toward the Shack. We noticed at least ten drunks on our way down, passed out on the dirt hill. On the far side of the pool, five or six jeeps raced up and down the hills doing donuts. Two fat, ugly naked guys wrestled on the narrow pool deck, while thirty drunken dudes stood on the ground below the deck, cheering and dousing the duo with beer, red wine, and Johnny Walker. When we got closer to the action, I noticed inside the Sugar Shack another gang of drug addicts as they played cards, Monopoly, and Risk (one of the great all-time strategic games in Parker Brothers history).

My sudden shock slowly developed into a gargantuan fear of being fired from my position at the pool. I would then face a court martial, be found guilty, and get sentenced to hard labor in the infamous Long Binh Jail, ironically located just up the hill from where I now stood. I silently wondered how lengthy a sentence I'd serve in LBJ for the numerous infractions I'd witnessed.

I searched the crowd for the party's host—the transportation ass whose name I couldn't even remember. I knew the first day I met what's-his-name that he was a con man and a classic bullshitter. Why hadn't I pressed him earlier with more questions about the party and how many guys would attend?

I surveyed the mass of out-of-control male humanity, trying to locate the slimeball responsible for turning me into some hulking dude's bitch inside the walls of LBJ. As I searched, the more acts of insanity I witnessed, and the more I freaked out. For instance, I saw a naked degenerate curled up on a shower floor, puke running from his mouth, two perverts in wet boxer shorts pissed on his head while they howled like wolves.

At some point, I looked in an open window of the Shack just in time to catch the tail end of an intellectual conversation between two obnoxious speed freaks playing Monopoly:

"Screw you, man!" the shorter freak screamed. "I had a hotel on Marvin Gardens—where is it, asshole?"

"You don't even own Marvin Gardens, bitch!" the second freak chimed in. "Roll the dice dick-wad or I'm quittin', dude."

"Quit, you little baby!" Freak One yelled as he stood up, prepared to do battle. "You're smokin' too much crank, dude. Lighten up man; don't mean nothin'."

Freak Two flicked the little metal dog game piece onto the floor with his finger. Then, like schoolyard kids fighting over a peanut butter and jelly sandwich, the two speed freaks grabbed each other and started wrestling around the room, bumping into the group playing cards.

I jumped on top of the picnic table next to the snack bar to have a better view of the chaos. At the same time, I heard a collision behind me and turned to see two jeeps that had crashed into each other. Just then, I felt someone grab my leg.

Looking down, I saw Sleepy, wasted out of his mind, staring up at me. He attempted to speak above the racket. "Pete, you gotta get these nut-jobs outta here, man. I can't sleep and some stinkin' fat-ass is crashed in my bunk—he stinks like shit, man." Sleepy was begging me. "Make 'em all leave so I can crash, man."

I just shook my head and flashed him the peace sign, hoping he'd go away. The last thing that concerned me at that moment was Wade "Sleepy" Fossett getting a good night's rest.

I heard a bizarre squeal coming from the pool deck and looked just in time to see some gangly black guy screaming and beating his chest like Johnny Weissmuller, then diving into the pool headfirst. When he surfaced, blood flowed from his forehead. When he noticed the blood running down his face, the dude started laughing.

Just then, I spotted "Mr. Transportation" sprawled out in a beach chair on the far side of the pool deck. I raced over to confront him. He was tripping on LSD and drinking wine directly from the bottle.

"Whalon, where you been, man?" he asked in that all-to-familiar druggie tone, common among the junkies and speed freaks. "This is like the Woodstock of Long Binh, dude. Thanks man for lettin' us party here—you're too cool, dude—way too cool." He stood up and shoved me into the pool.

The cool water helped clear my throbbing head. I realized that I could do absolutely nothing to bring this carnival under control. Also, I didn't want to be labeled a puss or bitch for busting up a spectacular bash. I climbed out of the water, smiling at the punk with no name.

"What have you been takin', man?" I asked the fried burnout. "You're like way gone. Come here, dude."

I stuck out my hand. When he grabbed it, I yanked his arm, sending him stumbling into the pool. The countless mob of buffoons poolside cheered and belched in appreciation.

I then grabbed Mr. Transportation's half-empty bottle of Bali Hi wine and began chugging it. When I finished, I threw the bottle against the large steel filter on the far side of the pool; the glass shattered into a thousand pieces. The chumps applauded again. I raised both arms in the air, flashing double peace signs, and then descended the pool stairs as the inebriated throng roared even louder. Idiots cheering a fool, I thought.

At that point, I realized the mayhem would end when it ended—and not based on my timing. I walked toward the

Sugar Shack and noticed my three apprentices standing off to the side of the deck, eyes bugging out in disbelief. I figured I might as well get some mileage out of this debacle and give them a memorable tale to tell their grandchildren. I strolled over, with a smug grin on my face.

"Should've been here for the happening last month," I said with a wink and a smile. "Twice as radical, dudes." I flashed them the peace sign, turned, and disappeared into the Shack.

Chapter XXV

Someday We'll Be Together

(Diana Ross & the Supremes, 1969)

During the day following the "Bash at the Bayou," word quickly spread throughout the Transportation, Signal, and MP battalions about its magnitude. Like an urban legend, the event developed an ever-more outrageous story of its own making. Inflated reports of between 1,500 and 2,000 drunken soldiers partying until the wee hours of the morning circulated throughout Long Binh.

When the exaggerated stories surfaced, I naturally worried that they'd reach my CC or Lieutenant Wicker and that I might face serious consequences. But to my welcomed surprise, they instead bestowed on me instant "legend" status as the Cal dude who threw the biggest and wildest party in Long Binh history. Only a few people knew that I was unaware of the party until it had spiraled completely out of control.

Adding fuel to this wildfire, Eric Lazear (Mr. Transportation), an incurable sensationalist, also embellished the events and the size of the party, giving me all the credit for its huge success. Eric's motivation for not taking recognition was to insulate himself from possible fallout from his superiors. However, most of the transportation lifers were at the party, drunk on their asses.

The day after the bash, I never left the Bayou. I didn't want to take the chance of going to the company area and having a run-in with Sergeant Lloyd, Captain Fuller, or Lieutenant Wicker—if they didn't see me, they couldn't confront me. Even though I now belonged to B Company, I knew Lloyd and Fuller could still screw me over. The Army could *always* find a way to mess with you if it so desired.

The second day after the party, I decided to eat lunch at the C Company mess hall to see if I could get a feel for my status. The reaction of strangers on my walk to the company took me by complete surprise.

"Hey dude," a well-built, black GI yelled from across the street, "that pool thing was a blast, when's the next one?"

"Shit man," another guy remarked as he passed me, "how'd you get so many dudes in the valley—get some nasty whores next time, man."

"Are you the guard from the pool?" a guy asked as he ran over to me. "So cool man, so cool—I got so wasted there—what's your name, man—keep on partyin' hard, man. I shit you not, man."

By the time I reached the mess hall, six GIs had stopped me, wanting to know about the next celebration. Although I had absolutely no intention of having another event that size at the pool, I lied and told them, "Next month some time—check with me later." I felt like the starting quarterback at UCLA, after he'd thrown the winning touchdown pass in the Rose Bowl, taking a stroll around campus—everybody wanted to know me and be my friend.

As I entered the mess hall, my inflated ego and I were riding high. The fifteen or so guys there sat and inhaled the day's special, leathery macaroni topped with fluorescent orange-yellow processed cheese. When the soldiers spotted me, they simultaneously started cheering and clapping. A little embarrassed, I smiled and flashed the peace sign. When I walked through the chow line, the greasy cooks began giving me double helpings of everything (as if that was a good thing).

I spotted Harper eating at a table in a corner and joined him. "Harp, did you hear about the thing at the pool the other night?" I was curious to get Saigon Bill's take on the situation.

"That's all everybody has been talking about here, Whalon," Harp said, then laughed. "What happened down there—what'd you do, dude?" He was displaying that familiar country grin and pointing his fork at me.

"Shit, I don't know—nothing," I confessed, shrugging my shoulders. "This phony dude I met playin' cards asked if he could have a few friends down for a going-away party for some lifer, and I came back from the movies at the 24th and saw seven or eight hundred idiots drinking and fighting and acting like delinquents. I kinda sat back and prayed for it to end—shit, I didn't do anything, man."

I still wasn't quite sure whether to worry or rejoice about the events that had unfolded. Harper eased my paranoia: "Man, what in hell are you worried about Pedro? The lifers here don't give a rat's ass about what happens at the pool when the sun goes down. They're too busy hiding in their hooches, hoping some freaked out junkie or juicer don't frag their ass. Everybody in the company is askin' about that new dude from California who threw the out-of-control shindig and when he's throwin' another one—shit man, you're the Man of the Hour. Enjoy it, dude, and lighten up." Bill chomped on a carrot stick as he talked.

"I guess it's cool, but there ain't gonna be no more gigantic parties in the Bayou—that's for sure, man," I emphatically stated, pointing my spoon at Harper. "I ain't losin' my gravy train over a bunch of psychotic rednecks I don't even know."

Still, Harper's words had helped ease my concerns. I decided to just go with the flow and see what transpired over the next few days. While Harp and I sat eating the nauseating goop on our plates, guys kept coming over to tell me what a fantastic time they had or to make sure I posted a notice about the next one. One guy even told me that he had heard about a "Bayou Blowout," scheduled for the last Saturday of every month. I assured the beady-eyed kid that he had been misinformed.

248

After eating lunch, I said 'bye to Harp and headed for the pool. As I passed the CO's office, Corporal Haskell called out to me. "Hey Pete, wait up—you've got a message here," he said. The corporal handed me a folded piece of paper.

My anxiety returned. I assumed it had to do with the party in some way, which would mean bad news.

"Thanks Haskell—see ya later." I stuffed the note in my pocket, not wanting to read it until I got to the pool.

"Hey Whalon," Haskell called, as I began to trot away, "heard you threw a wild one the other night. I'll be at the next one, dude."

I turned to see Haskell flashing me the peace sign. I waved without speaking and nervously hustled my butt back to the Bayou.

As I sat by myself in the far corner of the pool deck, I slowly unfolded the paper. The contents caught me off guard. The message came from John Soranno, my buddy who had tricked me into going to the recruiter's office with him on that fateful day in June of '68. I had forgiven John long ago and even retracted my vow to empty a magazine from my M16 into his body. I knew he had gone to Vietnam, but had no idea where he went.

The message was short and to the point: "I caught shrapnel in the foot—not bad enough to send me home but I get to pick my next assignment in Nam—my mom told me that you are at Long Binh now—I will be coming to Long Binh to work at the 24th Evac Hospital. Should be there by Jan. 10—let's party hard, Whale-on!"

I couldn't believe it! John would be stationed at the 24th Evac, less than half a mile from the pool. The message had been sitting in the CO's office for over a week; today was January 9. John Soranno, my best friend from the world, would arrive in Long Binh the next day!

The news elated me and I let out a loud scream. Both Buddy and Sleepy came running from the Shack, wondering what had happened.

"What the hell is wrong, Pete?" Sleepy asked while rubbing his eyes. "You scared the shit outta me."

"My buddy from the world is comin' to Long Binh tomorrow—he'll be stationed at the 24th—I can't believe this, man."

The two guards flashed me their "who-gives-a-crap" frown, grumbled some curse words, and then returned to the Shack.

That night, I barely slept; the anticipation overwhelmed me. Pete and John back together again, in Vietnam! Watch out lifers, gooks, round-eyes, wimps, fairies, rednecks, lowlifes, hustlers, and freaks—the Redondo Beach Boys ride again!

On January 10, I stayed in the Bayou all day, anxiously awaiting John's arrival. By 10:00 p.m., I gave up and went to bed. At 4:30 the next afternoon, I noticed a stranger in faded fatigues coming over the hill, heading toward the pool. I knew by the familiar gait it was John.

I ducked behind a chair on the pool deck as he approached. I picked up a magazine to hold in front of my face and placed Monte's football, which had been resting at my feet, by my side. As John stepped on the walkway below the pool, I jumped up and fired the football down at his head. He deflected it with his hand and screamed at me, "Asswipe, Whalon—this is your gig! You two-bit scammer! Unbelievable, man." John started laughing as he climbed the stairs leading to the pool deck.

As soon as he reached the top, I grabbed his fatigue shirt and pulled him into the water, holding him under for about fifteen seconds. When I let go, he popped up coughing and gagging. "That's for tricking me to the recruiter's office, Kinky—that's why I'm in this hellhole. You're lucky I don't have an M16 in my hands." We both laughed. John and I climbed out of the pool and walked over to where Sleepy, Buddy, and Monte sat playing hearts.

"Guys, this is John, my numba one amigo from the world. He grew up on the same block as me—he's gonna be stationed at the 24th." Everybody shook hands.

Over the next hour, John and I caught up on the preceding eighteen months of our lives.

John had been a medic assigned to the 11th Cavalry when his unit got involved in a wicked firefight. As he pulled a wounded comrade to safety, a grenade exploded nearby, sending shrapnel into his foot. The wound was pretty serious, but caused no significant permanent damage. John had spent two weeks in an Army field hospital before transferring to Long Binh; he had about six months left in country.

We sat on the pool deck drinking beer and smoking some Cambodian Red as we talked. John couldn't believe how blessed I had been to get assigned to Saigon, then to land duty as a lifeguard.

"Jeez, Whalon, you got all the luck, man—this is so far-out. Whose dick did you suck to get this gig?"

I told him the story of Lieutenant Wicker and his bizarre obsession with California and the beach cities.

Obviously envious, John said, "Let me meet this lifer, dude—I'll tell him I'm the *mayor* of Redondo and take your place—I'll tell him I got *twin* sisters he can bang."

Later that evening, I walked with John to the 24th. He promised to return to the pool in the next day or two. He

251

wanted to get settled and, as he put it, "Get some pity-love from the round-eyed nurses." John was understandably proud of his wound and the Purple Heart that followed it.

Over the next two weeks, John came to the pool every evening after his shift. Assigned to Ward 4, the head-trauma section, he worked six days a week from 6:00 a.m. to 6:00 p.m. He would give the other guards and me daily updates on the nurses in the ward, and his sense of humor helped him come up with pornographic nicknames for them all. The five nurses on the day shift were "Hum-Job," "Sweet-Knockers," "Wet Lips," "Ass-'n-a-Half," and "Ball-Breaker." He affectionately dubbed the three night-shift nurses "Humper," "Flat-Ass," and "I-HO" ("instant hard-on").

Over the next few months, we lived vicariously through John's tales about rubbing up against Wet Lips's ass or rubbing Sweet-K's tit with his elbow. John and I also conducted long, serious strategy sessions about moving in together when we got home and throwing the rowdiest parties with wild chicks. Of course, we'd mesmerize these chicks with our harrowing war stories. (John graciously told me I could borrow some of his tales from the bush.)

Sleepy, Buddy, Monte, and I had become good friends during our time in the Bayou, and John fit right in with our clique. The cast of bizarre characters that visited the Bayou daily and all the bullshit they shoveled amazed John. After a week, I became acutely aware that John's hellish experiences in the bush had changed him in profound ways. He was suspicious of strangers and had developed a nasty habit of physically challenging anyone, except me, he believed was "rippin' his ass." I never questioned his behavioral changes, but seldom left him alone at the pool for long periods of time. His time in Nam had hardened him in ways I couldn't begin to comprehend. I assumed that he'd revert to his old carefree, prank-playing, chick-chasing self when he returned to civilian life.

One night during his third week at the 24th, John arrived at the pool with what he termed "the best news of your pitiful, wasted, perverted life, Whalon." He had met an ear, nose, and throat doctor in his ward and informed him about a friend—me—with a deviated septum. John knew well the breathing difficulties I suffered due to my long-standing nose injury and how badly I wanted it corrected. The doctor thought he could possibly help me, and he instructed John to have me come see him the next day.

At first I was thrilled to hear the news, as I had always wanted to have my nose fixed and complete breathing restored. John had made my appointment for 9:00 a.m. the following day. That night, lying in my bunk, I weighed the pros and cons of having a young, inexperienced Army doctor in Vietnam bang on my nose in an attempt to open my breathing passages. I drifted off to sleep without making a decision. However, I leaned toward having the nose job.

Nightmares about hideous, disfiguring results from the surgery terrified me. In one memorable dream, I awoke on the operating table with nurses and doctors cackling hysterically at me. I shrieked in horror when I looked in the mirror floating above my bed and saw how the three-eyed surgeon had attached my nose to my forehead, upside down.

Chapter XXVI

A Hard Day's Night

(Beatles, 1964)

I didn't sleep well that night. I awoke tired and apprehensive about my appointment with the nose doc. I kept picturing myself emerging from the operating room with a mangled nose, disfigured for life. I'd fit in fine as a freak in a Barnum & Bailey sideshow. I had made jokes my entire life about circus freaks—now I'd be one!

Despite my disturbing nightmare, I opted for the nose job and took my chances. I planned to meet John in his ward at 8:45 a.m., and he'd show me to the doctor's office. I had visited John's ward seven or eight times over the previous three weeks and had met most of the nurses. (Nothing brightened my day like talking to a real live round-eye.)

I met John on time and he walked me to Doctor Palmer's small office. Once we arrived, I tried the door. It was locked so I took a seat on the bench outside.

John had to hustle back to the ward to work. In his typical way, he fired a few parting shots before leaving. "'Bout time you get that twisted honker repaired," John joked, attempting to lighten my mood. "Hope the doc doesn't make it worse—you're ugly enough without your beak pointin' sideways, Whalon. Stop by after he gives you the bad news." John hurried off, loudly laughing all the way down the long hallway.

I sat quietly on the bench and considered my situation. My parents couldn't afford the surgery stateside, and I really wanted to breathe properly through my nose again. It was also a pain in the ass explaining the details to everyone who asked, "What happened to your nose?" I hoped that I'd have confidence in the Army doctor John recommended.

"Hi, are you Pete? I'm Captain Palmer."

I looked up to see a baby-faced physician smiling down at me. His youthful appearance did nothing to calm my apprehension. I stood up and shook his waiting hand; he had a limp handshake and a clammy palm. He reminded me of Jesse Booly, one of the wimpy guys I callously made fun of back in high school. I thought about lying and telling him my name was Harry Hasselback and hustling my ass back to the Bayou. Instead, I nodded my head and followed the doctor into his office. He sat down behind his desk and gestured to the chair directly in front of him.

"Take a seat, Pete. Now, what's the problem with your nose?"

I proceeded to explain my situation. "I broke my nose four times playing sports," I said, pointing to the bend in my beak. "Now I can barely breathe through it. I'd like to have a nose job and get my breathing back." To demonstrate my problem, I attempted to take a deep breath using only my nose.

"Pete, it's not called a nose job," he said, talking to me as if I was a ten-year-old child. "You have a deviated septum; it is caused by..." The physician gave me a four-minute lecture on why I couldn't breathe. I looked at him intently, giving the false impression that I was listening. Meanwhile, a trigger deep in the recesses of my youthful mind clicked every time an adult began lecturing to me. The mechanism instantly shut down the concentration and attention-span portions of my brain. I tuned back in just in time to hear his rejection of my surgery.

"Pete, I'm afraid I cannot perform surgery for cosmetic reasons or for minor discomfort." Palmer politely smiled at me, waiting for a reply.

I couldn't believe it! What had this childlike quack told me? John had assured me that I just had to ask politely for the operation. I hadn't realized I needed to convince the doctor of the need for the surgery. The time came to use the poignant speech I had painstakingly prepared for presentation to the doctor at the Army Induction Center on my first day as a soldier. The "Nose Plan" had returned!

"Doctor Palmer," I began, leaning forward, "I'm afraid I didn't give you enough information about my situation. First of all, I didn't mention that I broke my nose again about a month ago playing water football at the swimming pool where I work (a spur-of-the-moment lie I added to the plan). For as long as I can remember, I haven't had a complete night's sleep. Breathing through my mouth causes dry sore throats and I wake up coughing ten to twenty times a night. In addition, I often experience severe sinus pain when I get a cold or the flu. Plus, I can't smell smoke, in case a fire breaks out. This is not for cosmetic reasons at all. Sir—my nose doesn't function properly." I tried in vain to produce a tear or two for dramatic effect but came up dry.

Then, like a slimy used-car salesman selling a lemon to a blue-haired grandma, I went for the kill with an ad-lib line: "Doctor Palmer, I intend on making the Army my career." I mentally forced the food in my stomach to stay down. "I'm going to reenlist at the end of my tour and I would really like to have my breathing restored to avoid any complications in the process. I'd be forever grateful if you'd perform the surgery, thank you sir." I frowned, wrinkled my forehead, and rubbed my left eye as if a little moisture had affected my vision.

"Pete," Palmer said, flashing me a paternal smile, "I'm glad you explained your situation in more detail. I do need justification for the surgery. In your situation, I believe surgery is warranted. I'd be glad to repair your septum for you. By the way, the reenlistment part was a little over the top." He laughed and I smiled.

256

"Let's see...we can schedule the surgery for Wednesday, which is the day after tomorrow. You'll need to be admitted on Tuesday. After surgery, you'll probably be staying in the ward three or four days. Can you get released from your work assignment? I'll give you a letter for your CO to sign."

A sudden chill made me shiver. I was elated and petrified at the same time. Surgery the day after tomorrow! I had assumed I'd undergo it months from now—giving me plenty of time to chicken out. No, Doctor Palmer wanted an answer now.

"Sure, that sounds good." I heard the words but wondered whether I had spoken them.

"Great," he said, then stood and handed me a form. "Take this to Ward 4 and they'll schedule you to be admitted tomorrow. I'll see you in surgery on Wednesday morning." The physician walked around his desk and opened the door for me.

"Thanks, Doctor Palmer—see you Wednesday—oh Doctor, your first name isn't Jesse, is it?" He smiled and closed the door behind me, not answering my question. I knew Jesse Booly didn't have enough smarts to become a doctor anyway.

I sat on the bench outside the doctor's office, trying to clear my head. I now wished I had listened to him as he explained my situation and the procedure for surgery. I made a mental note to begin seriously working on improving my listening skills.

After a few minutes, I got up and walked back to John's ward. After I recounted the details of my meeting, John informed me that I'd be recuperating in his area. He promised to score me lots of pain pills and said he'd try to swing a sponge bath from Nurse Sweet-Knockers.

I told John not to drop by the pool that evening. I wanted to go to bed early and abstain from alcohol and weed so I'd have a positive attitude and be well rested for surgery. He called me a pansy and I called him a Brownie.

John then introduced me to the scary head nurse (Ball-Breaker) who processed my paperwork for admittance the following day. While John stayed at the far end of the ward helping a patient, I seized the opportunity to repay him for some of his past shenanigans. Just before I headed back to the Bayou, I slyly confided a bit in Ball-Breaker.

"I hope John is doing okay here. Has he had any problems with the other GIs?" I feigned a look of deep concern.

"No—not at all," she said with a confused look on her face. "Why?" Ball-Breaker had taken the bait.

"Since John is a little slow, he sometimes gets picked on. In high school I had to watch out for him 'cuz he got his ass kicked a lot. John's not retarded, but just a bit slow if you know what I mean." I winked at the nurse and tapped the side of my head with my forefinger. "Back in the world, my friends and I protected him from the bullies who teased him and called him a retard. Don't tell him I told you—he's kinda sensitive about his condition." I strained to keep from laughing out loud. The wide-eyed nurse didn't reply, but she did shake her head in understanding and gave me a wink.

"Thanks. See you tomorrow, Nurse Andoe." I turned and strolled out the door, waving to John as I exited.

The next afternoon, I reported to Ward 4 at four o'clock as directed. My surgery was scheduled for seven the next morning.

John spotted me when I entered the ward. He rushed over to confront me. "Asshole, why'd you tell Ball-Breaker I'm a retard?" John tried to act upset but his smile gave him away.

"Because you are. I didn't tell her you're a retard. I would never do that. I told her you're slow." Now we were both smiling. John had done the same thing to me many times back in California, providing such background to chicks I had just met, for instance.

"Yeah, well Whalon," John proclaimed with pride, "I told her you lost your left nut in a bodysurfing accident, asshole." A true believer in a speedy payback, John *always* got even.

We both began giggling. It was just like being back in Redondo, trying to out-scam each other with juvenile pranks and immature lies about the other's personal traits and sexuality. God, I missed being back in the world!

John showed me to my bed, then explained the process leading up to the nose job. I'd eat a meal at five, then fast until after the operation. At four the next morning, I'd be moved to pre-op and injected with morphine. The doctor would perform the surgery under local anesthesia. This meant that although I'd be heavily drugged to avoid pain, I'd be awake during the operation. This disturbing revelation did nothing to relieve my fears.

Despite my anxieties about dying or disfigurement, I had an ethical question for John. During my talk with Dr. Palmer, the physician instructed me to shave my moustache before surgery. When I queried John about this, he boomed out his advice. "Screw him! He just wants the moustache off to make it easier for him to cut on you. You ain't gonna see him again until you're on the table, and by then, it will be too late—screw him and keep it, man."

John didn't have to tell me twice. I had shaved my stash only once since coming to Nam. I got so much crap from everybody about how I looked like a baby—sissy— retard—little girl—and on and on and on, that I swore I'd never shave my moustache again—as long as I lived. (In

259

fact, I haven't shaved it since that traumatic experience back in 1969.)

With the persistent, twisted thoughts of potential disfiguration and mutilation, I couldn't get to sleep. When the nurse arrived at 3:30 a.m. to move me to pre-op, I was wide awake in bed, forming bubbles with my siliva and then blowing them off my tongue (a difficult skill to perform, and which many of my friends envied). They wheeled my bed down the hall to a small room where I'd stay until 6:30.

A few minutes later, a slender black nurse and a grouchy doctor came in and informed me of their roles in my surgery. The attractive nurse then injected me with morphine. Within ten minutes, my mind traveled to another glorious, magnificent galaxy—Nirvana! Mysteriously, I now understood the ambiguity of the universe. I possessed the answers to all of man's unresolved questions. I yearned desperately to pass on my revelations to the less fortunate and explain the meaning and beauty of life to hospital staff. I had just started to climb out of bed, intent on spreading the word, when a petite nurse rushed in and stopped me in my tracks.

"Get back in bed!" she barked like a drill sergeant. "Where in the world do you think you're going mister? Just relax, please. Did the morphine kick in yet?" The nurse seemed overly concerned—didn't she realize that I knew precisely what I was doing and why?

"Do you have any Bob Dylan albums here?" I politely asked. "I'd like to hear 'Desolation Row' or 'Maggie's Farm'! Can I get some blackberry Jell-O or Corn Flakes or a Tootsie Roll?" Man, this morphine shit is an ass-kicker, I thought. Why didn't everybody take this stuff all the time? "What's your name, Miss Nurse—are you from California?"

I had so much that I wanted to say and do that I couldn't contain myself. The nurse had obviously seen the effects of morphine many times before. She told me not to talk so much and just close my eyes and rest. I shut my eyes and thought of one of my favorite songs, an anthem to the men stationed in Nam—"We Gotta Get Out of This Place." I couldn't remember all the words so I just hummed the tune.

"Nurse, do you like the Animals?" I asked. "I don't mean real animals like dogs and jellyfish. I mean the group. The singer is Eric Burdon, the short ugly dude from England." I couldn't believe my razor-sharp mind. "Who is your favorite group, Mrs. Nurse? Did you ever see *Riot in Cell Block 11?* That's a great movie…"

"Pete, Pete, wake up." I felt someone shaking my shoulder. I opened my eyes and saw four or five people standing over me, wearing surgical masks. I started laughing. Where in the hell was I?

"Pete, are you okay?" one of the masked men asked.

"Yeah—where am I?" I had no clue what was going on.

"You are in surgery," one of the females informed me. "You're having your deviated septum corrected by Dr. Palmer. Now let me explain what's going to happen. The doctor will be here soon. The operation will take about forty minutes. You'll be awake during the operation but shouldn't feel any pain. If you feel anything, let me know right away and we'll give you more anesthesia. Also, you'll notice your head being pushed back when the doctor uses his instruments on your nose. We're going to cover your eyes with a thin layer of gauze. It is to protect them. You'll still be able to see light. Do you have any questions?" The nurse had a soothing voice and was very deliberate and precise on the procedures.

"No. I'm cool. Not cool as in cold, but cool as in cool. Can I have one more shot of morphine, pretty please?" I asked.

The masked woman shook her head and said, "No!"

The drug had somehow given me an out-of-body sensation. I lay totally calm, fully aware of my surroundings, and prepared for the operation. It seemed as if the staff was about to operate on someone else, as I watched from a ringside seat inside the patient's head. My most pressing concern was what the hospital would serve for dinner in the ward that evening.

The door opened and Doctor Palmer walked in. He greeted me and then matter-of-factly posed a question. "Didn't I tell you to shave that hair on your lip?—too late now." John had been right!

For the next forty or so minutes, I heard the clunk of hammer to bone, followed by short crisp cracks. *Tap, tap. Tap, tap, crack—tap, tap. Crack, crack.* I was intellectually aware that it was the sound of my nose breaking, but it had no ill effect on me physically or psychologically. At one point, I felt a slight sensation (not pain) and, seizing the opportunity, requested more morphine. My mind advanced in overdrive—I concluded that if I felt a sensation, pain would soon follow. Therefore I'd ask for anesthesia in advance, preventing the onset of pain. Instantly, one of the operating staff produced a syringe and injected my upper-right arm. Man, that shit is amazing, I thought.

As time passed, my wits remained clear and I stayed totally alert. Much to the displeasure of Palmer, I even joined in on some of the operating-room banter.

The operation finished, I politely thanked Doctor Palmer and his staff. I joked that if I ever needed another nose job, I'd contact them. Two of the female assistants wheeled me back to the ward and turned me over to the orderly on duty, John Soranno.

"Dude, you look like shit, man!" he exclaimed. "Your face is bad—holy shit, Batman—did you get the number of the steamroller that ran over your nose?" I was sure John had rehearsed his lines in advance, waiting to unload them on me. Though I still felt pleasantly high, my euphoria slowly started wearing off.

"Hey John, get me some more morphine and some grub." I wanted the glorious high that I had experienced earlier returned as soon as possible.

"You can't get morphine now, idiot," John informed me. "It's only for the operation. And you can't eat for two hours. You'll puke your guts out, man, and I ain't cleaning up after your dead ass. I'll get you some Valium later, when Hum-Job goes to lunch. She always leaves her med keys in the drawer. Hey tonight, me, Ray, and the Chief are gonna sit on the bunker and smoke some opium. I'll come get you at seven. I gotta do rounds with Hum-Job. I'll see you in a little bit. God, you look like Sonny Liston caught you banging his wife—bad dude, really bad!" John flashed me the peace sign and walked to the far end of the ward to attend to a dude screaming like a madman.

Reality began setting in fast and I felt more discomfort and throbbing by the minute. The gory details of the operation remained crystal clear in my mind. The sound of the hammer striking and breaking my nose hadn't fazed me during the operation, but now it began to creep me out. I closed my eyes, hoping to fall asleep.

In less than five minutes, John started shaking my arm to wake me. "Hey Pete, you have to go outside until four this afternoon." It was 10:15 a.m.

"What are you talking about?" I asked. "Why?" He couldn't mean me. I had just come from surgery. It must be one of his poorly timed practical jokes.

263

"All noncritical patients, like you, have to vacate the ward from ten to four every day so we can change the beds and clean up the ward. Here, take these, Pete. You'll be wasted in no time." He handed me two white pills. "They're Valium, man. You'll be feeling no pain in ten minutes—I shit you not, man."

Without question, I swallowed the pills with a drink of water, eager to make the escape from reality as soon as possible.

"What in the world am I supposed to do 'til four?" I whined. I was feeling really lousy now and just wanted sleep.

"Go to the dayroom and shoot pool or sleep on a bench somewhere—shit, I don't know—walk around the hospital and scare people. Try to find some other freakazoids like you." As usual, he was no help.

"This is ridiculous, John. I just had major surgery and I feel like shit. Ask the nurse if I can stay in bed. I don't care if you don't change my sheets." I griped like a three-year-old kid who needed a nap.

"Get your ass out of bed, you big baby," he said loud enough for the ward nurse to hear. "You're in better shape than most guys in here." John pulled off my blanket and pointed to the door. "I get off early today," he whispered into my ear. "I'll come get you at six-thirty tonight. Have fun, Frankenstein."

John moved to the next bunk as I dragged myself outside.

I sat down on an outdoor bench just outside the ward, hoping the pain would go away and I could get some sleep sitting up. A tall stocky corporal with crooked teeth passed by and gave me a peculiar look. Less than a minute later, he passed again and stared at me, squinting his eyes. A minute later, he was back. This time, he stopped.

"Hey man, what happened to you? Have you seen your mug, dude? Did you get shot or somethin'?" He gawked at my face with shock and concern. For some strange reason, I hadn't thought about looking in a mirror after the operation.

"No, man, I had a nose job," I said defensively.

"Wow, cool man—go look at yourself—what a trip, dude." He was laughing and having a great time looking at the monster. "Your face is all messed up, man." He flashed me the peace sign and walked off.

Then I really began freaking out. I hurried back into the ward and went in a bathroom to take a look.

"Shit!" I screamed. Who is that hideous alien in the mirror? I thought. My eyes had almost swollen shut. My whole face shone deep purple and black; the thick gauze covering my nose and moustache was bright red from the blood. It looked as though the offensive line of the Los Angeles Rams had taken turns pummeling my head. John came into the bathroom as I examined what was once my face.

"Don't worry, Pete—the swelling will go down in a year or two. Nice facial colors, like a rainbow." He started singing the Rolling Stones' tune, "She's a Rainbow." He was having great fun at my expense and I couldn't blame him. However, the Valium started kicking in and my outlook on life once again improved.

"John, get a camera," I said, newly inspired by a combination of the Valium and a sudden brainstorm. "We've got to get some pictures of me. When I get back to the world, I can tell chicks a bullshit story and say that I got shot in the face by a sapper or jumped on a grenade to save my platoon. Get a camera and meet me outside on the bench." He agreed and scooted off to retrieve a camera from his hooch.

265

Feeling terrific again, I returned to the bench outside and waited for him to come back with the camera. I made a mental note to ask John for more Valium later. Soon he approached me with his Kodak Instamatic.

"Smile, Pete, you're on Vietnam camera." John prodded, "Say cheese!" He quickly snapped four pictures. "Listen, I need to get back to work; see you later, Whalon."

He disappeared inside to finish his shift and I plopped my ass back down on the bench. The blazing sun climbed high, and so did I.

During most of the next few hours, I stalked the halls of the 24th and engaged myself in conversations with other patients, GIs, and anyone else in the area who would talk to me. Almost everyone I chatted with had difficulty looking at my face. Just to mess with their heads, I'd ask them how I looked. The most common response was "Not too bad." Yeah, right, I thought. Around 2:30 p.m., I visited the dayroom and tried to read a magazine. However, because of surgery-related swelling around the eyes, my vision was too blurry to make out the small print.

At 3:30, I went back inside and asked Nurse Hum-Job if I could get in bed. I felt like dingo shit again and had forgotten to ask John for more Valium. My nose ached and throbbed, and my facial bones felt as though someone had squeezed them in a vise. Hum-Job very sympathetically instructed me to go back outside until four like everybody else. "Rules are rules, Private Whalon!" she squawked like a wounded crow.

I wanted to squash my wet and bloody nose-packing in her smug face. Instead I said, "Okay, thank you." Meanwhile I thought, up your ass, you round-eyed witch-bitch!

That evening at 6:30, John returned to Ward 4 with two of his abnormal buddies to pick me up. They were on their way to the top of Bunker 12, next to John's hooch in a company area. Wicked pain pierced my face and lack of food left me as weak as a mouse. In the past twenty-four hours I had eaten only a container of cold Campbell's tomato soup sucked through a flex-straw. My head ached from the combination of prescription and nonprescription drugs and my vision went slightly out of focus. My better judgment begged me to stay in bed. However, I knew if I didn't go with the "Three Stooges," I'd never live down the "sissy" label they would pin on me. So to preserve the perception of my manhood, I mustered all my strength and followed John and his two goofy friends to the top of Bunker 12. For the next six hours, we smoked weed, a little opium, and bolted down shooters of Jack Daniels. I had just lived one of the most physically miserable days of my life, but I uttered not one complaint for the entire time we spent on top of the bunker that night.

When the merriment and agony ended, I stumbled my way back to Ward 4 and silently slipped under the clean sheets on my bed. I was in severe pain, wasted out of my mind, starving, and semi-delusional; however, I felt oddly proud that I had toughed out the ordeal and therefore avoided lifelong ridicule from my best friend, John Soranno.

I drifted off to sleep, secure in the belief that tomorrow would bring a better day.

267

Chapter XXVII

Hooked on a Feeling

(B.J. Thomas, 1968)

The second day after my operation, Nurse Ball-Breaker cheerfully informed me that the hospital would release me the next morning. Despite her seeming geniality, I knew she had taken a quick dislike to me. Apparently Nurse Andoe didn't appreciate my acerbic wit and pathetic military attitude.

I attempted using flattery to convince her to let me stay a day or two longer in the ward. However, like the bitch she was, Ball-Breaker stood her ground. "Balls" compassionately educated me on the reality of my situation: "These beds are needed by seriously injured locals and soldiers, she scolded, wagging her plump finger in my swollen face. Not for cosmetic surgery patients like you, Private Whalon!"

The next morning, I packed my few belongings, received a much-needed bottle of Valium from John, and headed back to the pool. My face remained a severely discolored swollen mess. A nurse had changed the bloody bandages covering my nose and replaced them with clean, white gauze.

I actually looked forward to shocking the lifeguards with my worse-than-expected appearance. As I walked down the hill into the Bayou, I could see Sleepy hosing off the pool deck and Monte and Buddy tossing around a football in the area in front of the pool.

I popped a couple Valium into my mouth and let out a howl, signaling my return. "It's party time, assholes!" I bellowed from a distance with both arms raised.

Monte looked up, smiled, and tossed me the football. I made no attempt to catch it for fear of having the pigskin slip through my hands and strike me in the nose. My honker felt so sensitive to the slightest pressure that even a small breeze caused me pain.

Monte jogged toward me, then stopped abruptly. "Holy crap, Whale—what happened?" he asked, turning away. "What did they do to you, man? I thought it was just a nose job." He looked at me, and then turned away again.

"It *is* a nose job, dude," I said, pointing to my surgically repaired snout. "Is it ugly? I haven't seen myself," I lied, curious to see if he'd voice an honest opinion about my hideous appearance.

"It's worse than ugly, man," he observed, making me smile with his bluntness. "You look like a safe fell on your face from the twentieth floor. Does it hurt?" He squirmed in discomfort, unable to look directly into my swollen, blackened eyes.

"Not as long as I eat these for breakfast, lunch, and dinner," I replied, grinning, then showed him the bottle of "happy pills" provided by "Dr. Feelgood," John Soranno.

By that time, Sleepy and Buddy had joined us. They looked just as concerned and horrified at the amount of damage to my facial features. They stood there frozen, not quite sure what to say. I made it easy for them.

"Look guys—I know I look like afterbirth, but all the swelling will go away in a week or two," I explained in my most fatherly voice. "I'll finally be able to breathe without swallowin' bugs. Now catch me up, am I still a guard?" The four of us began moving toward the Sugar Shack.

We all went inside the Shack to get out of the heat and talk about the events of the past few days. It felt terrific to be home again, hanging with my boys.

269

For the next two weeks, I remained a carnival sideshow for visitors to the Bayou. As with the "half-man, half-lizard" act at a carnival, everybody wanted his picture taken with the frightening, eerie-looking lifeguard from California. As the swelling subsided and the discoloration faded, the demand for souvenir photos lessened. Since I knew the damage wasn't permanent, I had no problem playing the part of Circus Freak for the GI tourists.

Life for us at the pool settled into a routine of leisure and idleness, devoid of Army rules and regulations. We stayed truly out of sight, out of mind as far as the Army and its minions of lifers were concerned. Rarely did anyone above the rank of corporal visit the Bayou. Word had spread quickly that if you wanted a place to do your drugs of choice and avoid getting hassled, you went to the Bayou, just below LBJ. The valley became a hangout for malcontents, radicals, misfits, oddballs, nonconformists, and drug addicts from the surrounding companies. Although I rarely used drugs other than weed, nearly every group of addicts was represented in the Bayou—each with its own peculiar behavior and abnormal personalities.

Fortunately for us, heroin addicts rarely showed up at the Bayou. By far, they constituted the most miserable, demoralizing users to deal with at Long Binh. They concerned themselves solely with obtaining their next vial of "skag." Luckily for us, they didn't care for lounging and sunning themselves under the scorching sun. In fact, this lifeless pack of irritable zombies enjoyed only smoking heroin. Ill-tempered losers, their drug of choice also made them stupefyingly lazy. A neglect of basic hygiene was the junkie's worst trait. Pungent body odor, filthy hair, unbrushed teeth, and soiled, stained clothing characterized this inert group.

Heroin scared the shit out of me. I had seen what it had done to so many cherries who innocently took a simple toke off someone's powder-filled cigarette—within days they became addicted. I refused to let the addicts smoke their "crank" in the Bayou. And since their heroin addiction required hits hourly, it was exceptionally inconvenient for them to return to their hooches from the Bayou for a simple toke.

Simultaneously, I detested and felt deep sorrow for these lost souls. Someday they'd return home, hollow remnants of the young, strapping boys sent to Nam. Physically and emotionally, they'd be almost unrecognizable to their loving families. Sadly, junkies commonly disappeared on their day of departure from Vietnam. They'd hide out in a fellow addict's room, not wanting to be separated from the ever-flowing, inexpensive cache of the white devil. This terrifying act *alone* sufficiently convinced me never—under any circumstances—to take even one small hit of their poison. In Vietnam, the hopeless junkie was truly the most pathetic GI of all.

Observing the speed freaks hanging out at the pool reminded me of a monkey cage at the zoo. The sudden, perpetual movements and never-ending chatter were trademarks of this nerve-wracking group. As with most drugs, anyone could easily obtain liquid speed in Nam. After a simple request to a mama-san, she'd fill the order the next day. The speed came in small glass vials from France. One vial (often poured into a twelve-ounce can of Coke or Pepsi) would keep a person "speeding" for about eighteen hours. Anyone could easily identify speed freaks. They talked incessantly, rarely consumed food, looked as skinny as super models, and had open sores on their arms and legs affectionately called "speed bumps." The bumps appeared because the addicts ate so little; therefore they lacked nutrition and basic vitamins. Common among the group of heavy users were guys who had been overweight their entire lives. Speed provided an effortless way for the lard-asses to lose weight, since it suppressed the appetite.

I occasionally took speed as a novelty to break the monotony of everyday life in Nam. However, I knew well the potential dangers of daily use. Initially the drug brought on feelings of euphoria and well-being. However, after a month or so of abuse, those feelings got replaced with depression, irritability, paranoia, malnutrition, and obsessive-compulsive behavior.

There was nothing more comical than listening to a group of speed freaks engaged in a marathon session of Monopoly in the Sugar Shack. They'd sometimes argue for an hour or more over a single roll of the dice. I was lying on my bunk one day when an argument erupted between two speed freaks involved in a hotly contested Monopoly game in the Shack. Toby and Skeeter were notorious in the Bayou for their hilarious, insane, and intense arguments over meaningless aspects of the Parker Brothers board game.

"Hey Skeets, you got an eleven!" Toby hollered at Skeeter, just across the table from him. "You landed on Boardwalk, fool!"

"Bullshit," Skeeter fired back. "I landed on Luxury Tax, ass—not Boardwalk."

"You were on Water Works, ass-face," Toby grumbled as he stood up. "Eleven puts your thimble on Boardwalk—count man—1-2-3-4..."

"I was on Ventnor Avenue, not Water Works—you count, shithead." Skeeter jumped to his feet to show he wouldn't let Toby intimidate him.

"You're fulla shit, cheater—pay me. I got two houses—you own me six hundred dollars! Pay up or you're outta of the game, cheater." Toby had crossed the line with Skeeter. He lambasted him with the forbidden word among Monopoly-playing speeders.

"Will you guys shut up for once and roll—whose turn is it?" Sleepy, who was also playing, tried to get the game moving again.

"Stay out of this, man," Toby demanded. "Pay or you're outta the game, Skeeter the big fat cheater."

"You can't kick me out—let's vote. How many think I'm right?" Skeeter raised his hand, pleading to the three others in the game for support. They soon settled the immediate controversy, but I knew it wouldn't be too long before another disagreement flared up again.

Usually a game ended after a couple of hours when some speeder swept the board clean or knocked over the table. Rarely did the speed freaks complete a game with a winner being declared. They'd call each other depraved names and storm out of the Sugar Shack, only to return within the hour and start a new game.

I attempted to play with a group of speeders only one time, and predictably ended up quitting. In this incident, an MP from some redneck shit-hole in Tennessee accused me of sneaking a Get out of Jail Free card from the Chance pile. When I attempted to explain politely his mistake (he carried a pistol at all times), the MP indignantly proclaimed: "Look dude, just 'cuz you live here and you're some hotshot lifeguard from California, doesn't mean you can cheat us! You've been cheating the whole time with your sneaky moves and rollin' the dice." He picked up the dice and held them inches from my face as if this act proved his contention.

"Ya caught me, you hick copper," I said, and handed him all my money and properties. When I left the table, an argument ensued among the psychos about how they'd distribute my wealth.

Speeders continually amazed me at how intelligent they considered themselves after they downed some speed. As if they had swallowed a complete set of *The*

Encyclopedia Britannica, the freaks instantly became versed on subjects they previously knew nothing about. Nothing enlightened me more than when a high school dropout from Biloxi, Mississippi lectured me on the giant "man-eating" clam from the South Pacific, or on how Paul Revere became a silversmith in colonial America.

It was a grueling experience getting cornered by a speeder intent on displaying his newfound wisdom. A "wired" speed freak never looked for a conversation, just someone who'd listen to his never-ending drivel. A person found it almost impossible to excuse himself and get away from the monolog. I discovered that the best way to get speeders to find another victim was pretending to fall asleep. If you were lucky, after ten minutes or so of yapping to your closed eyes and exaggerated snores (for dramatic effect), they'd stride off in search of another set of ears.

Although speed freaks were more entertaining than junkies and a great deal more fun to watch, their lives—like those of all drug addicts—took on a pitiful, almost meaningless existence.

Another dangerous group of druggies, to themselves and others, were the "downers." Their drug of choice—again a French product—was known as BTs. The BTs came packaged in small foil containers, like Fizzies. They were the equivalent to "Reds," the most popular downer in the United States at the time, with effects similar to those of drunkenness: loss of basic motor skills, slurred speech, and total lack of inhibitions. Most fights between GIs in Vietnam usually involved drunks or BT abusers.

One day shortly after I arrived at Long Binh, a redneck in C Company passed out on the ground with two BTs in his hand. His dog Sam, a tough stray that no other dogs in the battalion would mess with, walked up and ate the two tablets out of the redneck's palm. Within minutes, Sam passed out next to his fallen master. When Sam woke up, eight hours later, the poor drugged-out pooch could only walk sideways. Thereafter, everyone affectionately called him "Sidewalk Sam."

By far, the heads made up the largest subculture of drug users in Vietnam. Grass was plentiful and powerful in Vietnam. Most of the GIs who smoked the "devil-weed" kept their stash in plain sight. It was common knowledge that lifers rarely did anything to curb drug use among the enlisted men. Having pot on hand was the equivalent of providing a dish of candy on your coffee table at home. A good GI host always had a large Ritz Cracker can full of CBR and a few bongs on hand for visitors to his hooch.

Also crazy, and the most obnoxious, were the juicers—the alkies. These guys got drunk every night, rain or shine. Most of the heavy juicers refrained from all drugs and spent their off-hours in the EM and NCO clubs on post. There, surrounded by fellow drinkers, they could listen to country-western music, their favorite.

Most GIs neatly fit into one of these five groups, although some compulsive personalities took all drugs and washed them down with a pint of Jack Daniels. And there existed also the straight guys, usually family men, churchgoers, or a combination of both. For the most part, these varied groups coexisted with limited problems.

In the evening, after closing time at the Bayou, our group consisted mostly of weed smokers and moderate drinkers. The junkies and downers stayed close to their hooches, while the speed freaks roamed all over the company area in a relentless search of some non-speeding soul with an open ear.

One of the tragedies of the Vietnam War, insuring the inevitable failure of the conflict, was unchecked drug use among GIs. Plainly put, the career men conducting military operations in Vietnam had no clue on how to prevent drug use among GIs. There was also a glaring lack of forethought given to the deleterious effects of drugs on the troops. Due to both an absence of knowledge on the part of the military command and a lack of desire to control the use of drugs, the problem spiraled out of control to epidemic proportions. The residue of this crisis came in the form of thousands of broken young men, now addicts, returning to the cities and towns of America. Men—the walking dead!—who for one year had eluded death at the hands of the Vietcong returned home critically wounded by drugs.

Chapter XXVIII
Black Is Black
(Los Bravos, 1966)

In the late '60s and early '70s, the Black Power movement was in full swing throughout the United States as well as in Vietnam. At Long Binh, in early 1970, problems between black and white GIs had gone from bad to worse. For the most part, in our battalion, blacks hung out with blacks and whites hung out with whites. Down in the Bayou, we had few difficulties with blacks vs. whites for one simple reason: rarely did blacks visit the pool during operating hours. In the company area, it proved a vastly different situation.

B Company was home to the "pole climbers" at Long Binh. Their primary assignment was to repair the damaged phone wires strung from pole to pole throughout the post. For some reason that I never understood, B Company consisted of about 75% black guys. Due to its racial imbalance, B Company became the hangout and unofficial headquarters for militant blacks from the other companies in the battalion.

Charlie Hardy, my old buddy from Saigon, had become one of the leaders of the militant blacks over the course of his first three months at Long Binh. At some point during that period, Charlie had stopped talking to the group of guys that had come with him from the warehouse—with the exception of Willie Stuart, the only other black transferred from Saigon. With his new status as a black leader, and as one of the toughest guys involved in the group, I think Hardy believed he could no longer speak to his white dudes—even his close friends from Saigon. He'd slightly nod his head when I walked by, but never said a word. I had the strong feeling that Charlie had told his followers that I was a cool white dude and to leave me alone and not hassle me. No member of the militants of their group ever singled me out; neither did they physically or verbally assault me for being white. Although Willie Stuart was a fringe member of the group, he'd occasionally talk to us, as long as there were no other blacks around. I missed bullshitting and drinking with Charlie and Willie; however, I accepted the reality of the racial climate behind these developments.

In March of 1970, tensions between the "brothers" and the white dudes escalated into violence and near riots in the battalion. One incident I witnessed occurred during a sweltering evening at C Company. I happened to be in the company area visiting some friends at the time. About twelve of us were sitting in a circle in our beach chairs outside a hooch, casually talking and smoking weed, when all hell broke loose.

From the black skies above came a hailstorm of jagged gravel rocks. The airborne stones peppered us and the area surrounding our circle. It took our startled cluster a few seconds to process what was happening. When our group finally realized that a bombardment of rocks was targeting us, we took off running through and between hooches 7 and 8, toward D Company and perceived safety. Someone had launched the rocks from the far side of Company B toward our weed-smoking klatch. The darkness prevented us from seeing exactly where the missiles were coming from, but I instinctively knew the blacks from B Company had thrown the rocks. This wasn't the first air assault of its kind in the company. Trouble had reached the boiling point weeks before and I knew then that it would worsen.

Fortunately, I didn't get hit, but five others from our freaked-out stampede didn't have such luck. Two guys had gotten hit in the face, and three more on their legs and arms. One poor sap from another battalion, visiting a friend in our company, bled profusely from his head. We rushed him to the CO's office for medical attention. The corporal on duty called for an ambulance and for the MPs. Within minutes, the battalion streets filled with MP jeeps. With loudspeakers blaring and MPs charging into the hooches, they ordered everyone out of B and C Companies and into the street.

"Attention—all personnel—out of your hooches now, and into the street," the MP captain's voice commanded through his megaphone. "Do not carry any weapons, and place your hands on your heads—you have two minutes."

Some MPs entered the hooches and began a room-to-room search, making sure everyone hustled outside to the chaotic street. They pounded on the doors with their fists. If no one answered within five seconds, they kicked in the door. (These macho guys lived for this stuff.)

An MP—and a frequent visitor to the Bayou—spotted me and called me over to his jeep. "Where's the guy who got shot, Pete?" he asked me.

"Nobody got shot, man." I informed him. "Some guys from B Company just chucked some rocks at us and a few guys got nailed. Who said a dude got shot?" I asked.

"I don't know," he said, shaking his head. "I gotta go; see you at the pool tomorrow." The MP ran to the captain's jeep at the top of the street. After passing on the information, the captain called for his guys to pull out and return to their company. As soon as the MPs left, all personnel quietly returned to their hooches. I said good-bye to Judge and Goodman and jogged toward the Bayou and safety.

I'd learn later that the corporal, high on speed when he called the MPs, had given them the impression that someone had been shot with a rifle. When the captain heading up the MP assault found out that it was just a rock-throwing incident and not a shooting, he called off the search and pulled out of the area. The captain stopped by the CO's office on his way out of the company. He chewed out the speeding corporal, calling him a brainless hippie, then jumped in his jeep and sped off. No one had gotten seriously injured, although the guy who caught one in the head required eight stitches to close his gash. Although we urged him to apply for a Purple Heart, which he later did, he never received one.

Throughout the battalion, the rock assault from Company B remained the hot topic of conversation the following week. Everyone thought it stemmed from racial tensions. Unfortunately that brought the redneck bigots out of their oily holes to add fuel to the raging fire.

Buck, a self-proclaimed leader of the "good ole boys" and a real slimeball, was the most blatant racist I had ever seen in my life. Nobody in C Company really liked him, but rednecks hung out together, so he always had a crowd close by to listen to his racist bullshit. Good ole boy Buck Coulter instantly began stirring up trouble as soon as he found out what had happened to our gathering. By the way, his claim to fame was "I can chug more brew than any two faggot druggies in this shit-hole!"

Most of the guys in the battalion made fun of "Buck-hole" (his nickname) behind his back. However, due to his drunken threats and crazed stare, rarely did anyone challenge Buck to his pockmarked face. He was one of those psychos you avoided completely.

Word spread throughout the battalion that Buck had plans to get even for the stoning on some of his "white boys." Five days after the air raid, some guy at the pool told me that Buck planned to get his revenge later in the evening. My gut told me to play it safe and stay clear of the company area that evening, but my curiosity and fear of missing the confrontation overpowered my apprehension. I went to visit Schrunk and Harper at 7:00 p.m. The three of us huddled safely in Schrunk's room, leaving to make frequent trips up the street to Buck's hooch. We hoped to learn what asinine stunt he had decided to pull.

Buck got sloppy drunk every night of the week. He would holler and curse at everybody and everything. He was the classic obnoxious, irritating redneck boozer—a self-righteous disciple of the George Wallace school on race relations.

At about 8:30 that night we heard the first incoherent screaming from up the way. We ran to the entrance of the hooch just in time to see Buck stumble to the middle of the street. He gripped a bottle of Johnny Walker in one hand and swung his prized Confederate sword (supposedly used in the Battle of Gettysburg) in the other.

The battalion drunk screamed at the top of his lungs: "Gutless jungle bunnies, I'll slaughter you assholes—I shit you not!" Buck paused to spit up some liquid. "Get your asses over here—I'll cut off your brainless heads with my rebel blade! Long live Robert E. Lee!"

Buck heaved his empty bottle at the first hooch in Company B. It hit some sandbags and quietly fell unbroken to the ground.

"You don't mess with whitey and get away with it, assholes. You tar babies are gonna feel the cold steel of my blade tonight, I shit you not—long live the Confederacy!"

One of the sergeants from the NCO hooches heard the commotion, ventured into "no-man's-land" for lifers, and confronted Lunatic Buck. We couldn't hear what the sergeant said, but Buck handed him the sword and, without saying a word, meekly disappeared into his hooch.

The sergeant stayed out in front of Buck's hooch for about ten minutes, until an MP jeep pulled up. He talked to the MP sergeant for a few minutes, then headed back to his hooch. About every fifteen minutes after the two sergeants had their conversation, an MP jeep cruised up and down the street between B and C Companies, flashing its spotlight on Buck's dwelling. I hung around for another half hour, then returned to the Bayou. It looked as if serious trouble had been averted and that nothing would happen after all.

The next morning, as I sat in the mess hall eating a bowl of Cheerios, Schrunk came hustling up to me.

"Did you hear about Buck?" Schrunk asked with wide eyes. "He got his ass kicked last night about two in the morning. That's one asshole that deserved it," Dave said while grabbing a piece of rye toast from my tray. He went on to explain.

Apparently three or four black guys from B Company hid in the dark down by the honey pots (outhouses) waiting for Buck to take a piss. With the amount of beer and booze he drank nightly, they knew it would be only a matter of time before their quarry showed up to release some of the Budweiser from his bladder. They were waiting when he exited the outhouse. They threw a blanket over Buck's head and proceeded to kick and beat the shit out of him. They also used his blood to scrawl a message on the mirror for his buddies: "You're next redneck!"

Buck's roommate discovered him when the roommate went to check on him after thirty minutes had passed. Good ole Buck Coulter lay in a pool of blood, still drunk, moaning like a baby with dirty diapers. Someone called an ambulance, which rushed him to the 24th Evac. Buck was placed in John's ward since most of the serious damage involved the face area. The redneck's injuries consisted of a broken nose, two knocked-out teeth, two black eyes, fractured ribs and twenty-seven stitches to his face and head. According to John, "The dude's head smelled like shit." I assumed that his attackers had shoved Coulter's head into the shit-hole of the latrine.

Two days later, the swollen-faced Buck was back at Company C, looking like a guy who had gone fifteen rounds with Floyd Patterson. That night, true to his twisted character, Buck wandered outside his hooch again, drinking and cussing out the blacks at the top of his lungs. The guy was not only a stupid drunk; he also had a serious death wish. Later that night, five "brothers" brazenly entered Buck's room, threw his roommate out in the street naked, and beat the shit out of Buck Coulter for the second time that week. Once again an ambulance came to haul his pummeled carcass off to the 24th Evac.

This time, Buck never made it to John's ward, and he never returned to C Company. Two rumors soon began circulating around the area after his second thumping. First, due to the severity of his wounds, Buck was evacuated to Okinawa that night in critical condition. Second, he died from the beating and was shipped home, listed as a "friendly-fire" casualty. Most likely, Buck got sent to an off-base hospital and later transferred to another unit for his own safety. His terrified roommate would never answer questions about Buck's fate, for fear of ending up just as his buddy had. In fact, as a result of an extreme fear for his life, the roommate convinced the CO to transfer him to another company on the far side of Long Binh.

Nobody really missed Buck or his unbearable behavior very much. The black pole climbers had delivered a clear and powerful message to the surrounding companies— mess with us and you'll end up like Buck Coulter! From that point on, I rarely visited the company area after dark.

Chapter XXIX

Did You Ever Have to Make Up Your Mind?

(Lovin' Spoonful, 1966)

At some point in the late '60s, the military instituted a policy called the "early-out" program for GIs serving in Vietnam. It allowed a GI to voluntarily extend his one-year Nam tour. The advantage in an extension for the GI was having five months dropped from his two-year or three-year enlistment. Any participating GI leaving Vietnam with less than 150 days remaining in his enlistment would receive an early-out discharge. The lure of having 149 days less to serve was a powerful incentive for many GIs. It was also an option I mentally wrestled with in April of 1970.

My Vietnam tour was scheduled to end on June 10, 1970. If I decided to leave Nam at that time, I'd return to the States to be stationed there until my discharge date of August 30, 1971. If I extended in Nam for six months, then extended a second time for another 110 days, I'd be released from the Army on or about March 31, 1971.

I'd have never considered an extension in Vietnam except for one obvious fact: I worked at a swimming pool practically unsupervised, and had total freedom to come and go as I pleased. In addition, the most enticing lure for me was getting home in time for the Southern California summer. I treasured the summertime there—bikinis, hot pants, tan chicks, and ice cold beer. Getting out in March would give me plenty of time to grow my hair, get a tan, get an apartment, and begin my life again.

Since I had great difficulty grappling with the decision to extend, I solicited advice from everybody I knew and obtained some valuable suggestions.

"Dude, only loser lifers and messed-up junkies extend," Judge informed me. "Which one are you Whalebone?"

"I got a better idea, Whalon," Goodman advised. "Put an M16 to your head, put it on automatic, and pull the trigger—that makes more sense to me!"

"Lifer, lifer, lifer, lifer, lifer..." Harper just laughed and continued to call me lifer until I walked away.

"Yeah, volunteer to stay in Vietnam when you could go back to the world and bang round-eyes," Stuart mocked. "Yeah, that's a sensible decision, Whalon. I can't believe you'd extend, man. You white dudes are nuts."

Since my Saigon buddies offered no positive comments, I solicited counsel from the neighborhood junkies.

"Cool, dude—that's so cool," Rocky encouraged. "Really Pete, I shit you not, dude—very cool. Why go home when drugs are this cheap?"

"Great move, man—why leave this druggie paradise?" A junkie cook who was a friend remarked. "I'm gonna stay here forever, man. They'll have to drag my ass out."

Two other junkies in C Company offered their advice. "You gotta do your own thing—peace, brother—you got any skag, man?" and "I'd do the same thing if I was in your boots, man—this place is like drug heaven."

It was a tie—mindless junkies for extending— rational Fab 50 members for going home. Although I valued the opinion of my friends much more than that of some drugged-out crankers, I chose to extend my tour. The deciding factor was my firm belief that it didn't matter where they stationed me; I couldn't begin my "real life" again until I was discharged from the Army. So I'd voluntarily extend and gut out another ten months in this shit-hole, for the ultimate reward of experiencing another glorious summer in Redondo Beach, California.

Complications stood in the way. I needed the blessing (and signature) of the Commander of Company C. He wasn't what I'd call a huge fan of my checkered military career, such as it was. On the brighter side, the chain of command rarely turned down extension requests. For every fool that extended it meant one less cherry shipped to Nam. I took the best approach and just submitted my papers and waited. On April 17, 1970, I handed my extension papers to Corporal Haskell. The corporal winked at me and told me not to worry; he'd put in a good word on my behalf. I thanked him and nervously trotted back to the Bayou.

Two days later, Haskell came to the pool and shook my hand. "Congrats, Pete, I guess," he said. "You're staying in country another six months. Your extension was approved."

I had mixed feelings. I was pleased to have this extension OK'd, but having another 180 days instantly added to my Nam tour created turmoil in the pit of my stomach. I hadn't informed my parents or friends back home of my intentions. I wanted to make sure my extension got approved before I attempted the difficult task of explaining why anybody in his right mind would choose to stay in Vietnam one more day than absolutely necessary.

For the next month, I attempted to persuade some of my friends from Saigon and the Bayou to extend with me. Blessed with a little more common sense than I, not one of them would even consider the possibility. It was understandable—they didn't sit poolside every day, soaking up rays, playing cards, and drinking beer.

Within sixty days of my approved extension, forty-nine of the Fab 50 would return to the world, having completed their one-year tours in Nam. All by his lonesome, Private Pete Whalon, United States Army, would carry the torch of the Fab 50 for another 290 days. Let the good times roll!

Chapter XXX
People Are Strange
(Doors, 1967)

One breezy evening in late September 1970, I sat by myself on the pool deck, listening to a Grand Funk Railroad tape. I began thinking of all the unusual characters I had met during the past sixteen months in country. Aside from my close friends, I had come in contact with hundreds, perhaps even thousands, of other young men like myself who couldn't wait to return home. As I fondly recalled some of those homesick soldiers, three stood out: Sheppard "the Butcher" Scolwick, Butter-Balls and Darby "the Dick" Pellco. They were among the most interesting and bizarre individuals I ever met.

Butcher Scolwick, from Upper New York State, was a scrawny, con-babbling, white cook for C Company. Over his left breast someone had tattooed the word "sweet"; over the right breast, the word "sour." His nickname was respectfully given to him because of his unique ability to provide the largest, thickest, most tender cuts of steak on Long Binh. Sheppard epitomized the classic New York hustler. He continually worked on schemes to earn a little extra cash or to trade supplies with another mess hall on post. Throughout Long Binh, Scolwick was notorious for his savvy deal-making ability. The Butcher took great pride in providing the boys in C Company with the best cuts of meat in Vietnam. Generally speaking, though I didn't care for con-chattering hotshots, I made an exception for Sheppard Scolwick. Even though I sometimes tired of his nonstop rap, he was quite generous and recounted unbelievable tales of his life on the streets of the Big Apple.

Shep loved hanging out at the pool with what he termed the "cool pool fools." On his frequent visits to the Bayou, Scolwick always arrived in a 2½-ton truck with the words "MESS HALL" stenciled on the driver door. Below that, scrawled in what resembled dripping blood, were the words "The Butcher." I assumed Shep had cut some deal with the CC to allow him to keep those words on an Army-issue truck. Shep would race down the embankment, kicking up a massive cloud of dust and dirt, blasting his horn all the way, and waving his tattooed arm out the window. On the top of his cab he had attached a loudspeaker wired to a microphone inside. Just before skidding to a halt inches from striking the Sugar Shack, Shep would howl over his speaker for all to hear: "The Butcher is in the Bayyyyoooouu!" He'd then leap out of his truck and unleash a bloodcurdling rebel yell. Those in the Bayou would traditionally give him a rousing standing ovation as he took a bow. Shep's Bayou visits were always filled with electricity. As a sign of appreciation for getting to hang out with the Bayou Bad Boys (another of his nicknames for us), he'd bring two or three boxes of rations from the mess hall every time he visited the Bayou. We always welcomed free food. The ever-hungry heads, constantly on the prowl for marijuana munchies, especially appreciated it.

Shep, who had also extended his tour in Vietnam, was the only guy in Company C who had lived in country longer than I, and he continually reminded me of it. Often as we talked in a group together, Shep would blurt out, "Ya know, I've been in country longer than Peety-boy." He proudly wore it as a badge of honor.

Scolwick was well into his second tour when he began smoking heroin. I had attempted many times to convince him to quit smoking the "white devil," but that proved impossible. It made me sick to my stomach to see anyone, especially one of my friends, addicted to crank. With only a few months remaining in his Nam tour, he'd become hopelessly addicted to "junk." The Butcher of Long Binh had become a junkie!

One evening about six, Shep raced his truck up to the Sugar Shack in a cloud of dust. He wanted me to take a ride with him to the other side of Long Binh. Shep told me he planned to swap some T-bone steaks with another mess hall in exchange for ten cases of Coors beer. He wanted to throw a barbeque for the boys at his hooch later that evening, complete with some tea girls to spice things up. I easily agreed to go, as I had accompanied Shep many times when he had delivered supplies to other battalions. I always found it a unique experience when traveling in Butcher's world.

As we drove up the hill and turned left on Long Binh's main highway, Shep had to swing wide to avoid hitting a mama-san carrying a basket of laundry. As usual, he drove too fast, and the wide turn sent the back wheels of our truck over the embankment and into the trench in front of LBJ. The truck slowly slid backwards down the short hill, leaving us stuck in the sand. Shep tried to pull out but the sand wouldn't allow it; the truck's tires couldn't get enough traction to extract us. Via his megaphone, the guard in tower 6 at LBJ—stationed just above where our truck rested— ordered us to get out of the truck with our hands up.

"Both of you step out of the vehicle now!" the guard yelled through his megaphone. "Raise your hands above your heads, and face me." Apparently he thought we had initiated some kind of elaborate jail break.

I started to climb out of the truck when Shep grabbed hold of my arm. Sweating profusely, he looked exceptionally nervous. I had never seen the look of utter fear in his face before.

"Pete," Shep said in a panicked voice, "hide these in your pocket, man. I can't get caught driving with this shit or I'll end up in there. I've been busted too many times. I'll end up someone's bitch in LBJ!" He pointed toward the infamous jail just behind us. "I go home in under ninety days, dude—help me, man, please," he begged. "The Butcher needs your help, man. You owe me." Shep had pulled out between fifteen and twenty small vials of heroin from his fatigue pocket and began shoving them toward me.

My mind raced, trying to form a response. Finally I blurted out, "Screw you, man—I ain't getting' busted with crank vials, shithead!" I pushed Shep's hand away. "Throw 'em out the window before the MPs get here—shit, what's wrong with you?—get rid of that garbage, man. You know I hate that shit!"

Over his loud speaker, the rifle-toting guard in the tower then told us that if we didn't exit the vehicle, he'd unload his M16 into our truck.

"Please, man," Shep, near tears, pleaded. "Take the shit and put it in your pocket; they won't check you 'cuz you weren't driving. I'm dead if they catch me—they always check the drivers. I'm a 'short-timer,' man. Please Whalon. I can't do time in LBJ."

Shep hyperventilated as he spoke. Like a chump, I grabbed the vials from his sweaty palm and shoved them into my fatigue pocket.

"You owe me big, Scolwick—BIG, asshole! And you can bet your ass I'm gonna collect."

We exited the truck at the same time, just as two MP jeeps screeched to a stop in front of us. I was now sweating more than Shep! I suddenly realized I had made a monumental mistake in putting the vials into my pocket.

The MP sergeant in the closest vehicle waved us over to his jeep. "You guys look loaded," the MP said as he got out of the jeep. "You guys been smoking 'Red' or 'speeding'? Don't lie to me, assholes." He flashed us the classic MP smile military cops made when they smelled blood.

I came dangerously close to pissing in my Army-issue boxers. I wanted to grab The Butcher by his chicken neck and squeeze until his eyes popped out of their sockets. Deciding not to call attention to myself, I kept quiet to allow Shep to answer the sergeant.

"We ain't loaded, sergeant," Shep replied. "I don't do drugs, sir." Unfortunately, Shep, like most junkies, always looked loaded. His emaciated appearance and snow-white face were a dead giveaway.

MPs knew a junkie when they saw one. "All right, assholes," the MP sergeant said as he slapped his hand on the hood of his jeep, "empty your pockets here, junkies!"

I started having difficulty breathing. Private Pete Whalon, who had cleverly scammed his way through the Army for over two years, would now end up in LBJ, for possession of an obscene amount of heroin. I glared at Shep, who mouthed the word "sorry" to me. Sorry!

I decided that I had to drop a dime on Shep to save my ass—I had to rat—and hope the MPs believed me. It was my only chance to survive this nightmare. I couldn't do time in LBJ! Those savage animals inside would eat my "candy-ass" alive on the first day.

Shep started emptying his pockets but I stayed frozen in place. My mind desperately raced in an attempt to come up with a better solution than ratting on him.

"Hey Whalon, you too, dude—put it on the hood," said the sergeant who had been driving the other jeep. Having exited the vehicle, he slapped his jeep loudly with a nightstick. God, I hated MPs.

Just as I was about to begin spilling my guts and pointing the finger at Shep, a third jeep came roaring up to where we stood. I recognized the MP captain who drove it.

"What the hell is goin' on here?" the captain asked the two sergeants.

The sergeants both saluted the captain. The MP sergeant who had gotten out of the first jeep answered the officer. "Their truck slid into the trench, sir. We were just about to check their pockets. This one is a junkie." He pointed to Scolwick. The dutiful sergeant stood at attention, waiting for a reply from the captain.

"It's all right, sergeant," the captain said as he smiled and patted me on the back. "This is the soldier who works at the pool." He pointed toward the Bayou. "Whalon's a good guy. He let me swim late one night after closing. Let them go and call a tow to get this truck out of the ditch."

The captain returned the sergeants' salutes, got back in his jeep, and drove off.

So that was where I recognized him from! I then remembered that the captain had come to the pool one night after ten, asking if he could swim some laps. I turned on the pool lights and let him swim for an hour. When he finished with the laps, the captain climbed out of the water, thanked me, and drove off in his jeep. At the time, I had no idea he was an MP officer.

"Shit, Whalon—why didn't you tell me that you're the dude from the Bayou?" the second sergeant asked. "Shit, man—get outta here, dude. That was an unbelievable party at the pool a few months ago, man. Scolwick, you wait here for the tow truck to pull you out." Then the sergeant said to me in a friendly tone, "hey Whalon, when's the next party? That last one was a real ass-kicker—later, man."

The two sergeants hopped into their jeeps and drove off, leaving Shep and me alone on the side of the road. We both sweated profusely. My legs shook, I couldn't swallow, and my heart had slowed to about four hundred beats a minute.

Scolwick started smiling at our good fortune. "Don't mean nothin', Whalon. The Butcher's got it under control."

I checked to make sure no MPs lurked nearby. Out of view of the tower guard, I grabbed the vials in my pocket and handed them to Shep without saying a word, then turned to walk the 500 yards back to the Bayou.

"Don't sweat the small shit, Whalon!" he yelled to me.

Without turning around, I flashed Sheppard "The Butcher" Scolwick the double "bird" salute and on rubbery legs began jogging toward the Bayou.

I never knew his real name. He was simply known throughout the battalion as "Butter-Balls." Butter (as most guys referred to him) was easily seventy-five pounds overweight, wore thick Coke-bottle eyeglasses, and had skin as white as Casper the Friendly Ghost. He was also the only Caucasian "black" guy that I had ever met. Butter acted black, and hung out only with black dudes. I asked him one time why everybody treated him as if he were black. He gave me an incredulous look and responded: "Because I *am* black, fool!" On another occasion, I asked Butter his real name, hoping to finally uncover the mystery. He flashed the same look and replied, "Butter-Balls, fool!" He talked shit like the black guys, gave the "dap" handshake like the black guys, and would threaten to kick your "white ass" if you crossed his "black ass." Nobody was actually afraid of the portly Butter, but everyone truly feared the hoodlum faction of blacks he ran with. It was a complete mystery to everybody why the militant blacks welcomed this white dude into their inner circle.

The first time I met Butter, I sat reading *Stars and Stripes* (a military newspaper) in the mess hall and eating the slop du jour. I had just moved to the Sugar Shack the week before. Butter sat at another table with five or six black guys, and then he got up and walked over to me.

294

"Hey dude," Butter said in a sarcastic tone, "you the joker from the swimmin' pool?" He took a seat next to me and began eating the cornbread from my tray.

"Yeah, I just started a few weeks ago," I answered, wondering what this fat slob was doing eating my food. "I'm Pete Whalon, transferred from Saigon." I wanted to stuff his fat face in my lumpy mashed potatoes, but his scary-looking cheering section of black thugs in the back was egging him on. I decided to play it cool and see where he'd lead the conversation.

"Me and the peanut gallery," he gestured toward the two tables in the back, "are comin' down later for a swim—you got beer there?"

He finished my cornbread and began eating my cherry cobbler with his pudgy fingers. The black guys in back started getting louder. Everybody in the mess hall was watching our table, seeing how I'd react to this white "brother."

"No problem, man," I calmly replied. "About what time are you guys coming down?" I wanted to make sure I had time to go to the PX and pick up some more brew for my new friends.

"Later, pool boy." Butter didn't tell me when they'd arrive, but I assumed it would be after closing hours. He stood to leave, then reached and grabbed my glass of milk, chugged the remaining contents, and yelled to his mob in the back, "He's cool!" They erupted with hooting and hollering.

On their way out of the mess hall, one of the black guys from the back called to me, "Hey pool dude, thanks man." He flashed me the peace sign and walked out the door.

One of the guys sitting a few tables down from mine stopped by on his way out. "Hey man, don't even mess with those dudes," he warned. "Butter-Balls is an asshole, and the other dudes with him are vicious, man." He left without waiting for a response.

That evening about eight, Private Butter-Balls and thirteen black guys noisily stormed into the Bayou. At the time, I was the only lifeguard working at the pool. I stood on the pool deck, nervously awaiting their arrival. Most of the mob gave me a slight courtesy wave, then headed for the water. For the next two hours, they screamed obscenities, thrashed around in the water, and chugged the four cases of beer I had put on ice for them. Sufficiently drunk, and exhausted from wrestling in the water, the feral gang emerged from the pool and staggered back toward the company.

The black guy who had earlier thanked me in the mess hall lagged behind and walked over to where I sat in front of the Sugar Shack. "Hey man, I'm Shag," he said, offering me his fist for some dap. "Thanks for the use of the pool. Some of those guys are assholes, I know," he said, pointing to the pack stumbling up the dirt hill. "Don't mind Butter. It's the first time in his life he's ever been cool— know what I mean?" Shag winked at me. "What's your name, man?" He stuck out his hand for some more dap.

"I'm Pete Whalon." His sincerity showed and he appreciated the nighttime use of the pool. "You're welcome, Shag. Thanks." I don't know why I thanked him—probably out of relief that I had survived the ordeal unscathed.

"Later, Whalon." He took off running toward the hill to catch up with his buddies.

After that first night at the pool, Butter-Balls acted really cool and much friendlier toward me every time he visited the valley. Butter grew on me (like a rash) and I began to enjoy mixing it up verbally with him on his trips to the Bayou.

One day as I sat in the sun with Butter-Balls, he turned to me out of the blue and remarked: "Ya know, Whale, if we had room for one more white black guy, it'd be you—but we don't, so tough shit."

He started snorting and slapping me on the back.

C Company was home to the undisputed venereal-disease champion in Vietnam. Darby "the Dick" Pellco hailed from Lincoln, Nebraska. Darby proudly kept everybody posted on his ever-rising bouts with VD, and made it his badge of honor.

"Hey PW," Darby called to me one day. "That's eighteen, man. Had the 'clap' eighteen times, dude—cool huh? That's gotta be the Nam record." ("Clap" was the name we conveniently used for all kinds of venereal diseases.) Darby's chest would swell with pride at such moments when he could report having another case of the clap. His numerous genital infections stemmed not from a case of plain bad luck. A simple answer existed: Darby "the Dick" Pellco would screw any Vietnamese woman without hesitation. Old, young, ugly, sick, dirty, fat, skinny—it made no difference to "the Dick." He had to have it at least once every day.

It was standard practice (and a running joke) among all who knew of his condition to move aside when he came our way and call to him as if to a leper: "Hey Dick, got 'clap' today?" He'd giggle, flash the peace sign, and ask if you had seen the short squat whore from Company A, or the mama-san with the large birthmark on her neck that cleans hooch 7. Like a ravenous lion in constant search of his next prey, "the Dick" prowled the battalion area. Darby truly believed that as long as he could obtain penicillin, he had nothing to worry about. His addiction was perverse, pitiful, and comical all at the same time.

One afternoon as I wandered through Company C searching for Harper, I spotted Darby strolling out of his hooch, holding hands with one of the greasy mama-sans who worked in the mess hall. It was difficult for me to guess the age of older Vietnamese women, but this one looked at least seventy. Enveloped with wrinkles, she had crooked, black teeth and sported dirty white pants. I stopped and stared at Darby in utter disbelief.

I then called him over to me so the mama-san couldn't hear us talking. "Darby, dude, please man, tell me you didn't—are you shittin' me, dude?" I really didn't want to know but I couldn't control my burning curiosity.

He tittered like a schoolgirl, flashed me the peace sign, and gladly answered my question. "I just finished and it was bitchin', man." He disgustingly circled his lips with his tongue. "She's paid for until two. You want her for a while, Pete?" Darby asked, and then laughed.

He rushed back to her side, not waiting for my response. They both chuckled and pointed at me as they continued walking back to the mess hall, hand in hand. The vivid image of Darby "the Dick" Pellco and "Mess Hall Mama-San" leisurely strolling up the street, holding hands, still haunts me to this day!

Chapter XXXI
It's Over
(Roy Orbison, 1964)

In early November 1970, on a dreary, rainy day, I said adios to Frank Montecalvo and Buddy Beard. Their one-year tours in Nam had ended and they were headed home to America. I sullenly watched the jeep taking them to the Processing Center disappear from view. Wade "Sleepy" Fossett, the only remaining lifeguard besides me, was scheduled to leave Vietnam on December 1, 1970. Although I had tried many times, I couldn't convince any of them to extend their tour in Nam and stay with me down on the Bayou. I had decided that if the decision were left up to me, I'd work at the pool by myself. I didn't want to take a chance on having some druggie loser getting assigned to the Bayou.

In mid-November, I submitted my paperwork for the final extension of my Vietnam tour. Someone had informed me it was only a formality. However, since the time of my first extension, the C Company commander had changed and Corporal Haskell had completed his tour months before. Still, I had no reason to believe that a problem might exist with my 110-day final extension.

A week after submitting my papers to the CC, I was summoned to the office for a meeting with the new company commander, Captain Milton Quaintance. I naively believed he wanted to inform me of my extension approval in person, and thank me for extending my tour in Vietnam.

"Come in, Private Whalon," Captain Quaintance barked when I knocked on his door. "Please, take a seat." The captain was all business. I arrived prepared to be humble when he expressed his gratitude.

"Thank you, sir." I smartly saluted, removed my cap (I had worn my jungle fatigues to impress him), and sat down. I quickly realized that I had serious problems the instant he uttered his first chilling words.

"I've been reading over your less-than-stellar file, Private Whalon," the captain began as he thumbed through a stack of papers on his desk. "You've had a pretty soft ride in the Army so far, young man," Quaintance gruffly noted as he continued to intently stare at my paperwork. "Hawaii, Saigon, and then somehow you conned your way into the assignment as a lifeguard. Sounds more like R&R to me."

He looked up for the first time and wryly smiled at me. My mood was sinking faster than the Titanic.

"Here's the deal, Whalon: I'm required by the post commander to assign two men to the main post office for the Christmas mail rush. They get swamped over there with packages and cards during this time each year. If you don't volunteer for this assignment, I'll not approve your final extension. That means bucko, you'll be sent back to the world on December tenth to finish out your three years with the Army—it's your choice, Whalon." He leaned back and clasped his hands behind his neck. The captain's shit-eating grin was one I had seen many times before over the course of my time in the Army.

I mounted my impromptu defense. "Sir," I began, "Captain Fuller promised me that if I extended for six months, he'd approve my second extension and let me keep my assignment at the pool. That's the only reason I extended, sir. If I'd known I'd lose my job at the pool I'd be home now."

I instinctively knew that what his predecessor had promised didn't matter a hill of beans to Captain Quaintance. He was "old-school" Army and delighted in screwing young hippies like me. Most lifers believed that all GIs from California were useless hippies. Nowhere in 1970 was the

300

"generation gap" more evident than in the United States military.

"Fuller's back in the world now, private!" the captain growled, gazing directly into my eyes. I borrowed Bellotti's old trick and scratched one of my eyes with my middle finger. "I'm your company commander now—B Company transferred you back to C Company months ago, when you extended the first time. It is your choice, Whalon. I need an answer by 1700 tomorrow!" the captain boomed as he pounded the desk with his fist. "That's all Mr. Lifeguard!"

I stood, scratched my eye once more for spite, and walked out of the office. I knew from experience it would do absolutely no good to argue—it would just give this vindictive snake more satisfaction. Screw you, Captain Bligh!

I slowly began walking back to the Bayou, pondering my options. Almost eighteen months in country—for what? If I didn't take the post office assignment, I'd still have to serve out the remainder of my full three years back in the States, meaning I had spent an extra six months in Nam for absolutely no reason. I was too close to the end to let the loss of my pool gig stop me. I needed to keep my eye on the "prize." I wanted out of the Army now more than ever.

I turned around and marched right back into Captain Quaintance's office. He was combing the few strands of hair remaining on his bulbous head when I burst in.

"I'll take the post office job," I said, louder than necessary. I had intentionally refrained from using "sir." "When do I start?" I glared in his eyes, biting my tongue. (I wouldn't give this bully the satisfaction of appearing as though I gave a shit.

"I knew you'd cave in, Whalon," the captain replied, laughing. "Losers like you can't wait to get back to the world with your mommy and daddy. The Army is too damn tough for your type—long-haired, hippie losers."

At least I have hair, you bald-headed simpleton, I wanted to scream in his puffy face, but didn't. I bit down harder on my tongue and glared back at the gloating fool. I could do 110 days with a harpoon shoved up my ass, dude— standing on my head in a rice paddie and whistling the USC fight song, asshole. Bring it on, Captain Bligh, bring it on! My mind was screaming all this at the malevolent jackal lecturing me.

"Report here on Monday at 0730, private!" he roared. "You'll go over with the other loser that I assigned there. Also, check back tomorrow for a hooch assignment. You're moving back to the company area on Friday—party's over, Mr. Poolman. Party is O-V-E-R!" The captain raised his voice as he spelled out the last word. In an insignificant act of defiance, I saluted him with my left hand and exited the building.

As always, I tried to look on the bright side; my extension was approved. I had only 110 days until my return to Redondo Beach. I had been in country longer than anyone in C Company except Sheppard "The Butcher" Scolwick, who was scheduled to leave soon. My time spent in the Bayou had given me a huge measure of "unearned" status. I knew just about everybody in the battalion with the ability to pull strings for me, and still had run of the place. I'd be a martyr for taking the "bullet" and giving up my glorious assignment, just to get out of the Army five months early. By the time I reached the Bayou, I felt pretty good, although the reason mystified me somewhat.

I made it one of my first priorities to find a room in the company where I could live by myself. The rooms in the hooches were tiny and cramped, and I had gotten quite spoiled from living in the Sugar Shack. Living alone would ease a little of the pain.

That evening, I visited the company and began my quest for a room. With help from a Bayou regular, I learned about two junkies that roomed together and who had orders to return home in seven days. I visited them with a bag full of junk food from the PX and $100 cash. Keenly aware that junkies always went broke by the fifteenth of every month (it was November 21), and that they usually begged for loans to supply their habit, I knocked on the druggies' door.

"Who's there?" a raspy, coughing voice asked from inside.

"It's Whalon; I work at the pool. Can I talk to you guys?" I politely requested.

"Come in, man," a different voice from the room invited me. I opened the door to a surprisingly clean, neat room, and saw two guys sitting in beach chairs listening to the Zager & Evans song, "In the Year 2525." For some strange reason, that was a favorite song among junkies.

"I'm Pete Whalon." I extended my hand. "I'm the lifeguard at the pool. I've seen you guys around the company before," I lied. "You guys want some chips?"

I handed my bag of potato chips to the guy wearing sunglasses. Both junkies looked as if they hadn't gone out in the sun since grade school. Heroin addicts reminded me very much of Dracula: sunlight made them recoil in horror.

"Hi, I'm Roscoe Kreyche. My friends call me 'Cap', and this is Stu Kulp—what's up?" the bigger of the two asked.

I proceeded to tell them my sad story as I fed them candy, cookies, and more rippled potato chips (a favorite among the addicts). When the right time came, I pulled out five $20 MPC bills and spread them on the small table in the middle of the room. Their eyes bulged out.

I knew exactly what the junkies were thinking—a hundred bucks could keep them both high until they went home the next week. I guess I should've felt some guilt, but I didn't. We made a deal right then. They'd take all of their shit out of the room by Saturday night and I'd move in Sunday. They'd be on their own to find a place to stay until the following Friday, the day they'd return to the world. Roscoe and Stu would have no trouble finding other junkies to crash with, since the pair would be holding a fresh stash of "smack" for all to share.

The next morning, I reported to the CO's office as instructed. I assured the worried corporal that I had found a room and that I'd be moving in Sunday night. He was a little concerned but accepted my word that I'd be living in the company by Monday morning. Apparently Captain Quaintance had instructed him to make sure I moved out of the pool house no later than Sunday night. I wasn't aware at the time, but they had already found a replacement for my lifeguard position—some wannabe lifer, with zero personality.

On my last Saturday night staying at the Sugar Shack, I decided to go to the Enlisted Men's Club on the far side of the battalion. A couple of my friends wanted to treat me to all the beer I could drink, since it was my last official night as head lifeguard. Although I rarely went to the club, I thought it would take my mind off the uncertain future I faced.

We arrived at the club just as the Vietnamese band started to play. Most of the Vietnamese bands that performed on Long Binh had learned to play the popular American rock songs of the time. They'd often take requests from the drunken guys in the club. By far, the most popular and most requested song, and one that every band sang at least once each set, was "The Green, Green Grass of Home." It was a sentimental favorite of the GIs for obvious reasons.

The more the juicers drank, the more they wanted to hear "The Green, Green Grass of Home." And, of course, everybody sang along. Notably, the Vietnamese people had great difficulty in pronouncing their "Rs." So, when they sang the trendy song, it sounded more like "The Gween, Gween Gwass of Home." This became a standard joke among GIs when requesting the tune and singing along. Everybody loved to sing the Vietnamese pronunciation. There was nothing quite like a beer hall filled with 250 intoxicated GIs singing off-key and using no Rs in their words.

After two hours of swilling beer and requesting songs that had lots of Rs in them, I said good-bye to my two drunken friends and returned to the Bayou. Sleepy Fossett had received a two-week early-out and returned home four days earlier. I'd spend my last night poolside in total isolation.

I filled up a pipe with some killer weed and sat outside the Shack, recalling the memorable people and events from my past eighteen months in country. A wave of nostalgic sentimentality consumed me. It was one of the few times since landing in Vietnam that I had been completely alone. I finished my pipe and jumped into the invigorating pool water. I climbed onto an inflatable mat and quietly floated around the pool. I laughed to myself as I softly sang the latest Beatle hit, "Let It Be"—leaving out all of the Rs, of course.

When I find myself in times of twoble,

Motha Mawee come to me,

Speaking woods of wisdom,

Wet it be.

Chapter XXXII
Return to Sender
(Elvis Presley, 1962)

Sunday morning, I checked out a truck from the motor pool, drove to the Sugar Shack, and loaded all my worldly possessions. After loading the truck, I spent the next twenty minutes carving a few words on the wooden pool deck, just above the last stair. They read: "Whalon, Born on the Bayou, 69-70." I then drove to C Company and, with the help of a few friends, crammed everything into my miniature room. With no ceremony, or pomp and circumstance, the golden era of the Bayou and my memorable days in the Sugar Shack had ended. I sat sadly on my bunk, unable to identify the feelings that passed through me. It was as if I had lost a loved one. Well Pete, you had a good run, I thought to myself.

I began organizing my tiny living quarters. A few guys dropped by to see if it was really true—Whalon had abandoned the Bayou to live at Company C.

I went to a movie that night, then slipped back into my room for a good night's sleep. Private Whalon had to report for work the next morning at 0730—an especially discouraging prospect.

The next morning at seven-thirty, I slowly hiked up the hill from hooch 8 to the CC's office for assignment to the main post office on Long Binh. The company clerk, Corporal Higgs, stood pensively in the doorway. The other hippie assigned to the postal duty sat in the office filling out some papers. Corporal Higgs motioned me inside.

"Hi Whalon," Higgs greeted me, offering a handshake. "This is Private Mark Devilbiss. His friends call him 'Devil.' He'll be working with you at the PO. Devil is from Pocatello, Idaho."

Who gives a flying shit, I thought. I shook Mark's hand and then posed a question. "Hey Mark, who'd you crap on to get this shit detail?"

Mark just shrugged his shoulders. His shiny new fatigue uniform gave him away as a clueless cherry.

Higgs continued, "I don't know how long your assignment is for, but when I know, you'll know. Do what they tell you at the PO. You're assigned to them—don't screw up or Quaintance will jump down your shit. Any questions?"

Higgs carefully checked the clipboard in his hand, making sure he hadn't missed anything. My curiosity got the best of me.

"Yeah," I said in my most sarcastic voice, "what lifer got my job at the pool?"

The corporal didn't answer. A small truck drove up outside.

"That's your ride, kids—have fun. After today, you guys will have to walk to the PO and back. It's not far, you'll see." He seemed in a hurry to get rid of us.

Higgs quickly closed the office door behind us. Cherry Boy Devilbiss and I jumped into the cab of the truck. Mark had the unmistakable blank stare of a true rookie on his face—a mix of confusion and fear. I gazed out the window for the entire five-minute ride to the post office. I had no desire to answer inane questions from the frightened, pimple-faced newcomer.

We drove through the gate and up to a gigantic single-level, corrugated-metal structure. In front of the building, thirty or forty other "volunteers" milled around. Most of them were wide-eyed cherries about to experience their first shit detail in Hell. Our driver instructed us to wait with the group and then drove off.

I walked up to the building and looked inside. It was the size of a large airplane hangar. Along the back wall, thousands of canvas bags lay stacked at least six feet high. To the left and right, against the sides of the building, hundreds of boxes rested in haphazard piles. The center of the structure was open, with the names of the various Long Binh battalions brightly painted on the cement floor. I ambled back toward the group of fresh meat standing in small clusters. On the other side of the open yard sat dozens of parked trucks. All the vehicles had the words U.S. MAIL stenciled on their doors. I spied a herd of lifers—looking in our direction, no less—huddled in front of an outhouse sized shack marked "Main Office." The exposed yard area where we loitered equaled the length of two football fields. God, I missed the Bayou!

I noticed two lifers breaking from the group and heading our way. I smelled an orientation brewing. I tucked my hair under my cap, unsure if these mailmen would begin with a "tough-guy" routine and yell at me to get a haircut. To a dedicated lifer, spotting a GI with hair hanging past his ears was like a prospector discovering a mother lode of gold.

"Okay men," the eldest of the two sergeants shouted as he approached our group. "Get your cherry asses into the mail center. It's getting hot out here, and you're gonna need your energy—I shit you not."

The second sergeant, a hulking man with a thick moustache and a half-smoked cigar wedged between his lips, had already gone inside. We all moved into the building, stopping next to the mountain of mailbags.

"Take a seat on the floor, men," the cigar-smoking sergeant ordered. "I'm Master Sergeant Tobiason. This is a classic Army shit detail you've heard so much about. I can only assume you've all screwed up and your CC wanted to dump your ass on us. Trust me when I tell you that you don't want to screw up here. You'll end up cleaning shitters at LBJ." The sergeant blew a perfect smoke ring and continued. "During the Christmas mail rush, our incoming mail is ten times normal and outgoing is five times the load. See all these bags and boxes behind me? They'll all be sorted and sent on their way each day before you drag your ass outta here. You leave when you're done, and not before. If you think it's too hot or you're too tired to lift another box or you

308

feel sick and want to complain to me, I'll save you a trip to my office. My response will always be the same: tough shit, Cherry! If by some miracle you finish early one day, we'll take advantage of the empty warehouse and scrub it down from top to bottom. If you think about complaining to your CO back at the company, feel free, ladies—but remember, the reason you're here is because they don't like you—ain't life a bitch, ladies?" The sergeant was thoroughly enjoying himself. I had stayed in country too long to let his lifer bullshit intimidate me.

When Tobiason finished, the gray-haired sergeant took over. He split us up into small groups of six or seven and gave us our assignments for the week. He also informed us that job tasks would change weekly so we could learn all the duties at the facility. Like most aspects of Army life, it was really quite simple. We'd either unload mailbags and boxes from trucks, load mailbags and boxes onto trucks, or sort mail from different battalions and load it on trucks. The first two assignments were ball-busting, backbreaking ordeals; the other one, tedious and monotonous. They brought back fond memories of Warehouse 32.

Temperatures in the facility averaged above 110 degrees. By noon every day of my first week, I had exhausted myself from the sheer amount of physical energy expended loading and unloading packages. If we worked our asses off, and cut our breaks short, we usually finished by 7:00 p.m. By the time I returned to the company, ate dinner, and showered, bedtime had arrived. Hell itself had engulfed me.

On Monday of the second week, my group was taking a break when a cocky young sergeant with wild eyes walked up to us.

"Hello men. I'm Sergeant Lancaster and I need two more volunteers for the new night-shift crew..."

Before the sweating sergeant could get more words out of his mouth, I shot up my hand like an ass-kissing schoolboy. I didn't have to think about this one. It was a no-brainer. At night no pounding sun beat down on the building, turning it into the world's biggest sauna. Also, the assignment could never equal the grueling drudgery of the day shift.

"Hold on, Whalon. Let me finish." I kept my arm raised, not wanting to take the chance that the sergeant would forget who had his hand up first. I remembered in high school that all the "brains" kept their hands wiggling in the air even though the teacher didn't call on them. As he continued to talk, more hands shot up.

Fortunately for me, the sergeant believed in the old adage "first come, first served." By the time he had explained the night-shift duties, all seven members of our bunch had their hands waving in the air, struggling to get the sergeant's attention. Sorry cherries—too late!

"Well, let's see," he slowly said, prolonging the suspense. "Whalon, your hand was up first and next was Dexter in the back. You two guys go back to your company right now and report back here tonight at 6:00 o'clock sharp. You're on the night-shift now. I'll see you guys back here tonight." While the five loser cherries grumbled, I looked skyward and thanked God for the assist.

"See you tonight, Sergeant Lancaster—thanks," I responded, and then smiled.

I stood and hurried from the building before he could change his mind. I had no idea how tough the night shift would be, but I knew it couldn't be as dreadful as the day shift. Even if the night shift brought more work, at least the unrelenting daytime heat inside the tin oven wouldn't boil me alive. I returned to the company and took a short nap to refresh myself for the new working hours.

I returned to the post office by 5:30. The walk from my company took about twenty minutes. I wanted to be the first arrival of the new night-shift crew, just in case they overbooked and had to send someone back to days. Also, it was never too early to begin collecting Brownie points. In my book, playing the role of a kiss-ass brought no shame, so long as it provided the desired results.

At 6:05, Sergeant Lancaster entered the "Canvas Cave" (my new name for the sizeable building). The six new members of the night shift stood by unenthusiastically. Of course, no new assignment would be complete without the mandatory, droll orientation. I vowed to myself to act like a good boy for this one and pay attention to the sergeant. I even considered throwing in a logical, meaningful question just for fun. My compulsive desire for sarcastic retorts and witty observations would have to come under control for a while. I'd portray the model soldier for as long as necessary.

"Welcome to the night detail," Sergeant Lancaster began. "You guys made a wise decision volunteering for nights—I shit you not. See those bags over there?" He pointed to the middle of the building. There we viewed a large, wooden table with approximately twenty to twenty-five full canvas mail sacks scattered around it. Just in front of the table, empty canvas bags hung side by side on racks. Stenciled on the bags were the names of the various battalions on Long Binh. (Every battalion on Long Binh had its own mail sack.)

"Our job is to sort the fourth-class mail by battalions. Fourth-class mail consists of magazines, catalogs, newspapers, fliers, newsletters, reports, and any other junk mail. The day shift does not handle fourth-class." Lancaster sounded irritated at having to explain the night-shift duties. "We empty the full bags and distribute their content to the proper battalion bags. We then tie up the full battalion bags and stack them over there." He pointed to an area in the far corner of the Cave, where a large sign reading FOURTH-CLASS OUTGOING MAIL hung on the wall.

"When we're finished with all the fourth-class bags, we're done for the night and you can leave. The faster you work, the faster you get out of here—any questions?"

Had I heard him correctly? I wanted to make sure I had completely understood what he said. "Sergeant Lancaster, do you mean that when we divide all the mail in those bags, we're done with our shift?" I always instinctively knew that when something seemed too good to be true, it usually turned out that way.

"Yes, Whalon," he replied, obviously exasperated. "That is *exactly* what I mean."

There had to be a catch; I cautiously persisted. "Sergeant Lancaster, excuse me one more time. Are there more bags coming in tonight or is that it?" I pointed to the tiny pile of bags stacked around the table.

"That's it, Whalon—why, do you want more? Geez." He grinned at me and I smiled back as I shook my head no.

Maybe something was missing, but it looked to me as though six guys working at a swift pace could empty, distribute, and tie up those bags in less than four hours.

That first night in the Canvas Cave, it took us three hours and forty-five minutes to finish sorting all the fourth-class mail. The longest shift we worked during our first week lasted five hours. Somehow, someone had pushed me into the proverbial pile of shit, but once again I came out smelling like a dozen red roses!

Although Lancaster was a sergeant, no lifer blood coursed through his veins. He seemed as lazy as the rest of us. The sergeant would usually arrive at the Cave about 6:30 p.m., then stop at our sorting table and spend a few minutes shooting the shit with us as he rummaged around for *Penthouse* and *Playboy* magazines. Once Lancaster had found three or four to his liking, he'd retreat into his office for a little "quality time" with his Playmate of the Month. Since we wanted to finish the bags quickly and then leave, we had no need for him to motivate us with threats and insults.

It was wonderful having the days off. However, every time I ventured out into the sunshine, it made me nostalgic for the Bayou. One day, during my third week at the post office, I decided the time had come to visit the pool and meet the pickpocket who had swiped my lifeguard job. I compared my melancholy feelings about the loss of my lifeguard gig to those of a retired baseball superstar. The superstar missed playing baseball so much that, in the beginning, he couldn't visit the ballpark without trepidation. The Bayou was now my "ballpark," and I hadn't returned there since the Sunday I moved out.

I purposely visited the pool an hour before it opened so I could confront the thief without having a bunch of sunburned drunks interrupting us. As I approached the Sugar Shack, I could see someone in red swimming trunks hosing off the pool deck. He spotted me as I climbed the stairs to the deck and began moving my way.

I stuck out my hand and introduced myself. "Hi, I'm Pete Whalon," I greeted, as he shook my hand. "I was the lifeguard here before you. I thought I'd come down and see who took my place, that's all." I forced a smile.

He stood stone-faced. After an awkward pause, he responded, "I'm Sergeant Snow. Are you the idiot who put that there?" He pointed down at my creative deck carving. His gruff reply had the unmistakable tone of superiority. He didn't wait for me to answer. "They assigned me to the pool so I could straighten this place out and keep all the hippies and junkies from hanging out here." Snow then motioned for me to follow him into the Shack.

Once inside, the sergeant put his hands on his hips and noted, "As you can see, I threw out all the hippie shit you left behind," referring to the posters that had plastered the walls inside the Sugar Shack, and the bright, fluorescent-painted furniture I had crammed inside. (I knew I should've taken my Bob Dylan poster with me.) He had also removed all the neon black lights someone had shipped me from the States. What once reigned as a state-of-the-art party house and crash pad, oozing with '60s culture and counterculture, existed no more. In its place stood an insipid, open room, painted off-white, and furnished with only one standard Army-issue bunk and one small table with two chairs. It reminded me of Red's Live Bait Shack on the Redondo Pier. The old Sugar Shack had become a dwelling only the United

313

States Army could take pride in. It saddened and depressed me.

"Is there anything else, Private Whalon? I have lots of work to do before I open." Hey asshole, I *made* this place; there is no work to do, I thought.

The arrogant lifer was dismissing me. His smug attitude cried out for a crushing left hook to his square jaw. While I knew not to hit him, I had to say something to rattle his pretentious macho facade.

"That's cool, dude. I dig the early-lifer décor. Smells like anchovies in here though!" I slickly replied. (Something about raw sarcasm just warmed the cockles of my heart.)

I had intentionally called him "dude," knowing it would *really* piss him off. Then I added, "Oh, be extremely careful late at night down here. Those little dirt hills behind the pool are a hangout for druggies and juicers. They like to get wasted there, and most of 'em carry pistols in case anyone messes with 'em. Just don't piss them off and they'll leave you alone, probably." I quickly turned and started jogging toward the company.

My Camelot—the commune-like atmosphere, the gang of misfits, the deafening music, the intense water-football games, the marathon Monopoly sessions, and the ever-present individual, eccentric characters that made up the lifeblood of the Bayou—had vanished. "Snow-job" Snow had thoroughly sanitized my Xanadu and transformed it into a typical Army operation—operated under Army regulations, and run by a dedicated Army sergeant. The Bayou had croaked. As I often did in moments like this, I sought comfort in the words of a Bob Dylan tune—"The Times They Are a-Changin'." I sang it softly as I trotted along.

I stopped running when I reached the top of the hill. I regretted my decision to visit the pool. Uncertain of what to expect by going there, I found the ordeal had placed me in a state of mild depression. Providentially, I walked by the church where Dave Schrunk and I had spent our first night in Long Binh. It triggered fond memories.

Without thinking, I walked across the street and into the church. I knelt down in the pew where I had slept that initial night. Although I had entered the Army a practicing Catholic, I had attended church only a few times during my Vietnam tour. A sudden wave of guilt flashed through me as I silently recited the Lord's Prayer. I followed that with three Hail Marys, blessed myself with holy water, and then exited the church and headed toward my hooch.

Just before I entered it, a voice called to me: "Hey man, just a minute!" Turning around, I saw a long-limbed cherry boy running toward me. He reached me, out of breath, and shook my hand. "Are you Whalon, the dude from California who worked at the pool for the last year?" he asked, still trying to get his wind back.

"Yeah, but I'm not there anymore. Got screwed outta the job. Now I'm working at the post office," I said, not quite sure where the conversation would lead.

"I was talking to the cook, Scolwick, a few weeks ago, before he went home. He was tellin' me about that giant party you had there last year," he said with glazed eyes. "This cook dude said that you had over one thousand dudes there. Is that true, man? I was just wonderin' if he was tellin' the truth, that's all."

I felt like a washed-up ballplayer dealing with a snot-nosed kid asking me about the grand slam I hit in the 1955 World Series. I took this perfect opportunity to blow smoke up a young rookie's ass.

"Listen cherry," I said coolly, pointing my finger at him. "You seem like a cool dude so I'll tell you the truth about that night, but don't tell any lifers, okay? They're still after my ass for that blowout." The cherry boy shook his head as his eyes widened in anticipation. "Here's the gospel. We had fifteen hundred GIs, two hundred of the foxiest whores in Nam, five hundred cases of beer, and two hundred bottles of booze. We offered every drug known to man at this blowout—Purple Haze, Yellow Sunshine, Cambodian Red, smack, cocaine, opium, heroin, BTs, liquid speed, reds, whites, and mescaline. We placed the drugs on two tables, like a buffet. Some whacked-out speed freak stationed in Saigon brought a baby elephant in a giant dump truck and dumped him in the pool. He stayed in there all night thrashing around and spraying everybody with snot-water. Then we had to airlift that beast out with a Chinook the next morning. The shit that monster took in the pool was the size of a surfboard, dude." While I ad-libbed my bullshit tale, the cherry slowly nodded his head. "Apparently, somebody stole Peanuts the elephant from the zoo just for the bash. They say it was the biggest party in Nam history, dude—kinda like Woodstock, dude, without Joan Baez, Richie Havens, and Country Joe. Did thirty days in LBJ for that carnival, man" Without saying another word, I lightly smacked him on his cheek, flashed the peace sign, turned and walked into my hooch.

Years later, just like the thousands of people who lied about attending Woodstock, this bug-eyed cherry could tell his grandchildren about the night he attended the biggest and most outrageous party ever thrown by American soldiers in Vietnam.

Chapter XXXIII

Time Is on My Side

(Rolling Stones, 1964)

The "Six-Pack" (the pet name Sergeant Lancaster gave to the half dozen of us working the PO night shift) soon became quick and efficient at distributing the fourth-class mail. In fact, within two weeks, we rarely took longer than three hours to complete the job. That meant we could be in by 6:00 p.m. and out by 9:00 p.m. Also, in the two weeks before Christmas, we'd report for work, distribute the mail, and sometimes finish before the day shift had completed its mail distribution. Occasionally a large truck filled with sacks of mail would arrive late in the day. That required the day shift to distribute all mail before they quit for the day, which meant they had to work past our 9:00 p.m. quitting time.

After our second week, we moved the night-shift operation into a smaller building behind the Canvas Cave. On the evenings when we finished before the day shift, we quietly exited through the back door and climbed the fence separating us from the road behind the PO. The six of us feared that if the suckers on the day shift saw us they'd harbor resentment at our perceived good fortune. (They had been busting their butts since 8:00 a.m.) We joked that the entire gang would surround us, beat us to death with fourth-class junk mail, stuff us into canvas sacks, and send us to Timbuktu—or worse, Arkansas.

As a group, the Six-Pack had consciously treated Sergeant Lancaster very well. We often brought him cigarettes and bottles of Jack Daniels from the PX. All six of us were well aware of the "gravy train" we rode on, and wanted the free ride to continue. Meanwhile, incredibly lazy Lancaster never lifted a finger to help us. He knew we wouldn't complain for fear of getting kicked back to days. I respected Lancaster's savvy and admired the way the sergeant hustled us, casually mentioning that his booze or smokes supply had dwindled to desperately low levels.

One evening a few days before Christmas, Sergeant Lancaster strolled out of his office and joined us at the mail racks. "How's it goin' tonight, guys?" he said warmly. I sensed that he wanted to put in a PX order that we'd obediently deliver the next night. It was shakedown time at the PO, but I didn't care. The reward of staying on the night shift justified the minimal price we had to pay.

"Hope you guys finish early tonight," he slyly said. "Some of the guys here at the post office are havin' a Christmas party on Friday. I told them I'd supply the booze." Lancaster rubbed his chin as though deep in thought. "Let's see, I think I'll bring two bottles of Jack (Jack Daniels), two bottles of JW (Johnny Walker), and two bottles of Early Times. That should do it, I think." (Translation: "You six underlings get together and each buy me a bottle of booze and set it in my office tomorrow night".) "See you mail boys later!" He returned to his office to fantasize about *Playboy's* Miss December.

Although Sergeant Lancaster was an accomplished con man and two-bit hustler, his style appealed to me.

By mid-January, the influx of mail had slowed and many of the slaves on the day shift had returned to their companies for a new assignment. I had just over two months remaining in Vietnam. After January 1, I began mentally mapping out a strategy for the final days of my tour. I definitely didn't want to join my company and spend the last two months typing at the nerve-wracking Comm Center. I hoped that somehow I could remain at the post office, on the night shift, until the time came for me to leave Nam.

Lancaster had informed us in December that our assignment at the PO would end in early February. Like me, all the guys in our group had decided long ago that they preferred to stay at the PO as long as possible. It was a much better situation than anything we'd face back at our companies.

By the night of February 7, 1971, when Sergeant Lancaster called me into his office, I had exactly fifty days remaining in my checkered military career.

"Whalon, sit down," the sergeant said, then offered me a Coke. "How long you got left in country?" He looked at his *Penthouse* magazine off and on as we spoke.

"Fifty days, sergeant," I answered.

"Wow, you are 'short,' dude," he said smiling. "I get to keep two of you guys here 'til March 15th. The other four are being sent back to their companies this Friday. I haven't yet decided who stays. You wanna stay here and play mailman Whalon?" he asked, knowing the answer.

"Definitely, Sergeant Lancaster," I said, though I knew *special* conditions would soon follow.

"Okay, here's the deal. I'll let you stay and pick the other guy to work with, under one condition." He leaned forward, looking around to see if anyone was within earshot. "I've got guard duty next Wednesday and one more after that. They're my last ones scheduled until I go home in three months. You pull my two guard-duty shifts and you stay here. I can get a sub to cover for you at the PO those nights." Lancaster leaned back and clasped his hands behind his head. That was it, I thought. Two nights of guard duty and I keep this assignment.

"No problem, I'd love to take your guard duty," I responded. "Where do I sign?"

"Cool, Whalon. Now, who do you want to stay with you?" He said, about to conclude the deal. I knew he'd have chosen me anyway. He knew that I could control the other guys and that I made sure we completed everything before we left each evening. Getting rid of his guard duty was just a bonus for him.

"Keep Woodburn, but don't tell the other guys I got to pick, okay?" I didn't want to piss off the other four guys.

The next night at the end of our shift, Sergeant Lancaster came out to the work area and informed us of his decision to keep Woodburn and me on at the PO. The other four guys would return to their companies after the completion of our shift on Friday night.

I feigned surprise at the announcement and demonstrated the proper amount of humility. Private Darwin Woodburn acted genuinely surprised and made no attempt to hide his joy from the group. I don't believe the other guys appreciated Darwin's pumping his fist in the air, barking like a harpooned walrus, and shaking Sergeant Lancaster's hand vigorously. I had chosen Woodburn to stay with me because he was the quietest of the Six-Pack and he enjoyed listening to my bullshit stories about life in Redondo Beach.

At Long Binh, guard duty fell on all low-ranking soldiers once a month. Anyone higher than corporal covered this post less often. Each company had a list posted, letting everyone know when his guard-duty shifts would take place. It was standard practice for many GIs to pay someone to pull their duty. The guys with money paid the guys who needed money (usually junkies, cherries, or idiots) to take their place. Since my arrival at Long Binh, I'd pulled guard duty only one time. For some peculiar reason, lifeguards at the pool didn't have to stand guard duty. I never asked why, fearing that someone would realize the absurdity of the rule—and then try to change it.

The Wednesday evening of Lancaster's first guard-duty shift, I reported to the guard shack, just inside Gate 1. Guard-duty assignments lasted twelve hours, from 6:00 p.m. to 6:00 a.m. Each GI spent six hours in one of the bunkers surrounding the perimeter of Long Binh, then six hours in the guard shack—sleeping, playing cards, or just hanging out. Those in the guard shack were on standby, just in case any problems at the fence line arose. Basically, guard duty consisted of twelve hours of boredom and small talk.

The Vietcong rarely attacked Long Binh due to its massive size and vast number of troops stationed there. Each bunker held two guys at all times during the night. Usually, the two would take turns sleeping. I was assigned to the second shift, midnight to 6:00 a.m., in Bunker 33, with a redneck cherry. (I had developed a cruel habit of calling "redneck" everyone I didn't know, didn't like, or didn't understand.)

With two hours remaining until dawn and the end of our shift, I was pretending to doze. The bobble-head in the bunker with me had arrived in country only eleven days before. When he discovered that I had lived in country twenty-one months, he began asking dumb-ass rookie questions about the war, drugs, lifers, whores, and anything else that popped in his simple mind. I opened my eyes slightly and there stood "Goober" (the name I had chosen for him), staring at me.

I was just about to jump in his shit for freaking me out, when the distinct clatter of M16 fire broke the silence. It came from the next bunker down from us, about 200 yards away. We instinctively ducked, then peeked over the top row of sandbags to see what was happening. We could see only tracer rounds fired by the two guys in Bunker 34. Goober grabbed his M16 and pointed it toward the wire, ready to start blasting away like John Wayne.

"Hey Goob!" I yelled at the petrified rookie. "Sit down and wait for the sergeant, and put down that rifle before you shoot yourself in your country ass!"

I was scared shitless but I didn't want him to know. Sweat ran down his face as he gasped for air.

The firing stopped for a few seconds, then started again. Within five minutes, three choppers appeared overhead, shining bright lights down on the wire. The firing stopped when two jeeps pulled up to the bunker. I stayed down, occasionally taking a peek. I couldn't believe this was happening to me with only forty-four days left in country. I looked up and saw a jeep coming our way.

"Aim your 16 at the wire, Goobs," I said, pointing toward the oncoming jeep. "And look like you're ready for action—sergeant's comin'."

I grabbed my M16 and took the firing position toward the wire. The jeep skidded to a halt in front of our bunker and a sergeant got out.

"Relax men," the sergeant advised. "Those two idiots in 34 fired at a German Shepherd caught in the wire. All they had to do was fire off a flare and they could've seen the mutt struggling to free itself. Did you guys hear a dog barking or anything else?" he asked us.

"No, only the firing when it started," I reported. "Sergeant, did they kill the dog?"

"Nope, two hundred rounds into the wire and the dog doesn't have a scratch—idiots!" The sergeant laughed. "I have to go fill out reports. Keep up the good work, men." He got into his jeep and sped off.

I was glad the pooch had decided to cross in front of their bunker. I probably would've opened fire, just as they had done. Since I knew I wouldn't be able to get to sleep, I thought I'd use the time to freak out the cherry and pay him back for the hours of boring, mindless conversation he made me endure.

"Okay Goober, you gotta lighten up when the shit hits, man—this stuff happens all the time here." I intentionally lied, hoping to scare him into shitting his pants. "I thought you were going to cry, dude. You got over three hundred days left in this shit-hole, man. You're in Nam now, cherry boy, not back on the block banging Betty (a line I ripped off from my drill sergeant in basic) and smokin' dope with your fairy friends. This is for real, dude!" I pointed my finger in his dripping face and glared in his eyes. "You better grow up fast or the bush will eat you alive—I shit you not, cherry boy—I shit you not. Got it, Goobs?" The Duke would've been mighty proud of my bullshit speech to this redneck rook. I fought to stifle laughter.

"Yes sir, uh, I mean Pete." He stuttered and cowered in the corner of the bunker like a scolded puppy. "I'm sorry, thanks man. Don't be mad." Then I felt sorry for him. As a sign of my compassion and guilt, I decided to throw the quivering pooch a bone.

"Look dude, you did okay for new meat." I walked over and patted him on his back. "But just be aware of what is going on around you—and don't start smokin' smack when the junkies offer you some—it'll kill you, I swear to God." I tossed in a drug warning for good measure. "Let's get our shit together—we only got thirty-five minutes left on our shift." I forced a smile. "By the way, what's your real name?" I asked for the first time that night, getting soft in my old age.

"Alvin, Alvin Pumple the Third," he said sheepishly, extending his hand.

Sorry I asked, dude!

Chapter XXXIV
The Long and Winding Road
(Beatles, 1970)

By March 6, 1971, the day I turned twenty-two years old, I had spent twenty-two months of my life in the Republic of Vietnam. With only twenty-four days remaining in country, I began planning my homecoming. Like most GIs, I looked at my months spent in Nam as a complete waste of time. At that point in my young life, I had no clue of the valuable life lessons my service stint had instilled in me, nor of the immeasurable appreciation I unknowingly developed for the freedom granted me as a United States citizen. My petty concerns were much more mundane. I needed to get a Coppertone tan, grow my locks as long as possible, and purchase accessory items from the PX that would complement the state-of-the-art stereo system waiting for me back home. I had bought the stereo through the PX catalog and asked that the components be shipped directly to Redondo Beach. I couldn't wait to get home and open the boxes. Also, although most of my friends had stopped writing me months before, I decided to send letters to everyone whose address I still had. I wanted the word spread throughout the South Bay—Pete Whalon will be home on or about April 1, and he's ready to party!

I also wanted to collect money some absentminded bandits still in country owed me. As in Saigon, moochers at Long Binh had dubbed me a "soft touch" during the first few weeks of my arrival. Over time, I'd created something of a welfare state in the battalion. Many of the "friends" owing me money had long since gone home. However, there still lingered around the battalion a large contingent of derelicts who had conveniently forgotten to pay me back. I made a list of every guy I believed still in country who owed me money. I prioritized the names by their likelihood of paying me back.

Of course, the junkies and speed freaks occupied the bottom of my wish list. When completed, my detailed roster listed thirty-four names and an estimated debt of over $550. I modestly set my collection goal at $200.

I began my quest for cash on March 8. By March 15, one week later, I had contacted twenty-three debtors on my list and collected a grand total of $12. I also received an IOU (written on a Kleenex) for $20, payable on demand, if I ever visited Fairbanks, Alaska sometime after October of 1971. Three of the deadbeats I hunted down actually asked to borrow more money. That evening I threw the list away, officially ending my naive attempt to collect past loans.

With the aid of some generous gifts of booze, I had convinced Sergeant Lancaster to end my PO assignment on March 19—ten days before I was scheduled to report to the Processing Center for my freedom flight back to the world. I was supposed to work until March 28, the day before I had to report for processing. However, good old Sergeant Lancaster couldn't refuse my substantial bribe that consisted of free alcohol.

On March 20, I posted a large cardboard sign on the company bulletin board, informing everybody that I was selling all my possessions. I'd carry home with me only my photo album. Everything else went up for sale—two electric fans, one reel-to-reel Pioneer tape deck, three black-light fluorescent tubes, four foldout beach chairs, two footlockers covered with fluorescent paint, and six slightly torn posters (these featured Donovan, Bob Dylan, The Doors, the Woodstock festival, Joan Baez, and the greatest band in the history of rock 'n' roll, Creedence Clearwater Revival).

That evening, before I had sold one item, two junkies knocked on my door. I invited them in. The taller of the two got right to the point.

"I'm Easy Eddie and this is Twist," he said, pointing to his buddy who was wiping white powder from under his nose. "We wanna buy your room from you. How much you want?" he asked.

Not quite sure what he meant, I asked, "You want the whole room with everything in it?" As I circled my arm above my head.

"Yeah, everything including the room." Eddie circled his arm as I had done. "You leave in a little over a week, right?"

I nodded my head yes.

"We'll move in when you leave. How much you want?" Twist still hadn't said a word.

I decided to throw out an excessive amount and barter from there. "Four hundred," I calmly said, expecting horrified looks on their faces.

"Cool," Eddie replied. He looked at Twist, who nodded his head. The spokesman for this odd pair then pulled out a wad of MPC from his pocket and counted out twenty $20 bills in my hand.

"Thanks," I said. "I hit the road on the twenty-ninth. I'll be gone by eight in the morning. Come by before then and check out the room before I go. Does that sound okay?" I shrugged my shoulders to signify I had nothing else to say.

"Thanks man," Easy Eddie replied. Twist followed him from my room, never uttering a word.

"Junkies," I whispered to myself.

My last week in country was the most stressful seven days of my entire Vietnam tour. I attributed my unstable, irrational state of mind to a number of factors. First, with ten days remaining in country, I had decided to refrain from all drugs, including weed and alcohol. In addition, about the same time, I developed the uneasy feeling of constant paranoia. I started believing that something catastrophic would befall me and keep me from returning home. Maybe the lifers had placed me under surveillance months ago, recording my every move. And now, with only days remaining, they secretly prepared to bust me for drug use and send me to LBJ. Or maybe the Vietcong would lob a few random rounds inside Long Binh and, by dumb luck, one of them would hit my hooch, blowing me to pieces. What if a vengeful, knife-wielding mama-san, eager for reprisal because I had made a negative comment about her fatigue-washing abilities, decided to slit my throat as I slept? I intellectually knew my fears were irrational; however, that knowledge did nothing to relieve them. Another factor was what I believed to be an offshoot of the Stockholm Syndrome. (When kidnap victims, over a period of time, begin to sympathize with their captors.) Only in my case, the Army was my "captor." I wondered if I could survive and function outside of the Army community. That disgusting thought actually made me sick to my stomach.

Aside from my perceived potential catastrophes, a heavy, unanswered question weighed on my mind: What would I do, now that I'd soon enter civilian life? I had no idea. Amazingly, I had never seriously considered the next step in my life after the Army. I had been too busy living day to day to ponder the course of my future, and had spent the past twenty-two months avoiding deep thoughts and retrospection. If a problem faced me, I'd handle it just as most of the guys around me would: Get together with friends, smoke weed, and drink beer. What better way to deal with your problems? I thought. I convinced myself that when I got home, everything would take care of itself.

I spent the evening of March 28 alone in my room. All of my close friends had long since left, and I didn't want to suffer through the usual bullshit good-bye speeches: "Hey

327

man, if you're ever in Golden, Colorado, look me up." Or, "Hey Whalon, I'm comin' to California when I get out—can I stay with you?" (No thanks, dude—you're a drugged-out idiot!) And my personal favorite: "Whalon, will you carry these vials of 'smack' home with you and send 'em to me when I get out?" (Sure guy, no problem! Will you visit me and my boyfriend in Folsom?)

After a restless night's sleep, I got up, showered and, with duffle bag in hand, reported to the CO's office at eight as instructed. (The two junkies who purchased Casa de Whalon never showed up, so I just left my door unlocked for them.) Two other guys in the office, both from Company D, waited to go home. The company clerk drove us to the other side of Long Binh and dropped us off at the Replacement Center. A corporal sitting at a small desk in front of the holding area signed me in. At 8:48 a.m., he handed me a card with a four-digit number in the corner and the date stamped in the middle—March 29, 1971. He told me not to leave the facility and to be ready to board a bus when my number was called. He also told me that the wait could last as long as forty-eight hours. At this point, I could've spent forty-eight hours rolling nude on a mountain of razor blades while singing "Santa Lucia"!

At 4:15 on the morning of March 30, 1971, my number was called. I boarded the bus headed for the Bien Hoa Airbase, where I'd catch an airplane bound for Oakland, California. At 8:48 a.m. that same day, the airplane I sat in taxied onto the main landing strip, and then separated itself from the cement runway at Bien Hoa Airbase, Republic of Vietnam. This time, *everybody* cheered—I shit you not!

Chapter XXXV
Gween, Gween Gwass of Home
(Tom Jones, 1967)

The first hour of our "Freedom Flight" proved an unruly one. The young guys in the plane headed home were in high spirits. Raucous cheering and off-key singing sporadically erupted throughout the aircraft. The four "stews" (whose average age had to be somewhere in the mid-seventies) struggled to keep the GIs in their seats. They also pleaded, to no avail, for the rowdy boys to refrain from using profanity and stop throwing soldiers' caps down the aisle.

I sat back in my window seat, quietly enjoying the sophomoric antics of the euphoric group. This was New Year's Eve, Christmas Day, the 4th of July, and the last day of school, all rolled into one! After all, who could blame this collection of Vietnam veterans for celebrating such an epic event? We had survived an unpopular war and were now returning home to resume the life the military had snatched away from us. Thousands before us had come home in body bags, unceremoniously returned to their grieving families. If there was ever an appropriate occasion for celebration, this was it!

After an hour or so, all the guys had settled down and returned to their proper seats. I attempted to sleep but I felt too revved up to doze. I started to read one of a handful of magazines that I had carried with me onto the plane, but I found it impossible to concentrate. I asked one of the grey-haired stews for a pencil and some paper and began compiling an essential list of the ten things I wanted to do most when I got home. In no particular order, they were:

1. *Have a massive plate of my mom's spaghetti and meatballs, with a glass of milk.*

2. *Go bodysurfing at Avenue C.*

3. *Cruise the beach for chicks (preferably blonde and tanned).*

4. *Drink a 40-ounce bottle of Colt 45.*

5. *Get all my friends together and catch up on the past two years.*

6. *Set up the stereo equipment I had purchased and shipped directly home.*

7. *Buy a sports car. (Triumph-Fiat-MG. Fire-engine red!)*

8. *Take a long, hot shower.*

9. *Have breakfast at the Zig Zag coffee shop, with an extra order of hash browns.*

10. *Go to a Dodger game and eat at least four "Dodger Dogs."*

Compiling the list took about fifteen minutes. More than sixteen hours still remained until we touched down in Oakland. I closed my eyes and silently reflected on my past thirty-one months as an Army private. I also contemplated my present situation as a twenty-two-year-old Vietnam veteran, and what my plans for the future should include.

A decision I had made early in my Army career was the absolute necessity of a college education. I had come face-to-face with ignorance numerous times in the Army, and had found it utterly unappealing. During that period, I had come to the undeniable conclusion that the smarter you were, the better off you'd be in life. I decided to enroll at El Camino Junior College for the fall semester of 1971. My time in the Army also convinced me that whatever I decided to choose as a career, it should be something I enjoyed. Since I loved playing, watching, and talking about sports, I decided to major in physical education, and then pursue a career in the field. At that moment, it seemed like the perfect job for me. It took me ten minutes to decide my educational path.

With my future career out of the way, I began fantasizing about my homecoming and how I'd make up for the thirty-one wasted months spent in the service. As we had discussed on many evenings smoking weed in the Bayou, John Soranno and I planned to rent a "swinging" bachelor pad together as soon as I got home. It would be like Hugh Hefner and James Bond rooming together. The two Nam vets would party every night and dazzle young foxy chicks with our witty conversation and street savvy. A wide smile appeared on my face at the thought of John and me wearing brightly colored smoking jackets and holding chilled martinis as bikini-clad, nubile young chicks fawned over us. My life would overflow with a whole lot more fun very soon, I pleasantly thought.

The reality of leaving the Army and going home for good had put me in an extraordinarily blissful mood. I wanted to holler as loud as possible to the green-clad occupants of this "freedom bird," "I'm going home, I'm really going home!" Certainly, most of the guys on the plane shared the same passion about returning to the USA.

For the next two hours, I gazed out the window and chatted with the guy sitting next to me. I did manage to doze on and off during the long leg of our flight after our thirty-minute stop at the airport in Osaka, Japan. When the pilot finally announced that we'd land in Alaska to refuel (we wouldn't leave the plane), we erupted again in spontaneous cheering and applause. We had arrived in United States airspace! Our plane stayed on the ground in Alaska for about thirty minutes. As we took off from the Anchorage Airport, my mind wandered to my days in Saigon and Long Binh.

The remaining three hours of the flight I spent warmly reminiscing about my time in Nam. I'd never forget the exceptional people who became my good friends there. All of the incredible experiences and anomalous events suddenly seemed surreal to me. For the first time since joining the Army, I consciously contemplated the changes I had gone through, and how they'd affect my life.

As I sat in my seat, mentally struggling to objectively evaluate my metamorphosis, I realized that I was returning home a better person than when I had entered the Army. Not only had I filled out and gained some much-needed weight, I had also unconsciously formed strong opinions about many of the pressing issues of the day. Sometime during the past thirty-one months, I had transformed from an apathetic, smart-assed teenager who cared only about his next cheap thrill, into a considerate, compassionate young man who still cared only about his next cheap thrill. I couldn't decide whether these developments were a natural part of growing up, or the result of my extraordinary experiences in the Army, or a combination of both. My next revelation distressed me a little more. One undeniable conclusion I reached was that my Army experience had been a truly valuable one. I realized that I had learned many worthwhile lessons during my time in the service. Also, I had unconsciously developed numerous admirable character traits such as patience, thoughtfulness, loyalty, sincerity, and a true sense of what it meant to be a friend.

I was twenty-two years old, with my entire adult life ahead of me, and I felt more than ready to begin the mystical journey. I hadn't smoked any grass or had an alcoholic beverage in over ten days, but I felt higher than ever before. I couldn't wait to share my experiences with friends at home. The thought of walking through my front door and seeing relieved looks on my loving parents' faces exhilarated me.

Over the past twenty-two months, I had slowly developed an overwhelming appreciation for the "American way" and a deep understanding of what it meant to be an American. At that moment, I truly understood what an impact my experiences would have on the remainder of my life.

By the time the pilot instructed us to buckle our seatbelts for the descent into Oakland, I was ready to explode from the anticipation of returning home. I looked around and saw the same eagerness and enthusiasm on every beaming face. The youngest stewardess moved to the front of the plane and asked for our attention. After smiling at us broadly, the stew screamed, "Men, welcome home!" She pumped her fists in the air like a high-school cheerleader, and then made a request of the ecstatic soon-to-be-civilians on the plane. "Please join Irene, Millie, Barbara, and me, Ellen, in a little welcome-home song I'm sure you're all familiar with." And with that, the four stews, strategically standing in the aisle, simultaneously began singing "The Green, Green, Grass of Home." Although the four ladies correctly pronounced all the words of the classic tune, the entire group of off-key soldier-singers predictably eliminated all "Rs" from the lyrics. At the top of our voices, and with intense passion, we joined the thoughtful quartet of stews in song:

> *The old hometown looks the same,*
> *as I step down fum the twain,*
> *And theh to meet me is my Mama and Papa,*
> *Down the woad I look and theh wons Mawee,*
> *Hah of gold, and lips like chawees,*
> *It's good to touch the gween, gween gwass of home.*

333

Vietnam Vocabulary
Words
(The Bee Gees, 1968)

During every American war or conflict, the GIs stationed in the foreign countries develop a "second language." Soldiers in Vietnam proved no exception to this practice. A sub-language developed in the early years of the conflict, and this was passed on to all "cherries," making it easier for GIs to communicate with the locals, lifers and, most importantly, each other. Military personnel formed these phrases, words, and terms using combinations of slang, the Vietnamese language, and terminology imported from America. You'll also notice the French influence. (The French military fielded large forces in Vietnam in the '40s and '50s, and they made a profound impact on the culture and language.) The following is a list of words and phrases that will make it easier for you to understand "Nam-speak."

Jargon Used by both the Vietnamese and GIs

Baby-san: GI slang for a young Vietnamese child or baby. Vietnamese prostitutes also used this term to describe sexually naïve or virgin GIs.

Beaucoup (boo-coo): Large quantity, many. "GI have boo-coo American dollars."

Boom-boom: Make love; screw. Used by street whores to entice GIs.

Cheap Charlie: A small tipper to the Saigon bar girls; a cheapskate. "Cheap Charlie, numba ten!"

Chop-chop: Food, eating.

Coc dau (cock-a-dow): Hit, beat up, kill. "VC coc dau you, GI!" The GI might respond: "Me coc dau boo-coo VC, papa-san!"

Dee-dee mau (dee-dee): Leave now, go away. "GI, dee-dee!"

Fini: Done; over with; finished; dead.

Mama-san: Vietnamese woman; mother.

Numba one: The best, very good. "GI, numba one."

Numba ten: The worst, very bad. "GI, numba ten."

Papa-san: Vietnamese man; father; taxi drivers in Saigon.

Rau: Moustache.

Tee-tee: Very small or little; short period of time. Used by prostitutes referencing the size of a GI's penis.

Army Military Terms

Article 15: Disciplinary action taken by the Army for wrongdoing by a GI (usually for minor offenses).

AWOL: Absent without leave; leaving a unit without permission, which subjected a GI to possible disciplinary action.

Eleven bravo (11-b): The infantry, the guys "in the shit."

ETS: Estimated time of separation. Every soldier in Nam knew exactly how many days he had remaining in country. A common reference to this would be, for example, "54 and a wake-up," meaning the GI had only 54 days until he returned home.

GI: General inductee; any soldier below the rank of sergeant.

In country: Phrase used by GIs to refer to time spent in Nam. "How long have you been in country?"

Klicks or clicks: Distance of 1 kilometer.

M16: Rifle used by American GIs.

MPC (military payment currency): The money used by the military in Vietnam.

NCOIC: Noncommissioned officer in charge; the sergeant in charge of a unit or group of GIs.

R&R: Rest and relaxation. A GI was granted a seven-day R&R if he stayed in country for one year. R&R sites included Hawaii, Japan, Thailand, and Australia.

Sir: Used when addressing an officer—"Yes sir." Calling sergeants "sir" pissed off most of them.

GI Slang

Black market: Selling of prohibited goods by GIs to Vietnamese or by Vietnamese to GIs.

Bong: Homemade pipe used for smoking marijuana in Vietnam. Many of the GIs' bongs, made from Army supplies and food containers, were very creative and elaborate. Every grass smoker had a collection of bongs.

Boonies: The jungle; field; bush; remote areas of Nam.

Charlie (Chuck): VC; Vietcong soldier; the enemy.

Cherry: New guy in Vietnam. "Look at this shitload of cherries."

CBR (Cambodian Red): A type of very strong marijuana. Most "heads" wanted only CBR when they bought grass from a mama-san.

Dap: Handshake used by black soldiers as a greeting, often lasting up to five minutes. Hands, fingers, and arms were used in a series of slaps, snaps, and chest pounding. The sequence appeared to vary daily.

Dew: One nickname for marijuana. Others included weed, smoke, grass, MJ, Mary Jane, shit, pot, stash, joints, Js, doobies, Cambodian Red (CBR) and Laotian gold.

Dinks: Derogatory expression referring to Vietnamese, especially the enemy.

Fragging: Term used when a GI killed another GI, usually a superior. It meant throwing a grenade under the person's bunk when he slept. "I'm gonna frag that lifer someday!" Although the phrase was used often, the threat was rarely carried out.

Gooks: Derogatory term for Vietnamese people.

Head: Marijuana smoker.

Hooch: Structures where GIs lived. Usually made from sheets of tin and plywood.

Lifer: Derogatory term for career soldier, used mostly by GIs. "He's a damn lifer."

Round-eye: American woman.

Sky (book): To leave; to split.

Speed Freak (Speeder): Guys who took speed. Names for other drug users and abusers included Downer or Downs for guys who used downer drugs; Juicers, Alkies, or Drunks for alcohol drinkers; and Johnny Cash* or Junkies for heroin addicts. (*Refers to the Johnny Cash song, "Cocaine Blues.")

337

The world: The USA or any place other than Vietnam. "I go back to the world in 33 days."

Phrases Used by Lifers & GIs

Don't mean nothin': No big deal; no sweat off my back; that's okay. Used by GIs to rationalize a bad situation or blow off a lifer.

Get your shit together: Get ready; prepare yourself; straighten up; get your act together. Lifers in particular used this phrase when they chewed out GIs.

I got over on him (gettin' over): I fooled him; I tricked him; I got the best of him. A GI might say this to his buddies, after a sergeant who yelled at him is gone: "That cracker is always givin' me a ration of shit—I'm gonna get over on his ass someday—don't mean nothin' to me."

I shit you not: I'm not kidding; I'm telling the truth; I'm not lying. If a lifer chewed out a group of GIs for causing a problem, one might hear him scream something like this: "You men are gonna be in a world of hurt if I catch you again, I shit you not. Don't mean nothin' to me if you have to pull extra duty, I shit you not. You had better get your shit together men, I shit you not!"

World of hurt: Predominantly a lifer phrase; their way of telling a GI he would be in trouble if he didn't get his shit together.

Where Are They Now?

Gene Bellotti: Lives in Northern California, where he has his own company that provides precision woodwork for upscale homes.

Mark Goodman: Mark passed away in 2001. His wife, Karen, lives in Delaware.

Bill Harper: Still lives in North Carolina. He operates Island Ferry Adventures in Beaufort, NC.

Jerry Judge: Jerry now lives with his wife and granddaughter in North Carolina. He works as a systems representative for a large electrical manufacturing company.

Lee Mills: Resides in his original home state of Florida and travels the country as a consultant for a nuclear power company.

Bill Oswald: Moved to Southern California in 1996. Oswald is a college professor.

Larry Pratt: Stayed in Maine. He is a retired police officer.

Dave Schrunk: Still resides in Iowa. Works for John Deere Company.

Pete Whalon

Pete Whalon has called the Beach Cities region of Southern California home since the age of five. Pete stays in the area for the idyllic weather and tranquil beaches, though he must wear Coppertone outdoors because he freckles easily.

The author has written humorous stories most of his life. One published piece explains why cat owners are really more macho than dog owners. His writing has received Honorable Mention awards from *The Easy Reader* weekly.

Whalon retired in 2001. This is his debut memoir. He's now working on *The Vegas Zoo—If It's Super Bowl Weekend, I Must Be Lost in Vegas.*

CPSIA information can be obtained at www.ICGtesting.com
Printed in the USA
BVOW11s0641260515

401843BV00020B/190/P

9 780741 420459